KIDS' STUFF

TOYS AND THE
CHANGING WORLD OF
AMERICAN CHILDHOOD

GARY CROSS

HARVARD UNIVERSITY PRESS

Cambridge, Massachusetts, and London, England 1997

Library of Congress Cataloging-in-Publication Data

Cross, Gary.
   Kids' stuff : toys and the changing world
of American childhood / Gary Cross.
      p.   cm.
Includes bibliographical references and index.
ISBN 0-674-89830-3 (alk. paper)
1. Toy industry—United States—History.
2. Toys—Social aspects—United States.
I. Title.
HD9993.T693U63   1997
338.4'768872'0973—dc21   97-2655

Designed by Gwen Nefsky Frankfeldt

PREFACE

PLAY IS THE WORK of children, and toys are their tools. This is a truism of almost a century of child-development experts. But toys have been far more (and less) than this. They have told the young what the older generation valued and expected of them. They have told parents that the young seek recognition and freedom. And these messages transmitted through playthings have changed dramatically over the years, mirroring the history of childhood and childrearing. The commercial toy industry has facilitated, accelerated, and very often distorted this process. The history of playthings in modern America tells us much about childhood and the culture that surrounds it.

At no time in this history has there been more conflict about the role of toys in the lives of children than today. Toys evoke memories of adults' own youth and can create bonds between generations. But toys also produce anxieties that adults may be overindulging the young. New toys often suggest that manufacturers are manipulating children by creating unrestrained longings and values of which adults may not approve.

I wrote this book to clarify these conflicting attitudes about toys and to explain the change that has created these tensions. To do this, I went back to the origins of modern American childrearing and the birth of the modern American toy industry toward the end of the nineteenth century. The impact of the manufacturing and marketing of toys on child's play is central to the story. So too are modern ideas about raising children. But at the core of the book are the toys that American children have played with over the last hundred years. These playthings tell us much about the changing meanings of childhood and parenting and also shed light on the history of the modern consumer society.

When I began this project some colleagues may have thought I was going through a midlife crisis or even a second childhood by abandoning my "serious" scholarship for a "childish" topic like toys. Others, especially my family, may have figured I was taking revenge for having to endure a house full of toys for years. In fact, I jokingly told my children that my new book would be called "Too Many Toys: What's the Matter with the Kids on Edward Street." But if I began with a sharply critical eye, my perspective became more complex, subtle, and, I hope, more balanced as I went along.

In truth, this book grew out of a long-developing interest in the social significance of consumption and a belief that the critics of American popular culture have failed to explain it. My years of teaching courses in the history of American families made me aware of how abstract and inadequate was our understanding of twentieth-century parenting and childhood. A study of toys seemed to be a good way of addressing both issues.

The research itself was a lot of fun. But there is little personal nostalgia in the book. I do not collect toys, and I recall having few as a child (although my mother might dispute this claim). Still, I hope that this story of toys in modern America will help readers reflect on their own childhoods as well as those of their offspring.

Historians are notorious for thinking and writing in isolation. I am no exception. But a number of friends and colleagues led me to new sources and fresh ideas. Librarians and curators at the Margaret Woodbury Strong Museum—E. Scott Eberle, Christopher Clarke-Hazlett, Carol Sandler, and Helen Schwartz—were especially helpful. Kristin Peszka and the Please Touch Museum were most gracious in opening up their amazing collection of recent Toy Fair materials, and Charles McGovern of the National Museum of American History offered useful assistance. Participants in the International Toy Research Conference in June 1996 at Halmstad University in Sweden provided incisive criticism and wonderful encouragement.

Greta Pennell, Stephen Kline, and Brian Sutton-Smith gave me ideas that found their way into the book in various ways. Peter Pluntky and Kathy George provided a fine array of photographs from their collections. Among my fellow historians who read parts of the work or gave me valuable insight or information are Dana Frank, Miriam Formanek-Brunell, Ellen Furlough, Steven Gelber, T. J. Jackson Lears, Roland Marchand, and Paula Petrik. Even though I tried not to impose on my colleagues at the Pennsylvania State University, somehow Gary Gallagher, Paul Harvey, Philip Jenkins, Sally McMurry, Bill Pencak, Anne C. Rose, and Robert Proctor provided criticism and useful information. Grants from Penn State's Institute for the Arts and Humanistic Studies and the Research Office of my college got me to libraries and paid for many of the photographs. I am especially grateful to Ray Lombra, my dean of research. Despite his number-crunching habits as an economist, he still found a way to support this book.

Joyce Seltzer at Harvard University Press was a wonderful partner in this project, helping to shape the book in many ways. Cherie Anciero and Camille Smith, also of Harvard, were wonderful collaborators. My wife, Maru, for years before I ever had any interest in toys, understood what play and playthings mean to children and families. Her insights have kept me focused. My visits to Wal-Mart with my children, Elena and Alex, to do "toy research" have reminded me what this book is really about.

CONTENTS

KIDS' STUFF

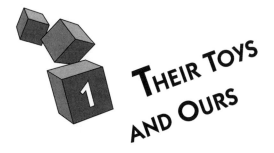

1 THEIR TOYS AND OURS

MOST OF US find ourselves at one time or another in a toy shop, looking for a gift for a child. Those of us who have not been in such stores since our youth can easily be bewildered, especially if we were born before the 1960s. Our favorite toys or games—fire engines, Tinkertoys, or baby dolls—have disappeared or are hidden in row after row of heroic fighters, fashion dolls, and exotic stuffed animals.

The more practical of us enter the store with a list of items desired by the child—this season's action figure, the newest Barbie, or the latest video game. Veteran toy shoppers may enjoy the inevitable transformations as Teenage Mutant Ninja Turtles give way to Mighty Morphin Power Rangers and Locket Surprise Barbie to Tropic Splash Barbie. But equally we may be appalled to think about the dozens of Ninja Turtles that an older boy just had to have a year earlier but that were then shunned by a younger brother who just had to have Power Rangers. Why don't kids pass down their toys as we remember giving our building blocks and dollhouses to our younger brothers and sisters? It is easy to wonder whether each year's must-have toys are really for children's play or whether their ever-changing forms represent other forces at work.

We often lament a loss of innocence in the young. We recall

playing ball in the street, holding "secret" meetings in treehouses, or pushing baby dolls in miniature wicker carriages. We assume that this is the way children "traditionally" played, that childhood "used to be" unchanging. We remember a less commercialized youth. Some of our wagons were handmade from scraps of lumber and discarded wheels, and grandmas sewed dolls' clothes. Even if most of our playthings were, in fact, manufactured, we had far fewer of them. Toys came at birthdays, Christmas, and Hanukkah. And, on those rare occasions when we bought them for ourselves, we did so with money saved from jobs and allowances, and at neighborhood toy stores or five-and-dimes. We window shopped for weeks before we had saved enough to make the plunge and buy. We knew the storekeepers and they knew us. Our parents understood when we should have a gun-and-holster set or a dress-up doll. Dolls and tea sets, electric trains and erector sets had been part of the rites of passage for generations of Americans. Parents understood the toys of children because they had been *their* toys once and were still so in memory.

These images contrast sharply with today's cornucopia of playthings. The toy store today is no longer a special place where customary gifts can be found but a well-organized warehouse for the experienced consumer. Only the merchandise excites. The sheer quantity from which to choose may well dull the imagination but encourages the filling of shopping carts. Gone are the "Mr. Hoopers" once nostalgically portrayed on *Sesame Street*, shopkeepers who patiently displayed each toy so that parents and kids could make a wise choice. Instead there are endless aisles with boxes piled high and clerks who look beyond the child for those price-code strips to be passed over their computer scanners. The desire for a toy comes not so much from reaching the age when children "naturally" got a bicycle or a dress-up doll as from advertising campaigns aimed to whet the child's appetite for more. Shopping for toys has become saddening, irritating, or bewildering to many adults.

Toymakers seem to be pied pipers leading our children away from us. They manufacture and endlessly promote fantasy war play that appears to teach violence as a way of resolving conflict. Toy manufacturers have made fortunes promoting sexist and unattainable images of women to young girls. Barbie's hourglass figure (at estimated projected measurements of 36"-18"-33") encourages little girls to have distorted expectations of their own bodies. Today's toys do not often convey the values that we wish our children to embrace and that we believe we learned with our toys in childhood.[1]

Occasionally parents protest and form organizations to combat these trends. In 1989 a group of parents and children from Louisville remodeled toy soldiers into firefighters and scuba divers. They turned Ninja Turtles into famous American women like Jane Addams and Rosa Parks. Children put on plays using scripts they wrote and scenery they constructed. The object was to turn passive play with violent toys into something creative and positive. Articles in *Parents' Magazine* ceaselessly offer obviously good advice: Buy "open-ended toys," not mere novelties. Find playthings depicting real adult work activities and toys that are truly "age-appropriate." But is such advice useful or realistic? By the time children are in kindergarten or even preschool, they want the G.I. Joes and Barbies that they see in TV advertisements and that other kids own. Mothers and fathers give in to their offspring's nagging and their fear of isolating their children from peers. Parents feel impotent to shape their children's play.[2]

Most adults doubt that children should be exposed to incessant change. It used to be that childhood was the dependable repository of our traditions such as Valentine's Day, Halloween, and the Fourth of July. Childhood symbolized the unchanging spirit of free play.

Now, however, the ever-transforming toy store offers novelty at every step of growing up. Being aware of the latest fad has come to define what it means to be a child. We do still give babies and toddlers traditional objects—rattles, teething rings, and push toys in the image of ageless clowns and circus animals. And we still listen to child psychologists and their popularizers in magazines who provide us with lists of time-tested toys. But as soon as our children are old enough to watch television (and advertisements), they want the new playthings they see glittering on the screen. We want to give the young the playthings that we remember, but they are hard to find on the overcrowded shelves of today's toy stores.

There have been disturbing changes in the making of playthings in the last few decades. Since the late 1960s many old toy companies, venerated for manufacturing toys passed from one generation to the next, have disappeared. The death of A. C. Gilbert in 1967 and the sale of his company shortly after ended a tradition of manufacturing boys' construction and science sets since 1913. Gilbert's most famous creation, the erector set, promised parents that their children would be preparing to join the adult world of engineering, industry, and science. Tinkertoys and Lincoln Logs, which appeared about the same time as the erector set, also declined in the 1970s. The old kitchen play sets, dollhouses, and baby dolls that were to teach girls the arts of housekeeping and childcare are also less in evidence today. Toys that seem to prepare children for adult life have become harder to find.[3]

Other old companies, such as Playskool and Fisher-Price, which had built trusted clientele around well-tested toys for small children, succumbed to the control of bigger corporations. Playskool and Fisher-Price specialized in so-called educational playthings. They offered age-appropriate toys, designed and approved by experts in child development. They advertised, if at all, in adult publications like *Parents' Magazine* and stressed that their toys were safe and prepared children for school. Their toys were largely free of novelty. Gradually, however, these companies abandoned this idealism. Finally, Playskool was taken over in 1984 by Hasbro and Fisher-Price in 1993 by Mattel, companies whose success has been in novelty toys. Old-style educational toys survive in the upscale children's and hobby shops where plain blocks and challenging craft sets still can be found. But they are not featured in the discount stores or warehouse toy marts where most toys are purchased.[4]

While many playthings before the 1970s trained children for adult roles or prepared preschoolers for education, others were whimsical novelties. For more than fifty years, Louis Marx manufactured thousands of playsets and mechanical toys that stressed fantasy and novelty. Marx toys were cheap, often recycling old themes. He used cartoon characters to sell his toys, and he mass marketed them through chain and department stores. A windup "crazy car" driven by a "college boy" one year would reappear with Mickey Mouse at the wheel in another year. But despite Marx's changing toy line, he was tradition-bound. Until the 1960s he used practically no advertising and his toys were often based on real life—parking garages and airports, for example. His toys appealed as much to adults as to children. However, his company too was caught in the crush of business buyouts and was sold to Quaker Oats in 1972, disappearing finally in 1979.[5]

The Gilberts, Playskools, and Marxes were toymakers of a different era. Although they offered very different types of toys, they all produced creative playthings that parents could delight in giving their children. This is much less true today. In their place have come a new breed of companies that specialize in novelty and appeal directly to the imaginations of children. By the mid-1980s the dominant toymakers were Mattel and Hasbro. Mattel originated in 1945 in California and made its mark with the Barbie doll. Hasbro, founded in 1923 in Providence, Rhode Island, grew rich with G.I. Joe action figures and through the acquisition of a host of smaller companies. Both these giants helped to transform an industry that had primarily addressed the needs and values of parents into one that appealed directly to the longings and imaginations of children.

Mattel and Hasbro pioneered television advertising in the 1950s on children's programs. Hasbro holds claim to the first (local) TV advertisements for toys (Mr. Potato Head in 1951). Mattel climbed to the top of the industry when it became a major advertiser on the Mickey Mouse Club in 1955. Their well-designed sales pitches presented not only the toys themselves but stories that told children how to play. These advertisements provided the scripts that suggested children's play and made the toys into props for their make-believe dramas. So successful was this form of advertising for sales that, by the early 1980s, these companies and others turned cartoon TV programs into half-hour commercials featuring specific toys as the cartoon characters. "G.I. Joe, A Great American Hero" (Hasbro) and "He-Man and Masters of the Universe" (Mattel) were typical animated stories of the struggle between the forces of good and evil, but their real purpose was to sell G.I. Joe and He-Man action figures. By providing children with a fantasy starring their favorite brand of superhero, Mattel and Hasbro made great inroads into the toy market.[6]

Mattel and Hasbro revolutionized the toy industry by turning toys into a product line that virtually demanded multiple purchases. Mattel spun endless fashion accessories around Barbie, and Hasbro launched its own arms race as G.I. Joe figures fought bad guys with an escalating array of space-age weapons. It was no fun unless a child's Barbie doll had friends like Ken or little sisters like Skipper. And G.I. Joe required both good guys and bad guys in order to play war. Toy companies rode the coattails of popular cartoon and movie characters, turning their images into playthings. Action figures, stuffed dolls, games, and eventually computer-operated video games were increasingly sold under character licenses.[7]

Mattel, Hasbro, and many imitators created toys that no longer reflected adult life as did Gilbert, or taught basic skills like Playskool, or even offered innocent whimsy as Louis Marx often did. Their toys led children into a new world of play, one which simulates activities more familiar in movies and television than at home or office. The popularity of traditional training and educational toys declined while fantasy/novelty playthings became increasingly central to children's lives. The toy lost much of its role as a conveyor of messages between parent and child or even as a source of shared enjoyment between the generations.

While old toy companies folded or were sold, the way consumers bought toys also changed. In the 1980s the discount stores and warehouse outlets beat out the department stores and toy shops in competition for the rising toy dollar. By 1992 Charles Lazarus's Toys "R" Us was dominant, with 126 stores abroad to add to its 497 American stores. These warehouses of playthings beckoned consumers to buy much and to buy often by charging less for each item. Toys "R" Us operated on the premise that toys could be sold all year round, not just at Christmas and Hanukkah, and accordingly marketed them in all seasons.[8]

For millions of children, new toys have become not only a year-round treat but a regular part of mealtime. Increased competition led fast-food chains to offer toy premiums to lure families with young children to their counters. McDonald's Happy Meals regularly include toys featuring characters from children's movies or miniature versions of Barbie, Hot Wheels, or other toy lines. In the late 1980s Wendy's Restaurants found that 84 percent of parents let their children help decide where to eat. Inevitably a major factor in the choice was the toy in the children's packaged meal. The miniature Barbies or Transformers offered in Happy Meals created a demand for the "real" thing at the store. The child's expectation that a plaything would come with every fast-food meal led most franchises to adopt this practice. The toy "prize" became as regular as the fast-food habit.[9]

Is it surprising that children have been inundated with toys and dolls? Retail sales rose from $4.2 billion in 1978 to $17.5 billion in 1993, not including the $3.97 billion for video games. Today's children have rooms filled with toys while many of their parents remember having only a shelf or two. American toymakers issue endless new products—three to six thousand new toys each year. And adults buy them at an increasingly brisk pace.[10]

The contrast between our toys and those of our offspring has many roots and reasons. The roots reach back much further than the 1970s to the last decades of the nineteenth century. And the reasons go beyond the toymakers and merchandisers to more profound cultural changes in the meaning of parenting and childhood.

The nostalgia for toys of earlier generations obscures certain continuities between past and present. For well over a century, ever since Americans became less self-sufficient and began purchasing most of the things they needed or wanted in stores, children's play has been shaped by the mass consumption economy and the manufacturers and salespeople behind it. Adults and children have shared in a commercial culture of play over the past hundred years even if the pace has been never as frenetic as it is today. The passing of the "useful" toys made by A. C. Gilbert, the educational playthings of the old Playskool, and even the charming whimsy of Louis Marx may suggest a loss of childhood innocence. But the Gilberts, Playskools, and Marxes were part of a commercial toy business that, in many ways, set the stage for contemporary TV toys with their quest for novelty and their capturing of the child's imagination.

Similarly, the useful, educational, and fantasy toys of the past expressed extremely diverse ideas and expectations about childhood that continue to shape the contemporary debate about playthings. The idea of learning through play with "ageless" blocks had nothing in common with the amusement of a cheap tin windup car with Popeye the Sailor Man at the wheel. There was a wide gap between the innocence of the Kewpie dolls of the 1910s and the tough-guy image of the Dick Tracy gun of the 1930s. Toys reflected a complex and rapidly changing world of popular culture and amusement long before the 1970s.

Many critics assume that toy companies alone are responsible for the quantity and cost of today's playthings. But the new world of toys is by no means simply the product of a profit-mad cabal of toy pushers discovering new ways of exploiting the child market. Playthings have always been subject to evolving and conflicting attitudes toward, and styles of, childrearing. Until the end of the nineteenth century, parents gave children few toys and those they did give reflected the convenience and taste of adults more than the desires and imagination of children. About 1900 a more child-centered approach arose that allowed youth their own material culture of play. The present surfeit of toys can be understood as the culmination of this century-long development. Toymakers certainly collaborated and cashed in on this trend, taking it further than many thoughtful parents wished it to go, but they did not create the overstuffed toybox by themselves.

The electric trains and baby dolls that adults remember as timeless classics were, in fact, products of childrearing ideas that emerged early in the twentieth century. The decline of these toys has more to do with changes in our society than with manipulation by toymakers. The erector set was supposed to teach boys to dream of becoming engineers and scientists at a time in American history when most adults had faith in a world of endless technological progress. The dollhouse and the baby doll taught the girl to be a modern homemaker and mother during the years when those roles were the expected futures of most American girls. But these roles were not timeless, and neither were the toys. Not even the teddy bear is a timeless plaything—even though children in many cultures and times have found soft and cuddly objects to hold and give them comfort. The bear began as a fad, sparked by the fame of Teddy Roosevelt, that amused adults as much as children.

Erector sets, baby dolls, and teddy bears reflected an American (especially middle-class) idea of childhood that dates from the beginning of the twentieth century. At that time, toys were to train children to be adults through imaginative play. Toys reflected parents' desire to give their kids a childhood free from work but still very much controlled by and shared with parents. Toymakers accommodated grown-ups with playthings that appealed to their goals and permitted them to stand between the toy business and their children's toys.

But by the late 1960s traditional cultural values were besieged and in flux. Parents were no longer very sure about what it meant to be a successful grown-up man or woman. As technology changed faster and faster, parents became less confident in their ability to predict the tools their children would need in adult life. Toys could not so easily serve as playful miniatures of those more complex tools. Kids played with computers but did not build toy electronics the way their fathers and grandfathers had once built models of factory machinery. The erector sets and baby dolls that had trained children to assume adult roles made less sense to parents who no longer knew what to train their children to become.

While early-twentieth-century toys had expressed the parents' toleration of the child's freedom in play, the new toys gave vent to a world of children's imagination in which adults had no real place. The modern toys that invite children into a fantasy world free of adults had their origins in playthings that were supposed to allow children to express themselves in ways embraced by adults. The Care Bears of the 1980s, whose story only children know, were the descendants of the teddy bears of the 1900s, whose magic was shared by adults and children. The disappearance of the certainties and shared feelings expressed in those earlier toys causes many parents to mourn the loss and to blame the toymakers of recent decades. This may be understandable but it obscures deeper truths.

The ever-expanding toy industry reflects a general American commitment to unrestrained markets and to constant change, a commitment at least a century old. Americans have long admired the new and have enriched those who produce it. For decades American parents have enjoyed sharing the world of consumption with their offspring. At first they did so knowing that they ultimately mediated between toys and their children. When the floodgates were opened and torrents of toys were presented directly to kids, parents found themselves merely providers of funds to buy toys.

Parents have long sought to protect children from the excesses of the consumer market. The toy industry offered toys intended to alleviate their fears. But the toy industry also discovered how to sell directly to children by tapping their imaginations in playthings inspired by characters in the mass media. The pace of this direct marketing was slow until after midcentury but has accelerated since the 1970s. The long-submerged tension between satisfying the parent, the child, and the need for profit has given way to a system in which the parent is an onlooker rather than an active participant.

The history of playthings tells us much about parents, children, and commerce and how they have interacted over time. Playthings may have always been a part of childhood, but their roles have changed in important ways. In order to understand these changes, we must return to the late nineteenth and early twentieth centuries, where we will find the antecedents of the toys that were familiar in our childhood as well as the roots of the novelties in our children's lives. An inquiry into the business of toy manufacturing and into the changing patterns of childrearing will help illuminate the nature and contents of today's toybox.

MODERN CHILDHOOD, MODERN TOYS

In 1892 the Marshall Field department store offered customers a thirty-six-page catalog crammed with playthings to fill the toybox of the American child.[1] Six pages were devoted to a dazzling array of cast-iron replicas of horses and wagons. The attractions of the surreys, pony express wagons, double trucks, pony phaetons, and hansoms may be lost to us, but these toys excited boys of late-Victorian America. Still more space was given to replicas of firefighting equipment and a large number of miniature steam engines. Twenty cast-iron and mechanical banks appealed to the imaginations (and attracted the pennies) of children of both sexes. While whimsical wheeled toys in the shapes of horses and farm animals rang bells when pulled by a toddler, building blocks promised to educate while amusing preschoolers.

The catalog favored boys' toys, but eight pages were devoted to dolls and doll furniture. Well-known French imports with their fashionable dresses appeared beside a wide assortment of American "lady" dolls. Tiny fashion sets, parlor furniture, metal kitchen stoves, washboards, and dustpans tantalized girls with visions of endless hours of doll play. The children of the poor could only dream of possessing these toys, but new manufacturing methods put them within the reach of the middle class. And thrifty parents were increasingly willing to fill toyboxes, giving their children permission to enjoy play.

In 1892 the beliefs that children had a right to play and needed specially manufactured objects for this purpose were still rather new. Only after the Civil War were there many American manufacturers who produced toys, and only from the beginning of the twentieth century did many American toymakers reach out to a mass market and use advertising to appeal to parents. Before the second half of the nineteenth century, toys were rare and often served the needs of adults more than the play of children. The modern toy is a distinct product of a new kind of toy business and a new childrearing ideal. The result by 1900 was not only more manufactured toys but toys that embodied positive attitudes toward children's play. Both manufacturers and parents sent the young the message that play was their job and playthings were their tools.

The modern toybox inherited much from the distant past. Archaeology reveals balls and dolls five thousand years old. What appear to be toy animals are found in graves from the western Indian Harappa culture of 2,800 BCE. Greek children of Horace's times had hobbyhorses, toy pets, and jointed dolls of wood and clay. Hoops and knucklebones (precursors of modern ball-and-jacks sets) were common in the ancient Mediterranean. And probably the play lives of children were much richer than these remains suggest. Few of the gourds or bits of wood that doubtless served as rattles, dolls, and toy animals have survived.[2]

After seeing these artifacts in museums, it is easy to conclude that toys through the ages have served common purposes. Anthropologists stress how toys in different times and places both imitate the adult world and protect children from its dangers and burdens. Dolls and toy weapons have always represented adult activity while remaining play objects, not child-sized adult tools. They have given children a feeling of adult power and significance without the danger, responsibility, or tedium of actual adulthood. As the anthropologist Brian Sutton-Smith notes, "Play schematizes life, it alludes to life, it does not imitate it in any very strict sense."[3]

The anthropologist Roland Caillois suggests that playthings address four distinct needs: mimicry, vertigo (or giddiness), competition, and chance. In some ways, these needs are two pairs of balanced opposites. A figure of a knight lets the child imitate the powerful and grown-up, while a top expresses the thrill of rapid motion. The same toy can serve both goals when a child builds and then destroys displays of toy soldiers or towers of blocks. Board games reward individual skill in competition while requiring players to accept the idea of chance and thus the unpredictability of life. Toys inevitably embody different combinations of these four needs. Cultures can be distinguished by their relative stress on competition or vertigo in their games and toys. Playthings teach the young and remind the old of the values and customs of their culture.[4]

But playthings have changed over time in dramatic ways. Until recently, children were obliged to work, helping parents with baby siblings and doing the housework that mothers had no time for. Children did have their times of play, and made toys and dolls from rocks, sticks, straw, and discarded crockery and cloth. But seldom did play involve a special space and time set aside for the free development of the child's imagination. And parents rarely gave specially made toys to their children. Showering children with playthings on birthdays and Christmas is a recent custom. Only modern affluence made manufactured toys possible in families beyond the ranks of the rich.

Only recently have adults relinquished control over most toys. It is difficult to distinguish ancient children's toys and dolls from objects intended to accompany the dead to the afterlife or icons designed to represent and embody the power of gods. In some preindustrial societies miniature figures first served adults in religious rites and then were passed on to children for play. And in many of these societies adults used dolls and toy soldiers for their own amusement. Given the relative scarcity of domestic decorations and pleasure objects, and the comparatively low recognition of children's needs, this should not be surprising. Doll historians may exaggerate when they equate *children's* dolls with civilization. But clearly a mark of modernity is the historical point when adults turn religious icons and amusements into children's play figures and recognize play as a special right of childhood.[5]

This suggests a final difference between traditional and modern playthings. Modern adults have ceded key elements of traditional play to their children. Slowly they gave up mimicking the gods with masks and dolls and using miniatures as idols. Eventually the supernatural beliefs attached to these objects were forgotten, leaving them to children's play. In modern times the doll that once embodied the power and personality of the god or departed relative has become a child's imaginary baby or playmate. The mask that represented a demon in religious rites and imbued its wearer with special powers has turned into the Halloween costume. Most adults also gradually rejected vertigo—the ecstatic dancing and singing common in ancient cultures that gave people the feeling of participating in a supernatural world. Instead, adult play came to stress competition and chance in games of calculation and rules rather than giddy triumph in contests of danger and power. Vertigo lives on among adult mountain climbers and bungee jumpers and in amusement parks, but most modern adults have ceased toying with the ecstatic or dangerous. Vertigo has largely been secularized, sanitized, and made safe for children. The jousting and fencing of medieval knights and courtiers have given way to rubber swords which children use to challenge one another on the field of play.

Playthings through the ages have served common purposes in introducing the young to the tools, experiences, and even emotional lives of their parents. But only in modern times have toys become primarily objects for children, props in a play world separated from adults. In the transformation of play and toys from medieval times to the mid-nineteenth century, toys gradually became specifically children's playthings.

Precursors of Modern Toys

The worlds of children and adults were far closer in medieval Europe than they are today. In part this meant that playthings initiated children into the adults' world. Medieval children played with miniatures representing their parents' lives. Boys anticipated adult roles by playing with sticks and hobbyhorses, toy knights, cannons, and even windmills. For girls there were dolls dressed as monks or as women in fashionable dresses. But the proximity of the cultures of youth and adult had also another meaning. "Child's play" also amused adults. Medieval Europeans viewed play as a periodic catharsis, a necessary release of tension, often associated with fairs or feast days, but not specifically with childhood. In Shakespeare's time "toy" meant anything frivolous or even simply a funny story. Medieval adults as well as children enjoyed games of tag and blindman's buff and played with hoops and sticks, stilts, and whistles.[6]

Many objects that we identify today with children's play originated as amusements for adults. Medieval churches displayed life-size manger scenes at Christmas to delight and edify their congregations; by the sixteenth century Italian and German craftspeople sold miniatures of these scenes for home display. In the fourteenth century jacks were mechanical wooden figures which struck bells in church towers; by the sixteenth century these objects of communal pleasure were miniaturized as string-pulled "jumping Jacks" and were sold widely as toys in central Europe. From about 1470 families cut out engravings of battles or of animals in natural settings and glued them on to pasteboard for display. They were not children's toys as such, but festive household decorations and home dramatizations. Gradually, however, these miniature scenes became children's playsets. Perhaps the earliest of these was the wooden Noah's Ark. This late-sixteenth-century German innovation offered religious training while allowing children to play with toy animals at home. Public (often church-supported) decorations and amusements were miniaturized for a domestic setting, where they served the enjoyment and edification of the whole family. Only after this stage did they pass to children for their own use.[7]

Other toys can be traced to the fascination of adults, mostly men, with mechanical movement. Automata in the form of mechanical figures or birds had been powered by water and even steam from the second century BCE in Alexandria, Egypt. During medieval religious festivals, life-size figures in the likeness of the Virgin Mary were automated by sand poured over power wheels. The eighteenth-century French artisans Jacques de Vaucanson and Pierre Jaquet-Droz fashioned mechanical angels, pecking birds, and other novelties that delighted adult aristocrats by singing or shuffling across the floor as if by magic. In the nineteenth century these objects trickled down to children as windup toys, and they survive today as remote-control robots.[8]

Many modern novelty toys have origins in the fads of medieval and Renaissance aristocrats. The simple cup-and-ball toy was a late-sixteenth-century amusement, enjoyed first by the French court and then passed down to children as an inexpensive present bought at fairs. Toy balloons were given to children when French aristocrats, celebrating the first hot-air balloon's ascension in 1783, grew tired of them.[9]

Fashion dolls also began their long history with adult women. In 1391 the French court sent the English queen a miniature female mannequin dressed in the latest French style. Indeed, the exchange of dolls among adult aristocratic women was common throughout the Middle Ages. The dolls not only charmed these ladies but informed them about the latest fashions (functioning much as style magazines do in modern times). In the seventeenth and eighteenth centuries clothing designers used these dolls to advertise Parisian styles throughout Europe. They were a major reason for French success in dominating women's fashion. Mothers gave the dolls to their young daughters when they no longer needed them for practical purposes.

The history of dollhouses follows a similar course. Doll cabinets, containing miniature furniture, date from 1558 in Saxon Germany. In the seventeenth century they were common decorations in the homes of wealthy Dutch and German merchants. These dollhouses were handmade and up to six feet high and eight feet long. In the early eighteenth century the Duchess Augusta Dorothea of Schwartzburg-Gotha had twenty doll cabinets built to display in miniature all aspects of her luxurious life. These replicas were not toys for children but models designed to amuse wealthy women and to exhibit their wealth and taste. Only at the end of the eighteenth century were they built specifically for girls, designed to instruct them in the arts of housekeeping.[10]

The historian Karl Grober notes that miniature soldiers served a similar purpose for men. Kings and other powerful aristocrats commissioned artisans to make lead or silver miniatures of their armies for their amusement. Only in 1578 did Nuremberg artisans produce tin versions of toy animals for children and, because of cost, only for children of rich families. Time and time again adult playthings and amusements were passed on to children after long use.[11]

If the amusements of adults gradually fell into the toybox, most belonged to the children of the rich. Few parents could commission skilled artisans to craft toys or dolls for their youngsters. Most surviving toys from before the nineteenth century were produced for children of the aristocracy or wealthy merchants. In 1572 the king of Saxony gave his son a wooden playset depicting hounds, stags, wild boars, foxes, wolves, and hares. The king's daughter received a doll's kitchen complete with dishes, meat plates, spoons, and furniture. These playthings reflected distinct sex roles but also displayed replicas of the luxuries of aristocratic society. Only the well-to-do could afford such handmade miniatures fashioned from expensive woods and precious metals.[12]

Poor children enjoyed roughly made rag-and-straw stuffed dolls. Animal wastes provided materials for balls and knucklebones in the Middle Ages. Children took pleasure in rolling discarded wooden wheel hoops across the ground with the skillful stroking of a stick across the top. And stray poles and blocks of wood were easily turned into stilts. Folk toys may have been simple, but they inspired modern toymakers to imitate them. And today many traditionally crafted toys have great snob appeal.[13]

Toys of aristocratic and folk origin both were handmade and thus relatively rare. Both groups of playthings survive in the modern toybox. But only when it became possible to mass market and manufacture cheap copies of these toys did they become available in large numbers. The modern toy industry has its distant roots in sixteenth-century Central Europe. At that time clusters of German villages became centers of specialized toy production. During long winters woodsmen and their families from Erzgebirge, the Groeder Valley, and Bohemia carved wooden animals inspired by local wildlife. In 1760 Andreas Hilpert of Nuremberg offered middle-class parents cheap tin imitations of expensive silver or lead toy armies. Thereafter, Nuremberg set the standard in toy soldiers. But the town also produced the "Nuremberg Kitchen," a mass-produced playset for training girls in the essentials of domestic work.[14]

Gradually toymaking became a well-organized business. In the sixteenth century, peddlers and other small-scale merchants purchased toys made by families and sold them at fairs and from door to door. Later, merchants centered in Nuremberg gained control over these traveling salespeople and forced artisans to adopt uniform designs and to specialize. Still, craft methods prevailed. Families made toys at home or in small shops until the end of the nineteenth century, when new machines and factories were introduced. In 1900 Germany was the world's greatest producer of toys, exporting 75 percent of its output and sending one quarter of that to the United States.[15]

Paralleling the rise of a rationalized toy industry was the introduction of new, cheaper materials. The invention of sheet metal stamping machines in 1815 eventually made possible the mass production of tin toys. By 1850 papier-mâché, "India" rubber, and simple molding machines lowered the cost of dolls. Porcelain doll heads were manufactured from the 1840s and bisque from 1870. Composition (a mixture of wood fiber, bran, and glue) began to replace china and other clay materials for dolls' heads in 1895. Paper dolls appeared in England about 1791, offering an inexpensive version of the three-dimensional fashion doll. Finally, simple mechanical contrivances also made dolls more lifelike. As early as 1823 dolls could say "mamma" when children squeezed simple bellows implanted in the bodies. Technical improvements, including weight-activated eyes and ball-jointed limbs, became common by 1850. These economic and technological changes made toys more accessible and more innovative.[16]

But changing attitudes toward children were also required to persuade parents to purchase toys and to give their children opportunities to play. Essential for this change was the view that children were distinct from adults and required a sheltered environment and special tools and activities to mature into effective adults. John Locke was the first to present this modern understanding of children. In *Some Thoughts Concerning Education* (1693) he defined the child's mind as a blank slate without any innate propensity toward evil. This view that environment and external influence shaped the child's character undermined the earlier belief that children were little demons or animals who had to be "broken" in order to live in civilized society. Play, according to Locke, was not the "devil's workshop," a surrender to the inner impulse of disorder and disobedience, but rather exploratory and expressive. Play was essential for children's development and enlightenment:

Recreation is as necessary, as Labour, or Food. But because there can be no *Recreation* without Delight, which depends not always on Reason, but oftener on Fancy, it must be permitted Children not only to divert themselves, but to do it after their own fashion . . . Gamesome humour which is wisely adapted by nature to their age and temper, should rather be encouraged to keep up their spirits and improve their strength and health, than curbed and restrained.

According to Locke, children should have a variety of toys. But he also insisted that these not be given to children all at once. Play had a practical purpose: to reveal those aptitudes in the child which parents ought to encourage. Locke's ideas were passed on to nineteenth-century parents via popular childrearing manuals. These books encouraged parents to find games and toys to guide the child's "progress" or training.[17]

Similarly, the eighteenth-century philosopher Jean-Jacques Rousseau held that small children were innocents whose naive simplicity was a virtue. Parents should encourage their spontaneity with an education that rewarded individual expression and personal development. Accordingly, Rousseau and his followers understood childhood as unique. Children were not miniature adults. They should be allowed a long childhood spent with those in their own age group. As Rousseau put it, "Nature wants children to be children before they are men. If we deliberately pervert this order, we shall get premature fruits which are neither ripe nor well-flavoured, and which soon decay." This was a revolutionary idea. The earlier view—concretely displayed in the child prodigy—was that the young should be introduced to adult life as soon as possible.[18]

But we cannot project modern attitudes or excesses about play onto Locke and Rousseau. They were hardly advocates of permissive parenting. Locke found fairytales too upsetting for children and believed that the offspring of the poor should work from the age of four in order to learn the tasks and discipline necessary to survive. His ideal was not free play but adult-controlled play. Rousseau's *Emile*, that manual for the education of boys, would today be considered authoritarian. Advocates of children's toys and games throughout the eighteenth and much of the nineteenth centuries stressed not spontaneity and imagination but moral and intellectual training. Toys were supposed to teach rationalist values and respect for property. These ideas reached only the literate and well-to-do. But they laid the foundation for the widely held modern idea that play and playthings are the child's way of learning how to be an adult. Toys did not cease serving the needs and imaginations of adults, but they began meeting adults' ideas about the needs of children.[19]

The Origins of the American Toybox

When we cross the Atlantic we find children who grew up in ways very similar to their European counterparts. In the colonies and the early American Republic, children had few toys and these remained within traditional European molds. Yet by the 1860s a nascent toy industry and a more child-centered family were beginning to reshape the meaning of play in the United States.

Colonial children enjoyed a mix of toys of aristocratic and folk origin. Their parents imported European dolls and even used them in trade with Native Americans. As early as 1733 English fashion dolls, brought by a ship's captain, were displayed at a Boston dressmaker's shop. A wooden horse on wheels from Sonneberg survives from the early-eighteenth-century childhood of a New York merchant's son. Affluent families favored imported toys, especially from Germany, from colonial times until World War I. Like their European counterparts, wealthy Americans commissioned cabinetmakers and other craftsmen to make dollhouses and Noah's Arks. Pennsylvania woodcarvers like Wilhelm Schimmel constructed rockinghorses, Noah's Arks, and Garden of Eden playsets in the tradition of their Swiss and South German ancestors. And examples of penny banks made of pottery go back at least to 1793, appealing especially to thrift-minded New England parents.

American children also made their own playthings as their European counterparts did. They improvised, creating fantasy worlds with whittled sticks, castoff bits of cloth, and clothespins. Cornhusks served as dolls and corncobs as building material for miniature log cabins or forts.[20]

As in Europe, American toys were relatively rare before the Civil War and many were designed as much for parents' needs as for the play of children. Teethers and rattles were supposed to quiet fussy babies. The few toys available for older children were supposed to distract them in that brief time before they could be put to work. Adults brought out playsets and dolls only on special holidays. For example, religious parents allowed their young to play with Noah's Arks only on Sundays or other religious days. With rare exceptions, early American parents did not look upon child's play as an important tool for learning adult roles. That was the purpose of the child's chores.

When toys did find their way into the hands of children, it was more often to the hands of boys than girls. In a survey of American portraits between 1830 and 1870, two-thirds of boys are shown with toys whereas only a fifth of girls are depicted with any playthings and these are mostly dolls. However, autobiographies of early-nineteenth-century American childhoods reveal that girls as well as boys climbed trees, coasted on sleds, and played mumblety-peg (a game testing skill at throwing a sharp knife).[21]

The industrialization that transformed American life in the generation after the Civil War changed the material worlds of children. Those lucky enough to visit toy shops or the new department and variety stores after 1865 were the first generation to imagine owning any significant number of playthings. But manufacturers thought first of the parents who would buy these toys. The nature of these toys and how they were presented to the adult customer tell us as much about childrearing ideals of the era as about the industry itself.

Only after the Civil War, when Americans directed their energies to rebuilding their families, did manufacturers begin producing toys in large numbers. Americans started applying techniques developed in other industries to mass-produce playthings. Makers of wood, metal, mechanical, and print and paper goods produced miniatures of their "adult" products or used waste materials to turn out modest batches of cheap children's playthings for Christmas. Pennsylvania upholsters made toy drums from scraps of fabric and wood. The McLoughlin Brothers used their experience as book printers to stamp out paper dolls and games. Samuel Leeds Allen manufactured farm equipment but diversified in 1889 with the famous Flexible Flyer, which, with its steerable handles, soon set the standard in sleds for winter fun.[22]

Because of simple construction, an extraordinary variety of toys could be cheaply produced. For example, in the 1860s, when cast iron began replacing tinplated toys, inexpensive and easily varied molds became available. In the 1870s manufacturers assembled cast-iron parts with bolts to make an extraordinary array of toy banks. Improved and cheaper brass clockwork mechanisms stimulated the production of a plethora of mechanical toys. J. & E. Stevens started an iron-founding business in 1843, but by 1850 they were producing a few toys. In 1869 Elisha Stevens joined with George Brown, a clock- and toymaker since 1856, to produce everything from five-cent toy watches to two-dollar iron fire engines. In 1868 Edward R. Ives, a son of a watchmaker from Plymouth, Connecticut, began manufacturing a vast array of windup toys, often on topical themes: fiddle players, performing bears, black preachers, General Grant smoking, and women's rights advocates.[23]

Even though new techniques allowed toymakers to offer an impressive array of products, the industry remained conservative. Most manufacturers produced toys only as a sideline. Playthings were almost an afterthought, hardly a certain source of profit to industrialists who well understood that parents were still unwilling or unable to devote much money to such frivolities. Generally American toymakers copied traditional homemade and handcrafted playthings much as European toymakers had long done. They introduced manufactured versions of homemade rattles, marbles, sleds, hobbyhorses, and wooden animal sets. Manufacturers mass-produced upper-class children's diversions (clockwork and sand-powered automata and fashion dolls, for example). They tapped into longings of middle-class American families for respectability and self-improvement by copying English "scientific" amusements, including magic lanterns (an early version of the slide projector). A few manufactured moralizing games of chance like the "Mansion of Happiness," which promised felicity for those players who successfully traversed the game board, avoiding spaces marked "dishonesty" and "anger." None of these playthings went beyond well-established parental expectations. They either fit adults' recollections of their own childhood playthings or met the goal of enlightened parents for educational play.[24]

The post–Civil War generation of toymakers did introduce some new concepts. These included sand molds for the growing family activity of seaside holidays. Children's roller skates followed soon after the adult version appeared in 1875. And manufacturers of adult velocipedes and bicycles also produced children's pedal vehicles. The popularity of these products reflected a new openness toward leisure among the hard-working business classes of New England and the growing belief of this group that recreation was good way to build ties between parents and children.[25] Still, these were only advance signs of much greater change to come later.

Not only were toy concepts generally conservative but toy manufacturers made little effort at marketing. Toymakers reflected the conventional production and marketing standards of the hardware trade. They shared little with the fashion clothing industry or with makers of souvenirs or other novelties. Most toys were standardized and changed relatively slowly. Toymakers made few appeals to the child's imagination and did not attempt to tap the sentimentality of parents. In fact, toys were often sold like general store dry goods. Sometimes toys shared wholesale catalog space with match holders and mousetraps. Even retail catalogs seldom displayed children using toys, nor did they feature brand names or use images of popular characters or celebrities to sell toys. Rather, catalogs let the objects speak for themselves.[26]

Manufacturers had not yet discovered the possibilities of selling personalities and imagination. Even if they had, few late-nineteenth-century parents would have approved of such toys. Toymakers sold objects whose purpose was conventional and well understood by the parents who purchased them. They were to be used by children to imitate adult roles, not to reenact the fantasy lives of heroes who had little to do with their own worlds.

The character of the toys and the advertising clearly reflected the fact that adults, not children, decided what toys would be purchased. Advertising copy stressed durability and educational value. The pull or mechanical toy was to distract the irritable or troublesome child. The mechanical bank, a big seller in the 1870s and 1880s, pleased adults because it taught children the valuable lesson of thrift while it entertained them. The mechanism, when wound and tripped by a coin, made a dog dance or a hunter shoot a wild bear. It coaxed "coins out of everybody's pocket" with the promise of entertainment.[27] The clockwork or sand-powered "tableaux" mass-produced by Albert Schoenhut from the 1870s, featuring moving figures of cobblers or peasants at work, not only were most meaningful to adults but were too expensive and fragile for free use by children. Enoch Rice's patented walking doll of 1862, which he dubbed the "Autoperipatetikos," was primarily a novelty attracting adults, as the pretentious name suggests. Stevens and Brown designed their mechanical toys to be child "quieters," dazzling the young child with the illusion that these windup figures moved on their own.

The rare topical "personality" incorporated in toys was far more likely to entertain the parent than the child. Mechanical figures, for example, featured grotesque or even frightening images (often in racist form) that may have given adults a mildly sadistic pleasure by scaring small children. This explains in part the popularity of the jack-in-the-box. In 1883 Ives and Blakeslee sold a clockwork toy portraying the defeated presidential candidate Samuel Tilden as "The Visiting Statesman," a bit of political satire that would have amused adults alone. These play objects gave children the sensation of being in charge as they wound up and directed their toys, but only adults understood the playthings' meaning. The joke was on the children.[28]

Even toys we might think clearly designed for young boys were advertised to adults. The Rifle Air Pistol, a toy that shot a "Steel dart" up to fifty feet, was advertised in 1875 as a "parlor game." One catalog in 1890 tried to sell an air rifle with the claim that it was "just the thing to make the neighbor's cat scratch and growl and doggy fly for home." This was not a toy for boys or even a "safe" weapon to prepare them for the manly skills of hunting or soldiering as the makers of the Daisy Air Rifle (or BB gun) would later claim. Boys may have been the ultimate recipients of these air-powered rifles, but in 1890 they were still sold to meet adult needs.[29]

Parents certainly expected playthings that imitated current adult roles. Not surprisingly, toys were primarily sex-stereotyped miniatures of contemporary adult tools and work settings. The Stevens and Brown catalog of 1872 offered toy hammers, saws, and even garden-tool sets for boys. The Ives company presented a full array of age-graded tool chests, toy printing presses, and steam engines in 1893. Girls' playthings were almost exclusively dolls and their accessories (including washing boards, coal hods and shovels, and irons for pressing clothes). Makers of metal toys like Stevens and Brown sold matched parlor furniture and tin kitchen sets, while others produced doll beds, carriages, and houses.[30]

Both boys' and girls' toys reflected conventional work roles and the tools that went with them. But they did so with no self-conscious effort to "train" the child. These toys were not often designed to encourage fantasy, nor were they linked to a wider world of popular culture. Playthings were largely miniatures of adult tools that allowed children to anticipate conventional adult roles.

Not only were toys miniatures of hardware and household goods, but manufacturers often sold them like dry goods. Excepting expensive foreign models, catalogs grouped dolls without trade names by material type (bisque, china, rubber, wood, and stockinet, a sock-like fabric stuffed with soft fiber). And heads, limbs, and bodies were often sold separately. Retailers assumed that parents would put the doll together (or buy parts to replace broken heads or limbs of older dolls). The customer was also expected to make (or more rarely purchase separately) the dolls' clothes. These handmade extras lowered the cost of toys for hard-pressed parents and allowed them and other relatives to contribute personally to children's play. Parents did not buy a toy line, a prepackaged set of dolls or play figures. They purchased generic parts for functional playthings much as a farmer would buy a mold board for his plow.

Finally, manufacturers targeted the middle-class, not the mass, market. Toymakers were relatively slow to widen the pool of customers with cheaper materials or production methods. The less affluent had their "penny toys" (wooden tops, tiny toy swords, and crude animals, for example), sold on the street or at newsstands. But makers of cast-iron mechanical toys and china dolls offered little to ordinary wage-earners. Clockwork novelties cost from one to about three dollars in an age when those amounts could easily be several days' wages. Few manufacturers saw much opportunity for sale to working-class parents who neither could afford these prices nor really wanted to encourage their children to play.[31]

Toymakers of the post–Civil War generation delivered what most middle-class parents expected in playthings for their children. They reflected a culture that respected the past, mechanical innovation, and utilitarian objects. Adults viewed the young and "their" toys as repositories of tradition. More practically, these parents understood playthings to be miniatures of the work-related objects of adults. There was little ambiguity about what should be saved from the past or learned about the present. And novelties of all kinds drew on the adult's sense of what was fun, not on the child's world of imagination or fantasy. But changes in the views of both toy producers and adult toy consumers were about to transform the play life of children.

Revolutions in Marketing and Childrearing

By 1900 playthings that had been rare were commonplace, and they increasingly appealed to the imagination and freedom of children. The dramatic upsurge of mass marketing in American society alongside the emergence of the child-centered family brought this change. Mechanized production and aggressive retailing may appear to have little to do with the building of family life around children. But the mass-marketed toy in the late Victorian nursery put these two worlds together.[32]

At the same time as general stores were selling child-sized coal hods and windup figures of adult celebrities, a revolution of mass production and marketing was taking place. After 1865 rapid industrialization delivered much more plentiful and varied goods to the consumer. New department stores, chain outlets, and mail-order catalogs made shopping a romantic adventure. New forms of advertising both stimulated demand and gave goods new meanings. Toward end of the nineteenth century these changes began to affect how toys were produced and sold.

Between 1860 and 1920 American manufacturing grew almost fourteenfold while the population merely tripled. A vast array of new machines increased output and made parts so precisely that they could be cheaply assembled into typewriters, wagons, and even toys. The result was that machine-made goods were often better and cheaper than homemade ones. Toys no longer depended on the invention and resources of parent or child but could be purchased at the nearby store. Probably even more important was the radical transformation of marketing. Webs of telegraph wire and railroads linked eastern factories to westward-moving consumers. Distant but efficient manufacturers drove local artisans out of the market and gave new power to large producers.[33]

From the late 1860s a veritable retail revolution began to eliminate general stores and many small specialty shops.[34] The department store led the way, making shopping into an exciting event. The first, A. T. Stewart's Marble Dry Goods Palace, which opened in New York in 1846, was followed by Lord and Taylor (1858), Macy's (1860), and Bloomingdale's (1872). These temples of consumption, located along train and trolley lines, attracted shoppers from all over New York City. Beginning in the 1870s department stores were built in the centers of cities across the nation. They attracted crowds of consumers with their eye-catching window displays and luxurious marble staircases and balconies. Open displays of goods, posted prices, newspaper advertising, free delivery, and liberal returns policies all encouraged spending.[35]

But in the 1880s most Americans still lived on farms or in small towns, far from the urban department stores. Montgomery Ward, a Chicago-based firm, began a mail-order business in 1872 to serve the needs of rural Americans. With the cooperation of the farmer's Grange movement, Ward built a catalog that by 1887 listed over 23,000 items, including toys. In that year Richard Sears and his partner Alvah Roebuck launched a catalog business selling watches by mail. Sears soon surpassed Ward, becoming the country folk's window on the new world of affluence. By 1916 the Sears catalog contained 1,636 pages crammed with pictures of goods of all kinds, also including toys.[36]

When Frank W. Woolworth opened his first variety store in 1879 in Lancaster, Pennsylvania, he created a third element in the retail revolution, the chain store. By combining low prices (eliminating the middleman) with convenient neighborhood outlets, Woolworth built a retailing empire. By 1909 there were 318 Woolworth's stores in the United States. Competitors included McCrory (1880), S. S. Kresge (1899), S. H. Kress (1906), and especially J. C. Penney (1902). These chain stores were far less elaborate than the mammoth department stores. But they were cheaply and quickly erected and conveniently located along the shopping arteries of the new suburbs and older market towns.

If the new stores and catalogs dazzled consumers with the promise of plenty, manufacturers still had to make them buy. As early as the 1850s innovative companies like Singer and McCormick tried to create brand-name identity by stamping their logos on their sewing machines and farm equipment. Later manufacturers won customers by packaging their flour, oatmeal, and other quite ordinary goods into colorful boxes with distinct trademarks. Newspapers and magazines also got out the manufacturers' message. In the 1890s Joseph Pulitzer built a newspaper combine by appealing to all members of the family. He introduced women's sections and sports pages and attracted advertisers of toys and other products with cut-rate ad prices. Similarly, Cyrus Curtis created a media empire by combining low-priced subscriptions with flashy advertisements. His *Ladies' Home Journal* and *Saturday Evening Post* became billboards to display new mass-marketed goods, ranging from safety razors and canned soup to candy bars, cars, and toys.[37]

Advertising agents developed new forms of persuasion. Once mere brokers of print space in newspapers, by the 1890s they had taken on the task of teaching consumers the glories of a new age of affluence. They informed Americans of the nutritional value of canned soup, the hygienic virtues of tooth brushing, and the pleasures of cigarettes. Advertising specialists used nostalgic themes and colorful personalities in order to establish a friendly image for impersonal corporations: the faces of wizened grandmothers sold coffee and cute Kewpies peddled Jell-O. Companies offered premiums of various kinds to persuade customers to try their products. Americans were sold on the virtues of affluence and spending. But advertisers also invited them to imagine themselves in new ways with the help of new goods—as modern, happy, important, and well-adjusted people.[38]

Toymakers were very much a part of this mass-market revolution. Like other manufacturers, toy companies expanded and rationalized production. Morton Converse, a maker of rockinghorses, wooden playsets, and puzzles, was a leader. In the 1880s, he introduced up-to-date cost-cutting machinery in his plant, created a formal planning department, and trained a highly specialized workforce. Converse made his Winchendon, Massachusetts, works into the "Nuremberg of America." In the 1890s other American toymakers introduced pressed steel and offset lithography to replace tinplate and hand-painted toys. By 1900 steel clockwork supplanted more fragile and expensive brass mechanisms. Increased mechanization, new materials, and innovative methods brought lower consumer prices and more toys to the American family. Many of these changes also reduced the time required for getting toys and games to retail shelves, allowing manufacturers to respond effectively to fads and current events.[39]

Inevitably these successes let the American toy industry win customers away from German and other imports. By the late 1870s Americans were taking the lead in cast-iron automata and banks. By 1890 American dollmakers like E. I. Horsman were making inroads in an industry long dominated by the French and Germans. American dollmakers began to replace ceramic dolls' heads with composition, a new, cheap, and relatively durable material made mostly of pressed sawdust, bran, and glue. Even though toy imports continued to grow until World War I shut down European suppliers, American toys were already developing their own distinct style and appeal. The wholesale value of American toys and games rose from $8.29 million in 1899 to $70.17 million in 1919, an astounding twelvefold increase in twenty years. The appearance of the trade journal *Playthings* in 1903 and the founding of the industry's own lobbying association, the Toy Manufacturers of the U.S.A., in 1916 signaled the growing self-confidence of American toymakers.[40]

Retailers too began to see the possibilities of an expanded toy market. F. A. O. Schwarz turned his modest toy shop of 1870 into a mammoth store offering 16,000 items by 1908. In 1875 Macy created the first toy section of a department store. In 1908 the Sigel-Cooper department store of Chicago offered a year-round toy department. Marshall Field joined them in 1912, followed rapidly by most other big department stores. Ward pictured toys in his catalog as early as 1885 and added dolls in 1886. Sears and Roebuck joined him with a small selection of dolls in 1895. While the Sears catalog of 1914 devoted only one of its 1,450 pages to toys and dolls, that number rose to 46 of 1,183 by 1931. Chain stores got into the act by offering cut-price toys. The Woolworth's chain eliminated the middleman by sending its own toy buyer to Germany in the 1890s. Soon thereafter, cheap American-made play novelties and dolls became a mainstay in dime stores.[41]

By the 1890s window displays at Christmas featured toys. The same artistry and imagination that went into romancing the market for fashion and furniture lured parents into department stores to buy the "latest thing" in toys. In 1909 *Playthings* advised retailers that window displays should stress "realism, originality and an artistic atmosphere" to pull in crowds. Especially to female customers, a display of a family gathered under the Christmas tree "must represent their ideal of themselves" and feature "articles that are desired by others." Toys, like fashionable clothing, were increasingly wrapped in the aura of romance and status.[42]

Toymakers themselves increasingly pursued expanding markets by offering diverse and constantly changing products. They created novel sales appeals that reflected and simulated the desires of modern consumers. The earliest tool to extend sales was the wholesale catalog, developed first in nineteenth-century Germany and appearing in the United States about 1860. These catalogs gave storekeepers access to a wide assortment of play goods and gradually displaced peddlers who had hawked toys from their carts. At first the catalogs were mostly price lists, often advertising toys from dozens of manufacturers. The jobbers who distributed them seldom identified goods by manufacturer for fear that larger stores would deal directly with toymakers. But gradually ambitious manufacturers found ways of bypassing the wholesale catalog and directly reaching retailer and consumer. Not only did they produce their own catalogs by the 1870s, but they adopted sales gimmicks used throughout the American consumer sector—brand-name logos, distinctive lines of products, and advertising.[43]

Especially after 1910, eager toy companies took out advertisements in a variety of popular family, women's, do-it-yourself, and even children's (especially boys') magazines. *Playthings* editors were early advocates of magazine promotions. Toy advertising copy, they advised in 1912, should be brief; a picture should "telegraph" the idea. And it should be directed toward the middle-class mother: "her woman's heart reads aright the heart of her child and knows what it most desires." In 1913 the Daisy Air Rifle company boasted to retailers that "We Advertise Daisies—You Sell Them." They promoted their rifles regularly in boys' magazines to make sure that "Daisies sell all the year round," not just at Christmas.[44]

These tactics also helped to change the character of the toy. Playthings increasingly presented a style or "personality" that customers easily identified with a specific company. Toys and dolls were no longer generic commodities like sacks of potatoes, nor were parents expected to assemble nondescript dolls' heads and limbs. Just as advertising and "friendly" trademarks created demand for Kellogg's Corn Flakes or Aunt Jemima Flour, so they made parents want a Horsman doll or an Ives fire truck.

Although the toy industry continued to sell primarily to adults, it increasingly recognized the potential of appealing directly to children. In 1913 *Toys and Novelties* rather cynically noted: "an advertisement to a child has no barriers to climb, no scruples to overcome." And *Playthings* declared: "the nervous temperament of the average American child and the rapidity with which it tires of things [ensures] a continuous outlet in this country" for toy sales. Another article instructed retailers on the value of displays "which enter far into the fields of fiction, of fairy lore, and of unrestrained fancy." These promotionals must appeal to children "to cause their wonderment, their desire for ownership and their immediate pleas to the kind friend who can and will buy almost anything the little yellow-topped boys cry for."[45]

Advertisements in popular magazines suggested that mothers take their offspring shopping with them. "Watch her, then you'll know which Horsman doll will bring her Christmas joy," suggested an ad in *McCall's*. A promotion for Knapp Toys in *Child's Life* taught children to show the ad to their parents. By the 1910s electric-train companies used boys' magazines to persuade children to order catalogs. "Take your Dad into partnership . . . Make him your pal" in the project of owning a Lionel train, suggested one ad. Few children were able to purchase toys with their own money. But toy companies recognized that in an era of growing permissiveness, children had influence over parent's spending.[46]

Just as American toymakers became more sophisticated in pushing the emotional buttons of American parents and children, they promoted American playthings over imported ones. When imports vanished during World War I and both patriotism and isolationism were on the rise, the Toy Manufacturers of the U.S.A. won permission from the government to keep producing toys. Despite government curtailment of other nonessentials, toymakers convinced officials that American-made toys were essential for building home-front morale. In anticipation of the return of German toys after the war, they pushed a buy-American campaign in 1918. Arcade Toys offered this homily:

> For pennies spent on little toys
> For U.S.'s own girls and boys
> In turn, of course, go back again
> To our own loyal work men.

Such patriotic appeals eased the way for American toymakers to win tariffs on foreign toys after the war. In 1914, 50 percent of toys sold in the United States were still imported. By 1939, 95 percent were American-made.[47]

In March 1916 *Playthings* advocated that July Fourth become a "second Christmas." Instead of dangerous fireworks, "give toys to the boys on Uncle Sam's Day." Uncle Sam was a "ready made Patron Saint of Fourth of July Toys." Industry leaders resurrected the idea with a new holiday, "Children's Day," for mid-June 1927. This time the symbol was to be Peter Pan as the summer version of Santa. Peter was to encourage wholesome summertime play and, of course, toy buying. As early as 1910 the toy trade press self-consciously pursued a strategy to make the industry less dependent upon Christmas sales. It boldly asserted that playthings were like women's fashions and men's sporting articles, objects to be purchased twelve months of the year. From the 1900s aggressive manufacturers and trade leaders tried to make gifts of play a regular part of a "healthy" child's growing up.[48]

Despite all this change, most toy companies remained small and conservative until after the mid-twentieth century. Retail markups were high (ideally four times the costs of production, according to one manual). Even *Playthings*, long noted for "progressive" marketing, advised against price cutting as a threat to the stability and profitability of the toy trade. Manufacturers generally stuck to limited product lines, restricting themselves to a comfortable niche in the market. Toymakers churned out mechanical banks and other common toys for decades with little alteration. Most continued to rely on wholesale jobbers like Butler Brothers and traveling sales agents to sell their products to retailers. Neighborhood toy shops held their own, despite the arrival of the chain or department stores. In fact, J. C. Penney offered no toys until 1921. Advertising in popular magazines was limited, even in holiday issues. Well into the twentieth century, knowledgeable retail sales staffs sold playthings directly to parents without advertising. And long after World War II, storekeepers kept toys in glass cases, protected from children's dirty fingers, but also separated from their longings to touch and possess.[49]

The toy industry was constrained by its limited marketing tools and by a prudent commitment to producing playthings that met parents' wishes. Still, the American toy industry certainly followed in the path of the mass-marketing revolution. The quantity, variety, and pace of production rose; sales outlets diversified; and, with trademarking and advertising, manufacturers reached out to the imaginations of consumers. All this meant more toys for children.

But the business success of toymakers would have been inconceivable without a new empathy of parents toward children's play. These feelings were rooted in new attitudes toward childrearing; and this new understanding of childhood was, in turn, profoundly connected to the marketing revolution. This revolution fundamentally transformed family life. As the modern factory, office, and store gradually pulled business out of the home, the family residence became a retreat from income-earning work. The transformation of the home from a workplace to a leisure place affected children profoundly. They were no longer automatically inducted into the labor force as they had been when work was done at home. And many of their traditional household duties disappeared with the spread of manufactured goods and new domestic technologies. It is true that in the late nineteenth century more of the young attended school. But they also had more time and energy for play.[50]

At the same time, a dramatic decrease in the number of children per household ironically also encouraged the sale of manufactured toys. In 1800 white American mothers bore an average of 7.04 children. That number dropped to 5.42 by 1851 and to 3.56 by 1900. The drift from the farm to the towns reduced the need for children as laborers. Because the commercial world required higher educational standards, children cost more to bring up, reducing the incentive to have large families. This decline of births had a class dimension. It tended to occur later in the working classes and among immigrants and blacks. In these groups income earned by children was often an important part of family survival. Nonetheless, the long-term trend of all American families was toward fewer offspring. For the individual child, reduction in family size meant that he or she was less likely to be surrounded by siblings and more likely to spend time alone and need distractions like toys. By the 1880s urban girls had reduced duties in the care of younger siblings. The result was both more time and greater need for doll play to teach child-care skills necessary for future maternal roles.[51]

These large-scale social and economic changes affected the way children learned values and skills. The training that traditionally had been part of work and interaction with siblings had to assume new forms. Play and toys became important parts of childrearing. From the 1830s the children of the affluent increasingly learned values and skills in the new refuge of the home. There, a small circle of family members gathered on Sunday evenings to play parlor games. Leisure increasingly replaced shared work to create family loyalties. Games and toys rather than work were supposed to train the child in the values of competition and honesty. In the home bereft of productive tasks and sometimes of baby siblings, playthings gave children a way to imitate adult roles.[52]

As families retreated into the domestic nest, parents tried to bind their children more closely to home and away from the play of the street and the authority of the peer group. Victorian middle-class parents attempted to break up "child societies," groups of youth that formed around apprentices at work or neighborhood gathering spots, free from the control of busy parents. In the mid-Victorian city these groups increasingly took on the cast of semi-criminal gangs. In the new economy middle-class parents (especially mothers) now had time to supervise their children's play. They wished their offspring to develop the character, discipline, and personal integrity that were essential for success as adults. Thus parents had an incentive to isolate their children from the anarchic influence of the street. Increasingly, middle-class homes provided space for nurseries and playrooms. Playthings served as "antidotes for loneliness" as they became substitutes for the free play of the "child society." Toys helped to make the home an attractive and acceptable alternative to the rowdyism of street society.[53]

When affluent Victorian parents withdrew their children from the wider society, they also attempted to shelter them from early contact with adult activities and experiences. Precocious children were now out of fashion. Families abandoned the custom of bringing young children on mothers' social visits or fathers' hunting trips as the idea of age-appropriate activity took hold. Ideally the young were isolated in age-based grades in school. The same segmentation took place in children's literature. Separate magazines for children, adolescents, and young adults all appeared in the nineteenth century. Toys had also to fit the age. Blocks and checkers would teach young children "gentle manners," argued William Dewees in 1826. Little boys should have access to rockinghorses only sparingly to avoid overexcitement unfitting for their age. Toys became tools of the parents' attempt to isolate and rear the child according to parental aims and ambitions.[54]

While toys served the parents' stern goals of training and isolating the child, by midcentury adults also began to recognize that their wealth and domestic comfort allowed their children a less regimented growing up than they had experienced. A "present for a good boy" more than physical punishment became the "progressive" parents' technique for shaping children's behavior.[55] Serious mothers began to question both their own austere upbringings and the competitive and materialistic worlds of their husbands. Some expressed these doubts in romantic notions about childhood as a time of imagination and freedom from the cares of the harsh business world. As a result, toys became more "playful" and more celebratory of childhood as the nineteenth century wore on.

While broad economic and social change surely set the context for the transformation of childrearing, powerful ideas also defined the new childhood. The followers of Locke and Rousseau tried to make play an educational exercise indirectly controlled by parents. But the moralizing content of that education gradually, even if never completely, gave way to a greater indulgence in the imagination and free activity of children. The influential New England Protestant reformer Horace Bushnell insisted in 1847 that the "genuinely Christian parent" should "show a generous sympathy with the plays of his children." The ideal of self-discipline, which had often guided the success of the early Victorian middle-class family, eased after midcentury, with a new stress on instinct and spontaneity in play.[56]

If nineteenth-century adults felt uneasy about enjoying pleasure themselves, they could experience it through their children. Victorian children's literature in particular reveals this trend. From the late 1840s the fairytales of Hans Christian Andersen began to supplant the moralistic tales of Puritan writers. Later Victorians celebrated the spontaneity of youth in Lewis Carroll's *Alice in Wonderland* (1865) and Thomas Aldrich's *The Story of a Bad Boy* (1870). The amusements and literary fantasy adults had traditionally enjoyed were increasingly shifted to children. Thus medieval tales of adventure and romance like Robin Hood and St. George became the preserve of children rather than their parents. When parents said yes to fun for children, they opened the way for a whole range of playthings that no longer taught the discipline and skill of adults but strove to capture the essence and spirit of youth.[57]

This loosening of the grip of parents over children's time in the second half of the nineteenth century was only relative to the past and was restricted to the comfortable classes. The image of free play hardly described the working-class or African-American childhood which even in 1900 was frequently over by age ten. Many American children, especially in rural areas, enjoyed relatively unorganized play with few toys, books, or other manufactured or commercial amusements into the twentieth century. These children used cans for "footballs" and played hopscotch on the street. For generations children have preserved, with little change, traditional games and songs. American children played blindman's buff and hide and seek just about as much in the 1950s as in 1900. Games like tag scarcely changed in three centuries. Still, the trend was clear. Parents increasingly accepted play rather than work to teach the young values and skills. And manufactured toys increasingly were the tools of this learning.[58]

Nevertheless, these emerging principles of childrearing from the mid-nineteenth century produced a legacy of contradictions that remains with us today. Childhood was to be a time of home-centered training, but the young used things produced outside the home. Children were to learn to be productive, not in work or in training for a parent's trade, but in purposive play. Parents became much more self-conscious about childrearing and about how to prepare the young for a complex and changing future, while also insisting that childhood was a time of imagination and protection from the adult world. Children were expected to learn the rational culture of self-control in the isolation of the nursery, while they were also encouraged to enjoy the spontaneity and the pleasures of youth. Toymakers accommodated these contradictions in the play-things they promoted and sold to adults. Toys were both vehicles to introduce the "real world" and fantasy objects shut off from that world in the child's "secret garden."

The New Toybox

The twin revolutions in mass marketing and childrearing came together in the contents of the late-Victorian toybox. While exploit-ing the new techniques of selling, toymakers manufactured play-things that incorporated new images of childhood and children. This is well illustrated by the evolution of two pioneering manu-facturers, Charles M. Crandall of New York and Albert Schoenhut of Philadelphia. They were leaders in the transition from the con-ventional production of European-style toys sold like dry goods to the mass production of distinctly American playthings advertised as novelties and appealing to the new ideas of childrearing.

As a toymaker, Charles Crandall was definitely ahead of his time. He was quick to adapt new technology to a changing market. When a croquet craze swept the Northeast in the late 1860s, tapping the longing for family togetherness and wholesome fun following the bitter divisions of the Civil War, Crandall was quick to turn his wood goods factory to the production of croquet sets. But he was best known for a new kind of children's building blocks that he marketed in 1867. Crandall found that the "tongue and groove" construction that had been recently invented to interlock the sides of wood boxes could also fasten together children's blocks. Machine-cut tabs alternating with grooves could easily and securely link blocks in a "thousand and one" ways. This was the ancestor of the modern Lego.[59]

Building blocks had taught basic reasoning to small children of an enlightened elite since Locke's day. But Crandall did more than provide a sophisticated version of this traditional learning tool. His toys appealed to a new, more playful image of childhood. By 1874 he was selling Expression Blocks, with which the child could create comical expressions by combining pieces representing parts of the face in various ways. His Wide Awake Alphabet Blocks of 1877 consisted of twenty-six little wooden men representing letters that could be interlocked in amusing patterns.

A year earlier he had introduced a jointed wood figure of "Ye Hero of '76" (complete with American flag) for the celebration of the nation's centennial. This novelty item was an adaptation of similarly jointed figures of acrobats and menagerie animals which could be manipulated into "almost numberless interesting and amusing positions." But the "Hero of '76" had the added appeal of timeliness. Crandall exploited contemporary racism when he manufactured "Two Jolly Blacks"—jointed figures which, when pulled on a wooden base, moved in distorted ways. And, like others after the Civil War, he was not above producing a toy cannon (operated by a rubber band) that could hit a "fort" made of Crandall blocks at twenty-five feet. By 1879 Crandall offered twenty-eight sets of interlocking building blocks and jointed figures. He showed his modern approach to marketing his toys when he advertised in the *American Agriculturalist,* an important magazine read by farming families in the 1870s. Crandall added variety, novelty, fantasy, humor, timeliness, and even appeals to boyish aggression to his range of educational blocks and wooden figures.[60]

One of Crandall's most daring toys was the District School, introduced in 1876. It was a facsimile of the floor plan of a country schoolhouse with flexible figures. Children, the advertising claimed:

will laugh over this group of teachers and scholars . . . Thousands of parents will recall with great delight their own experiences in child-

hood . . . The grave master seated by the desk, with his whisking stick
. . . ; the boys and girls, with books having REAL words which can be
used in helping the wee urchins at home to read; the "little lamb" that
has followed his young owner into the school; the "dunce" and his
cap; and the altogether comical appearance of the whole company
make this one of the most attractive toys of Crandall's invention.[61]

In many ways Crandall anticipated later toymakers. He promised
free play with interlocking pieces and touted his toys as "an educational advantage." Yet his playsets tended to program play and
encourage multiple purchases. He promised that children would
learn their ABCs while constructing grotesque figures out of the
images in blocks. The young were to play school while making the
teacher look funny. Crandall tapped into the contradictions of late-
Victorian childrearing—its didacticism and its underlying permissiveness.

Albert Schoenhut borrowed much from Charles Crandall. But he
went much further in diversifying his products. Schoenhut was a
German immigrant who arrived in Philadelphia in 1866 with a job
repairing toy pianos at Wanamaker's department store. This son of
a toymaker was soon importing German toys. By 1872 he had
acquired enough capital to establish his own company specializing
in fabricating high-quality toy pianos and other musical toys. This
hardly made Schoenhut special. Expensive novelties were a well-
established trade in Germany, and wealthy Americans were willing
to pay for such handcrafted luxuries. Although in the 1880s he
branched out to make wooden play shooting galleries and even real
firefighting equipment, his stock-in-trade remained toy musical instruments.[62]

Late in his career, however, Schoenhut made a major change in
business philosophy when he broke from his long-held dedication
to a limited line of traditional German-style musical toys. In 1902
he expanded his production to infant and toddler toys. Schoenhut's
first offering was the Polly Dolly, a large papier-mâché roly-poly
female figure with a weighted bottom. In itself this was a minor
innovation. But he turned this basic toy into a line of goods, with
models changing yearly. By 1909 he had manufactured seventy
Polly Dollies, including a Santa Claus and a Dutch girl and boy. The
Polly Dolly was advertised as a child's "first toy," a standard that

celebrated the playfulness of infancy. It invited the child to knock down the figure and watch it stand up again. This toy acknowledged infantile aggression and its need for expression, while also responding to a growing sentimentality toward small children by evoking images of a happy world of child's play in the eyes of the parents.[63]

In 1903 Schoenhut introduced his greatest success, the Humpty Dumpty Circus. This wooden playset with whimsical animals, clowns, and acrobats was designed for children who had outgrown their Polly Dollies. In some ways it was merely an elaboration of a traditional menagerie of wooden animals and wagon. Like Crandall's before him, Schoenhut's wooden animals and figures were jointed. But when Schoenhut introduced heavy rubber cords to attach head and limbs to the torso, children could pose Schoenhut's circus animals and clowns in "life like or grotesque attitudes." Moreover, Schoenhut's circus figures had a distinctive look. They were brightly painted figures with whimsical facial expressions.

Advertising stressed that these toys were educational, appealing to parental desires that children be well prepared for school: "In the Kindergarten the educational training of eye and hand are more and more appreciated the longer these toys are used, especially when the children are encouraged to work out their own ideas by means of the figures." But by the 1910 catalog the circus could no longer be called a kindergarten toy if it ever really had fit that didactic standard. The catalog that year featured a twenty-five-piece "circus" called Humpty Dumpty in Africa, complete with a likeness of Theodore Roosevelt with black guide that recalled Teddy's 1909 safari. This circus no longer let children "work out their own ideas." Rather, it told them how to play in reenacting the romantic adventures of a contemporary hero. This toy anticipated the modern action-figure playset.[64]

The Schoenhut company was also a leader in introducing character images into its circus and Polly Dolly lines. Among the earlier offerings were the faces of the German comic strip personalities, Max and Moritz (1907) and Tootsie Wootsie (1911). Schoenhut's 1911 catalog was also noteworthy for illustrations of happy children playing. The toy no longer was merely an object. Now it expressed the joys of youth. The advertising for the circus sets became progressively more engaging. In 1915 circuses were displayed in a series of "acts" beginning with the cheapest set and culminating in the final "act," a forty-four-piece circus complete with tent and ring. The appeal was supplemented with little poems: "Then there's the goat who is rather rude, with the awful flashy nigger dude." The circus sold in sets priced at from one to thirty-five dollars. The child participated in the fun of the spectacle and the promise of more with the purchase of expensive sets.[65]

The 1911 catalog offered an "unbreakable" wooden doll, another expansion of Schoenhut's line. Here Schoenhut made the full complement of contradictory appeals to parents. Advertising stressed the European lineage of these wooden dolls. Albert's grandfather had been a dollmaker as far back as 1796. At the same time, the catalog claimed that the new doll was modern. It did not have the traditional "doll face" but a countenance that was "artistically modelled" to look like a real child that its owner would want to play with. An advertisement in 1914 bragged that the Schoenhut doll was a "welcome American invention," not a foreign face alien to American youth, and promised that it would "gladden the hearts of our dear little ones." The Schoenhut company upgraded this line with a walking doll in 1917 despite its earlier pride in simple construction. In that year the company also hired Katherine Rauser as "couturier" of its dolls, drawing on an "un-American" desire for European snob appeal.[66]

In the 1910s the company appealed also to small boys and their fathers with a growing array of construction toys and wood cars and trucks. It also began to carry gun-and-target sets. The Big Game Hunter, recalling Teddy Roosevelt's exploits, came with air rifles equipped with wood bullets. In 1915 the Submarine and Dreadnought appeared in time to celebrate the naval war in Europe. Schoenhut, however, had not abandoned its upscale and educational market. The company still made toy pianos tuned to "concert pitch" with keys "properly spaced." Its advertising prominently displayed the trademark logo embossed on the piano's front as a symbol of quality and tradition.[67]

In the 1920s Schoenhut was one of the most important toy companies in the United States. It bragged of the five-and-a-half acres of floor space in its factories. Yet Schoenhut's toys were large and expensive, and thus had a limited market. The animals in the Humpty Dumpty Circus were six to eight inches high, and the circus tent was about three-and-a-half feet long. The Humpty Dumpty in Africa retailed for twelve dollars in 1911 (nearly a week's wages for an ordinary factory worker.) This placed Schoenhut at a disadvantage in a mass market, especially when faced with the flashy mechanical toys offered by upstarts like Louis Marx in the 1920s. The company may well have been a victim of its quality. Schoenhut toys easily survived one child's play and were passed on to the next. Today they are highly valued by collectors. In the 1920s Schoenhut tried to keep up with the times by licensing comic strip characters from "Bringing Up Father." It brought out a cheaper line of dolls. The company even produced smaller and cheaper circus animals to appeal to a less affluent market. But the Albert Schoenhut Company disappeared in 1934, a victim of the Depression.[68]

The experience of Schoenhut reflects a pattern that characterized many successful toy companies that emerged in the generation around 1900. Schoenhut transformed itself from a small producer of expensive toy pianos into a multi-line manufacturer of toys for all ages and both sexes. Schoenhut traded on its "quality" image and stuck to "unbreakable" construction and its reputation as a wood specialist. Yet it embraced many of the tricks for expanding markets that were common in other consumer-goods industries. It created a market niche with its Humpty Dumpty Circus. But it offered this "must have" classic in a wide price range. Schoenhut encouraged "add-ons" and "upgrades" with annual "model changes" in the line of wood animals, figures, and accessories. It appealed to parents by touting its approval by educators. But it also exploited adults' attraction to topical personalities like Teddy Roosevelt and popular fictional and comic characters. Schoenhut drew on the snob appeal of its German lineage while also bragging of its "American" inventiveness.

Perhaps more than anything else, Schoenhut toys projected an image of childish innocence and fantasy. These toys and dolls definitely were for children, not adults. And, while they promised education, they were not didactic but fun, and reflected an emerging image of the child as playful and capable of choice. These sales tactics were the stock-in-trade of a successful consumer industry in these years. But they worked because they tapped into the rich, often contradictory, notions that parents held about childrearing.

The Gift of Santa

Late Victorian toys were more than reflections of a new world of technology and aggressive marketing or even of changing modes of childrearing. They were first and foremost *gifts*. And they were usually presented at Christmas. The distinctively modern idea of Santa's sack of toys expresses well the linkage between these new worlds of consumerism and childhood.

The child's anxious anticipation of Santa's visit is really quite recent. Until the mid-1800s Christmas was not even celebrated in parts of the United States because of Puritan scruples against the "pagan" excesses of the winter festival of traditional Catholicism. The story of the nativity was not even taught in most Protestant Sunday Schools until the 1850s. To be sure, European celebrations were observed where Puritan influences were weak, especially in the Old South. But even there Christmas was largely a sharing of food and drink. Children and their playthings had no special role. When presents were exchanged, they were homemade, traditional, and often sweets or knitted items rather than playthings. After about 1820 the giving of playthings became more common, but few presents were manufactured toys before the Civil War. It was only between 1837 and 1890 that individual states began to recognize Christmas as a legal holiday. Only in the 1880s do we see fully expressed that wonderful contradiction: wide-eyed children unwrapping gifts of store-bought toy trumpets and dolls that in their imaginations had come from Santa's sack.[69]

Nevertheless, it is not true that commerce corrupted the family celebration of Christmas. The two were inextricably linked in the nineteenth century. In 1843 Charles Dickens told his English readers in "A Christmas Carol" that the miserly Scrooge had recovered his humanity when he learned to share his wealth and find happiness in the warmth of the family. This was not an indictment against a commercialized Christmas. The Christmas spirit meant the enjoyment (not merely sharing) of material goods that Scrooge could buy.

Family togetherness (praised in the scene of the Cratchits' Christmas dinner) merged with the celebration of the affluence that industrial capitalism brought. It was Scrooge's gifts after all that brought the Cratchits joy. His wealth unshared and unspent was evil and pathetic. But Scrooge, the archetypical capitalist, was redeemed through his learning to give and to enjoy. It was not hard for the reader to conclude that the accumulation of wealth was justified if it was well spent on Christmas gifts.[70]

The meaning of presents has changed greatly in modern times. Anthropologists tell us that all societies exchange gifts, symbolizing and affirming social ties. Gifts express messages of loyalty, solidarity, and even power between people on different rungs of the social ladder. In medieval England inferiors gave Christmas presents to superiors. In the American South before the Civil War, plantation owners sometimes gave their slaves gifts at Christmas. Leaders of competing kinship groups exchanged presents as tokens of peace.[71]

The market society that emerged fully in the nineteenth century deemphasized these bonds of hierarchy and group solidarity. Such sentiments were inconsistent with the modern notions of individual competition and impersonal commerce. Yet the gift continued to play a major role in holidays. But gift-giving, especially to children, served quite different purposes. The social bonds that presents affirmed were less between groups or unequal individuals within a community. Instead, gifts created emotional ties within the nuclear family. Thus Christmas ceased being a communal festival. Rather, it became a celebration of family home life. Symbols of this sentimental union of parents and children included the Christmas tree and yule log. These "traditional" tokens of family solidarity were widely adopted in the Anglo-American world only in the Victorian era. They reinforced the separation of family and outsiders and made the holiday one of domestic intimacy.[72]

Most important was the role played by the child in the new rituals of Christmas gift-giving. It was Tiny Tim who melted the heart of Scrooge. This emphasis on youth is rooted in deep antiquity. Christmas and New Year's are paired holidays appealing to the universal human need for renewal and rebirth and for a special time in which daily cares are suspended. But the child took on added significance in nineteenth-century observances. The young symbolized the intimacy and innocence of family against the increasingly impersonal society that surrounded it. The child became a visible reminder of the adult's own youth and the hope of the future. The child was also the fruit of the marital bond and a reason for family life. The child was received as innocent and deserving, separate and in need of protection from the faceless forces of industry and commerce. Parents gave selflessly to their children, with no expectation of profit as required in a business contract. They expressed their longing for an emotional life apart from the market in an act that was utterly contrary to economic behavior.[73]

The toy had become a wonderful expression of a complex blend of family ideals. The plaything itself was domesticated in modern times. The giant automata, nativity scenes, and even adult-sized carousels that had served as props of medieval village festivals were miniaturized, placed in the home, and eventually turned over to children. Icons of community solidarity became, as modern toys, the talismans of parent-child bonding.

At the same time, playthings gave expression to the joys of private affluence. Christmas had long given permission for extravagance—eating, drinking, and loafing—as did other Carnivalesque festivals. But in the nineteenth century these celebrations of indulgence were increasingly focused on the family, in parents pampering children. The shower of gifts became a way of demonstrating personal affluence. And it did so without seeming to deny the work ethic or "normal" values of thrift. The social critic Thorstein Veblen in 1898 gave this phenomenon a name—"vicarious consumption." He meant that American businessmen displayed their wealth by showering their wives with luxuries without undermining their images of themselves as thrifty and hard-working. The same principle fit parental gift-giving to children. When parents bestowed presents on their offspring, they also attempted to share their excitement with the wider world of new things. In effect, money earned in the market was transformed through the child's presents into a sentiment of family life radically separate from that market.[74]

These trends favored the practice of purchasing toys rather than hand-making them. As industrialism advanced and Americans took factory and office jobs, the skills and time that formerly had made possible handmade dolls and hobbyhorses disappeared. The farmer might have had weeks after the harvest to work on home-crafted toys. But urbanized employees had no such opportunity, and many lacked the skills and probably even the desire to try. Store-bought toys had more variety and expressed new ideas. These playthings attracted late nineteenth-century parents in the same way as did new ready-to-wear fashions.[75]

But commercial toys as Christmas gifts also produced ambivalence: How could manufactured playthings be an expression of personal love when they were no longer made by the hand of the giver? What, besides money with its origin in the marketplace, was involved to "personalize" the gift? What was an appropriate gift? How could such playthings, so obviously products of the faceless world of machines and commerce, express the very opposite, the unique family?[76]

It is here that the rise of Santa Claus can be understood. He represented the new sentimentality toward children but also the modern embrace of abundance in a new consumer culture. He removed the ambivalence parents felt about the connection between the worlds of home and market by disguising the commercial origins of Christmas toys. His helpers at the North Pole fashioned these playthings for good little boys and girls.

Santa changed dramatically with the coming of the child-centered family. The old Father Christmas, Christ Child (that is, Christ Kindel or Kris Kringle), and St. Nicholas (Sinter Klass), handed down from Europe, were far different characters from the personality portrayed in Clement Moore's famous poem of 1822, "A Visit from St. Nicholas." And that new Americanized Santa was firmly rooted in the American psyche only with Thomas Nast's cartoon of 1863 showing the familiar jolly fat man. The traditional English Father Christmas had no specific role as gift-giver. He vaguely represented the traditional twelve-day festival of merriment and excess. On the Continent, the Christ Child traditionally delivered gifts to the young (just as Christ was brought presents). St. Nicholas was a fourth-century bishop from Myra in what is now Turkey. In the Dutch setting he became Sinter Klass, a gift-giver on St. Nicholas Day, December 6. Dutch settlers in New York adopted this tradition, and by the early nineteenth century blended it with

English traditions of the jovial Father Christmas to create Santa Claus.[77]

Early versions of St. Nick were clearly instruments of parental control, used both to threaten and to reward children. In the Netherlands St. Nicholas appeared with the mysterious "Black Peter," who punished naughty children. Sometimes Dutch villagers played this role and actually used the switch on disobedient children. In some characterizations St. Nicholas's bag was half filled with gifts and half with switches. This image of Santa as judge survives in the twentieth century when parents warn children to be good or Santa will pass up their house on Christmas eve. But the emphasis gradually has shifted to the concept of Santa as all-forgiving benefactor. An essay in *Parents' Magazine* (1926) advised that "we must not make a policeman" of Santa Claus. If he "doesn't know that we didn't mean to be naughty—then who does? He must know that we want truly to be good most of the time, else why should he want so heavily to reward us."[78]

The new Santa also clearly represented abundance, from his bottomless bag of gifts to his cheery cheeks and plump belly. He recalled the ancient god of pleasure, Bacchus. Santa was and is a secular god, all knowing, prayed to (in letters at least), and capable of supernatural feats on Christmas Eve. But he brings a salvation in toys. Parents teach their children to believe that Santa will bring them heaps of toys which no one had to sacrifice or even pay for.[79]

Santa became an important part of parents' solution to the problem of manufactured toys. He essentially disguised the marketplace origin of gifts and suffused them with the mystery and magic of his workshop. He even hid the indulgence of parents from the children and to some extent from the parents themselves. After all, Santa, not Mommy and Daddy, brought this abundance. The custom of writing to Santa or presenting him with a list of wants helped parents to know what to buy at a time when traditional handmade gifts were no longer obvious choices. Again this disguised the linkage between commerce and childhood. From the 1880s his presents were wrapped (no longer looking like goods on the store shelf), adding to the mystery and hiding still more the commercial origins of toys.

But the real linkage of Santa and commerce was never fully obscured, and in the twentieth century the commercialization of Santa has become brazen. In 1875 F. A. O. Schwarz used a dressed-up Santa to promote seasonal toy sales. But Santa became a regular holiday feature of big city stores only in the mid-1890s. Even then he was relegated to toy departments in unadorned store basements, until his status rose in the 1910s, when toys were moved to more elegant surroundings on the higher floors. Publicity offices arranged for his arrival by train from the North Pole. Store officials escorted him from the station with great fanfare to a throne in toy departments attended by a court of elves. Santa had become part of the pageantry of the department store in its heyday. By the late 1920s Santa Claus even had his own talk shows on radio. Macy's Thanksgiving Parade ended with Santa's appearance, kicking off what *Playthings* called in 1930 the "buying season" for Christmas toys. Santa linked the magic of childhood with the gift of plenty. Without him, Christmas might have become more crassly materialistic and children more hard-nosed about their presents. But with him, all members of the family could forget just how materialistic they had become.[80]

By the last quarter of the nineteenth century playthings had become an important opportunity for business and an increasing concern of parents. No longer were they rare or merely afterthoughts of busy adults. As toys ceased to be the shared play objects of communities or baubles of adult amusement passed down absentmindedly to children, they became the possessions of the young. Even so, toys were almost always gifts from adults and thus reflected adults' ambivalence. Should the toy be preparation for the "real world" or an imaginative retreat from it? Through gifts of toys parents expressed their need to recall their own youth. Yet parents also sought to use toys to say "We are up-to-date and optimistic about the future." Some toys evoked feelings of nostalgia and others of fashion. Toy manufacturers tapped into this ambiguity. They offered education and fantasy, the past and the current.

By the beginning of the twentieth century the child's right to a toybox had been established, and for many, especially from the middle class, it was filled up. Many of the toys that adults now look back on with nostalgia and think of as timeless were in fact added to the box between 1900 and 1940. Some of these playthings were inspired by parents' ideas of the child's future; others by sentimental notions of the innocence of childhood; still others by the theories of educators and child-development specialists. In all their differences, these toys reflected not a golden age of childhood but ambiguous and even conflicting ideas about what childhood should be.

3 SHAPING THE CHILD'S FUTURE

As THE WORK, tools, and attitudes of adults were transformed in the nineteenth century, new toys appeared to imitate those changes. The playthings of the 1900s through the 1930s also responded to trends in adult life. Horse-and-buggy toys and Victorian sewing dolls were replaced by miniature cars and lovable baby dolls. But there was a subtle difference: the new toys of the early twentieth century trained as much for the future as for the present world of adults. In a time of unprecedented change, few serious middle-class parents could predict exactly what their children's lives would be like. But they were generally confident that the future world would be a "better" one *if* their children were properly prepared. This preparation would certainly not come from playing with the toys of the parents' generation. Toys had to be up-to-date, reflecting the latest technology available in business and in the home. But they had also to train for the future by inculcating values of optimism and responsibility, teaching children to look forward to their eventual roles as men and women in a new society.

Yet in the first decade of the twentieth century manufacturers began to address messages to young people's imaginations rather than just parents' concerns.[1] Toymakers realized that children had limited financial autonomy but also recognized their unlimited desires. As early as the 1870s *Youth's Companion* offered toys as payment for selling subscriptions to the magazine. Toymakers used such awards to introduce children to new lines of play products. For example, *American Boy* in 1916 offered erector sets, a Daisy Air Rifle, a rotary press, and even a Big Dick machine gun to boys who sold subscriptions. Girls, in 1912, could earn a Lettie Lane Doll House if they found three family friends to sign up for the *Ladies' Home Journal*.

Parents also began to give children allowances, less as payment for household chores than as a way to learn how to select and purchase consumer goods. Developing shopping skills was becoming an important part of growing up. Toymakers knew that many of these purchases would be playthings. They understood that by appealing to both the expectations of parents and the imaginations of children they could increase their sales. Even more promising were toys that claimed to unite parent and child in the shared joy of electric trains or modern dollhouses.[2]

These toys that trained for the future were not the old child quieters designed for toddlers. Rather they were manufactured for children old enough to understand their future roles and independent enough to take part in the purchasing decision. Young people in a less affluent age would have been working at age eleven or twelve, but now they were given toys to learn adult roles in play rather than at work. In the 1910s advertisements encouraged older boys to share model-railroad and construction-toy catalogs with friends and to join together to purchase more expensive equipment. By the early 1930s *Playthings* looked to toy consumers between the ages of ten and seventeen as a growth market. Science in schools had stimulated sales of toy microscopes, and model airplane clubs (sponsored by department stores) also sparked sales.[3]

The road to the future through play would be sharply divided for boys and girls. Toys designed for boys idealized technology, constant innovation, and the values of competition and teamwork. Those for girls were mostly dolls and were designed to train girls to become "modern" housewives and nurturing mothers, to cultivate personal relationships with friends, and to be charming and attractive to adults. The gender divide shaped the vision of the future: to boys it promised an exciting public world of mechanical progress, and to girls a personal life of warm relationships and fashion. The boys' toybox mirrored the world of science and industrial production, the girls' a consumerism of modern homemaking and personal vitality.

Toys for both sexes also taught the art, habit, and joy of spending. Boys and girls learned the pride of having a "complete set" of Buddy "L" trucks or Patsy dolls. Advertisers encouraged buying the next, more sophisticated, more "grown-up" toy. Toys celebrated the full range of consumer goods available to adults. The journalist James Fri wrote in glowing terms of the "seven acres" of toys displayed at the New York toy fair of 1937: "Every aspect of the more abundant American life has been reproduced in realistic miniatures, at low prices."[4] In their very different ways, girls and boys learned to keep up with the latest trends conforming to their future roles. The toys introduced in the years between 1900 and 1930 defined the childhoods of many Americans and helped shape their sense of self and society well into the midcentury.

Toys for Boys

Toys are often excellent witnesses to change, especially in gender roles. Boys imitated men in their use of playthings. And parents offered safe and small-scale renditions of male tools to allow boys to practice being grown up. For example, as "artistic" home gardening became popular among urban middle-class men soon after the Civil War, toy catalogs offered toy gardening tools mostly for young boys.[5] But the imitative character of toys began to change in the late nineteenth century. Manufactured playthings no longer were merely miniatures of adult male objects. Rather they were self-consciously imbedded with messages about gender roles, technology, and business. They were designed to teach expectations about the future.

Many boys' toys in the forty years after 1900 celebrated technological change. They closely reflected trends in transportation, science, and construction. It would be surprising if it had been otherwise, for this was surely the most dramatically innovative period in the history of machines. Improvements in electric power led to electric trolleys and the modern electric motor in 1888. The

1885 invention of the internal combustion engine made possible the automobile by 1886, the cheap Model-T Ford in 1908, and the practical gasoline farm tractor by 1913. The airplane's appearance in 1902 initiated the era of winged flight. The invention of roll photographic film in 1888 and the movie camera in 1892 gave the masses the personal snapshot and the entertainment of the moving picture. The radio appeared first as a "wireless telegraph" in 1896; then, in the fifteen years after the invention of the vacuum tube in 1906, the modern "voice" radio emerged. By 1925 there was even experimental television. Less heralded improvements in telephone exchanges and the advent of long-distance calls made this invention of 1876 a common household appliance by the 1900s. New light bulb design and improved generation of electric power in the 1900s led the way for a sixteenfold increase in the use of light bulbs between 1910 and 1930.[6]

Boys' playthings offered in miniature virtually every one of these innovations, from toy cars and airplanes to child-sized cameras and radios. More subtly, they reflected male fascination with a technological future. These toys appeared in the era of the founding of *Popular Mechanics* (1902) and similar magazines that offered ordinary men inspiring articles about new technology and the thrill of understanding and using these new gadgets. Popular books offered the young instruction in making electrical devices at home (tomato can batteries, for example). The 1900s saw the beginning of the do-it-yourself movement, when men took on the task of home improvement and repair in basement workshops. Not surprisingly, toys followed suit and encouraged boys to try their hands at constructing the gadgets of the new age. Chemistry sets and toy airports prepared boys for an optimistic world of new machines and business success.[7]

This was a period in which the media and educators encouraged fathers to spend more time with their sons. The pressures of work may have prevented many fathers from following this advice, and surveys showed that boys still preferred their mothers. But men did embrace the idea of playing with their sons, especially if the play cultivated male gender roles. And a key to that play was the shared celebration of technological progress in miniatures.[8]

From the 1910s to the 1960s model trains were the capstone toys for many middle-class American boys. The appeal of the train was even older. Cast-iron replicas of locomotives and pull-toy trains were common in the 1870s. Clockwork self-propelled trains appeared from 1880, and toymakers offered miniature steam locomotives as early as 1872. But the far more flexible and exciting electric train was a late invention. Joshua Lionel Cowen is credited with the first in 1901: a miniature electric trolley that used dry cell batteries. By 1906 Cowen had developed an electric transformer capable of adapting household current to his now more elaborate train sets. That development propelled his Lionel trains into long-lasting dominance. American Flyer, Hubley, Ives, and the cut-price Louis Marx were other producers. The heavy locomotives with their churning wheels made boys feel the power of the train; the replicas of coal cars, refrigerator cars, colorful boxcars, and cabooses gave boys a sense of being part of a real world of commerce and success; and the miniature roundhouses, railroad crossing signals, and other accessories completed the romance. These companies also offered younger boys windup trains, enticing them with electric power when they "grew up." The electric train industry associated age with buying up. As the boy grew older, Lionel's advertisements suggested, he should expect bigger models and more accessories in track, cars, signals, and stations.[9]

Catalogs from Ives and Lionel ran endorsements from railroad engineers and officials. Lionel's "20th Century Limited" was the one "that railroad men buy for their boys" and was "just like" the real thing. Little could compare with the miniworld of the electric train set. It miniaturized a society of men with powerful machines. And it was all there at the fingertips of the boy at the transformer. American Flyer appealed to the godlike thrill of a "remote control reverse motor" that "you can stop, start, or reverse . . . from a distant position." The 1932 "Texan" fulfilled "in every detail . . . the demand of discriminating boys."[10]

The father also had a responsibility for leading his son to this golden future. "The dads of today," noted a 1932 American Flyer catalog, "are different from the dads of yesterday in this way—you want your boy to have and enjoy things not possible in your day!" A shared fascination with the gadgetry of modernity was to build intergenerational friendship. "Accessory signal sets," noted an Ives pitch in 1923, "makes the lad the pal to dad."[11]

Automobile replicas showed a similar fascination with "the latest thing." Toy cars appeared about 1900 just as the American automobile industry was emerging. Years later established iron-toy makers like Hubley were still selling a full line of miniature surreys and figures of black men in dump carts. But soon after 1905 new toy companies fascinated young customers with their careful reproductions of contemporary cars and trucks. And Hubley soon followed suit. In 1911 Samuel Dowst used a linotype casting machine to produce toy cars. In 1922 Dowst introduced the brand name "Tootsietoy" (named after his granddaughter). Fred Lundahl of Moline Pressed Steel Company turned the manufacturing techniques he used to make cabs and fenders for trucks in the 1910s to produce his Buddy "L" line of durable toy trucks and construction vehicles. These companies and competitors (including Arcade, Keystone, Kenton, and Kingsbury) turned out replicas of up-to-date cars. Arcade's 1921 Yellow Taxicab was "so realistic, it seems to have rolled right off Fifth Avenue." By the mid-1920s specific models were reproduced: Tootsietoy's Flivver or Model T came in colors just as Henry Ford was adding color to his formerly all-black Model Ts. Many of these toys were heavy-duty, relatively large, and expensive with moveable steel and rubber wheels designed for active, imaginative play.[12]

In that age of "auto-mobility," the toy car had to appear to be self-powered. Batteries came only in the late 1930s. But "friction motors" propelled toy cars and trucks when the wheels were rubbed repeatedly against a hard surface. Invented in 1905, the "hill climbing friction" vehicle soon became very popular. Pedal-powered cars appeared first in 1903. Although they were expensive, their makers strove to imitate contemporary automobile styling and accessories down to the mud-guards and gas caps. In the 1910s and 1920s popular versions were widely featured in Sears and other catalogs. In 1911 Anderson Electric attempted to market the Autoette, a child-sized gasoline car for the "exhilaration of motoring without the attendant danger and expense." Toy companies also kept boys up-to-date with replicas of new farm and road construction equipment. Hubley offered a miniature of the Huber Road Roller (a steam roller) in 1928 and stressed that their "dump trucks really dump."[13]

Toy vehicles captured the variety of men's life of automobility, as drivers of status cars, as deliverers of useful goods, as roadmakers, and race car drivers. These were male machines that opened up a dynamic modern world to their drivers. Women were slow to take to the wheel. And, as advertisers and salesmen knew well, it was men who had the greatest say in automobile purchases. Vehicles were a wonderful expression of rapid technological change and male optimism about progress.[14]

The realism of these toys was not only in the appearance of self-propulsion and the up-to-date detail. It was also in the association of the toy with an event in the news. This was particularly evident in the fascination with airplanes. The Aero Flying Machine (a rubber-band windup) appeared in 1911 in *Playthings*. But a true aviation craze came only with Charles Lindbergh's solo flight across the Atlantic with the *Spirit of St. Louis* in 1927. Motor-powered models from Ideal Aeroplane were so popular that Gimbel's started a Model Airplane League in 1928 to organize youthful enthusiasts and buyers. In 1929 Keystone Toys celebrated the advent of U.S. air mail service with a replica of the first airmail plane. By owning a toy miniature, the child "participated" in the celebrated event. An advertisement for a model of the Graf Zeppelin in 1928 suggested that when boys bought and played with their miniature Zeppelin they would "Help make the Future Safe for Air Travel." Ideal Aeroplanes admonished boys: "Do as much as the Wright Brothers to help your country advance the knowledge and science of flying." The toy airplane offered young boys a heroic vision of participating in the technological miracle of fearless flying. It was a future to be shared by boys and men.[15]

Moline Pressed Steel, makers of the Buddy "L" line of miniature construction vehicles, expressed well this futurist fantasy of father-son bonding.[16] An advertising brochure told of the toy line's origin. It began when the father, noticing that his son, Buddy "L," was bored, had a miniature "express truck" made for him. Buddy immediately began to build a backyard city. As the boy's imagination and ambition expanded and as he grew tired of the first truck, the father gave him, in turn, a dump truck, derrick, steam shovel, sand loader, and overhead crane. As Buddy "L" got bigger, with the help of more construction toys, he "understood better the things that take place on a real construction job." He learned the power of machines.

But these toys taught him more. Because they were so much fun, they attracted all the boys in the neighborhood; and each boy took part at playing with all of Buddy's trucks. In fact, Buddy needed a second derrick for all to share. Finally Buddy's dad brought home a fire truck and for weeks the boys put out fires "in Nancy Jones's dollhouse." When the novelty wore off, the fire truck became part of the team of construction vehicles, serving as a wrecking truck. After watching how Buddy acted out the role of foreman on the construction site, dad added a "Flivver" truck that supervisors used in real life. Soon the other boys wanted similar trucks of their own. So dad brought home more Flivvers (even though Buddy retained exclusive ownership of a special coupe that foremen used). Buddy, like any "regular boy," did not care about girls' games. Still, he would play with girls "if he could do something like a man's work"—hauling dollhouse furniture, for example. Not surprisingly, the other boys also wanted the "pride in having a complete building outfit of their own." So Buddy's father "helped" their fathers by going into the business of manufacturing Buddy's wonderful toys.

The "Story of Buddy 'L'" appealed on many levels. It claimed that toy trucks relieved boredom, stimulated productive and instructive fantasy, helped make friends, established the prerogatives of leadership, confirmed masculine roles, and taught boys to be men. The underlying theme was that all fathers could be like Buddy's dad—givers of male progress.

Vehicles were not the only boys' toys that celebrated technological change and control. Since the early nineteenth century scientific novelties had claimed both to edify and to entertain. At first they were not specially designed for children. These "philosophical toys" taught the whole family the idea of progress. The kaleidoscope (1817), the magic lantern (a simple slide projector manufactured in the United States in 1830), and other gadgets of visual illusion amused affluent families at Sunday evening parties. The zoetrope consisted of a series of drawings on a strip of paper placed on an inside of a drum. When the drum was turned, the illusion of a moving picture was seen through slits in the cylinder. Like board and card games, these amusements were not strictly children's playthings, nor did they really encourage much scientific learning. Instead they promoted the idea of technological and scientific progress while serving as foci for family togetherness. Gradually, however, manufacturers cheapened and even miniaturized these gadgets, turning them into toys for children. Until the 1880s philosophical toys were sold mostly in optical shops. Only then did they become staples in the toy and game sections of department store catalogs.[17]

Parents bought miniature steam engines to teach and entertain their sons. The first patent was filed in 1867, and Russell Frisbie of Cromwell, Connecticut, manufactured the first toy steam engines in 1871. But it was William Weeden who popularized them. In the late 1870s, while serving as superintendent of the Waterbury Watch company, Weeden built miniature steam engines. They became well known when a prominent boys' magazine, *Youth's Companion*, awarded them to readers who sold subscriptions. This made Weeden's toys so popular that he set up a company in 1877. Others followed. In 1893 an advertisement for thirteen steam engines produced by Ives proclaimed "EDUCATE YOUR BOYS"; smaller letters below read, "and at the same time amuse them." Stevens and Brown claimed that their steam engines, which used alcohol for fuel, were "safe, novel, and durable."

In 1892, in a virtual celebration of the steam age, Marshall Field offered three pages of steam engines ranging in price from nine to ninety dollars. At those prices, these toys were obviously not designed for the wage-earner's son. Nor were they intended for the exclusive or unsupervised play of boys. Indeed they offered "amusement for parent and child." The range of accessories that the engine powered suggests several meanings of the toy: some were replicas of the latest machinery like pile drivers and dredges; others represented past technologies like windmills; still others were tableaux of Italian organ grinders or Irish jiggers, "always pleasing scenes for children." The toy steam engine powered the boy's imagination of technological progress, but it also drove nostalgic images of simples times that attracted a wider family audience.[18]

Toy steam engines first appeared nearly 150 years after the real thing. Curiously they reached their heyday just as steam was beginning to be displaced by internal combustion engines and electric motors. For many fathers, however, steam seemed still to represent power and progress in the 1890s. After all, diesel locomotives displaced steam only in the 1950s. Steam cars outnumbered internal combustion engines in 1900, only to disappear shortly after 1910. Toy steam engines shifted gradually from representing progress to embodying the nostalgia of parents and grandparents. Sears and other retailers were still selling a wide range of steam engines (costing from $1.25 to $9.45) in 1919 and would continue to do so beyond World War II. As the years went by, fathers doubtless bought their sons steam toys because their own fathers had bought these playthings for them.[19]

Steam toys, however, were the exception. Toymakers were quick to imitate the latest technology. A good example is the miniature electric battery. The Erlich Brothers offered working electric batteries as early as 1882, and Ives sold acid-free battery sets in 1893. Again these toys were not exclusively for children. An Ives battery was advertised as "great for parties." Some batteries powered miniature machines and, of course, trains. Other manufacturers offered playlike experimentation in the construction kits for wet and dry batteries. One firm sold X-ray sets and the "Little Electroplater," which carried out the exciting new industrial process of plating steel with nickel. In 1914 E. I. Horsman even distributed the "Electric Magneto," designed to amuse and invigorate while giving an electric shock that could "be graduated either to suit a child or a strong man." These toys celebrated the new power source of electricity and gave youth a chance to participate.[20]

Boys' toys also gloried in media and communications technology. Ward's 1903 array of toy cameras included both the older models that used dry plates and Kodak's new "Brownie Camera" (with roll film). The Reflectoscope of 1908 adapted the craze of collecting post cards to the old parlor pastime of magic lantern shows. Now boys were in charge of the projection of exciting images. J. J. Duck promised a wireless radio set capable of sending messages "thousands of miles" that "even boys of nine years are experts at." Toy phonographs and movie projectors also found their way into toy catalogs in the 1900s.[21]

All these toys attempted to minimize the barrier between the plaything and the real thing. They claimed not to be toys at all but rather miniature scientific instruments. They taught boys to admire the technologies of the future and allowed them to imagine themselves in control of modern power. These toys were functioning devices that ordinary people could understand and use, not molded plastic or make-believe images of a fantastic future as boys' toys became in the 1970s. Their mechanisms were exciting to boys in the 1900s. They offered not science fiction but the illusion of participating in the excitement of a here-and-now, new-and-different-but-real world.

Perhaps the best example of these trends is the extraordinary success of construction sets. Between 1901 and 1914 all of the building toys appeared that so much defined the boyhood of the American middle class until the 1960s. These included Meccano steel strips, Tinkertoy spools and sticks, Lincoln Logs, and, of course, erector sets. In many ways these toys were like the wooden block and interlocking wood playsets that Milton Bradley, Charles Crandall, and R. Bliss had manufactured from the 1860s. Indeed, there was great similarity between Joel Ellis's log cabin play house of the 1860s and the Lincoln Logs popularized by the famous architect's son John Lloyd Wright in 1916.[22] But these earlier toys were designed for toddlers and boys of primary school age. The Tinkertoys, created by Charles Pajeau in 1914, continued this tradition. But something had changed in the 1900s and 1910s. Increasing space in toy shops was devoted to more complex, even motorized, construction sets. These were clearly intended for older boys. Advertising stressed neither fantasy nor the development of bodily skills. Instead, these toys introduced the more mature child into the manly world of engineering.

By the 1900s older boys had free time to play when their predecessors had had to work. The proportion of American males between the ages of fourteen and nineteen at work decreased from 61 percent to 40 percent between 1890 and 1930. Middle-class boys of ten or even sixteen could look to sophisticated construction sets as fun, but also as practical training for modern careers in engineering and science. Such toys also appealed to parents who wanted their older sons to spend their playtime "wisely."[23]

In 1910 the makers of Tyro wooden construction blocks advertised their product as "constructive, scientific, amusing." A picture showed mother, father, and sister admiring a boy's masterpiece, a large house assembled with pegs that interlocked blocks. The Structo construction set was even more clearly directed toward the boy's ambition: "you don't have to wait until you grow up to get training in mechanical building." Structo bragged that "Fathers can't resist the fascination of Structo, because it does the real things that big men do in real life. It is not a toy. It is a miniature of the mechanical world for boys." The linkage of father and son contributed to the toy's realism. Tinkertoys appealed to a younger age range. But their manufacturer reached to the older boy when a Tinkertoy set came with a motor in 1919. Like Lego today, Tinkertoy sets appeared in the 1920s with parts to make specific things like ponies or radios. An interesting variation on the construction theme was the "U Make M" Home Toymaker that appeared in the Sears catalog in 1919. This was a toy to make toys and included a "real" scroll saw and soft wood that allowed boys to manufacture their own products by following "blueprints." It encouraged the boy to imitate the worker/manufacturer.[24]

There were many types of the construction toy.[25] But Albert C. Gilbert (1884–1961), inventor of the erector set in 1913, was the genius who best exploited its potential. Gilbert sold more than sets of miniature girders awkwardly bolted together to form imitations of modern railroad and industrial equipment. He sold himself as the simultaneous embodiment of the model boy and man.

Gilbert came from old American stock. An ancestor had been governor of the New Haven Colony. Albert Gilbert had been born in Salem, Oregon, and had spent part of his youth in Idaho, where he developed a love for hiking and hunting. Educated at Yale, he was a champion pole-vaulter and an Olympian in 1908. Meanwhile, he earned a medical degree. However, instead of practicing medicine, in 1909 he joined a friend in founding a company to manufacture magical tricks. They promised boys the "secrets of the world's greatest magicians at toy prices." Gilbert's big idea came in 1911.

On a train voyage between New Haven and New York, he later recalled, he noticed steel girders being erected for an electric railway. This presumably was the inspiration for the erector set. The reader may be skeptical, for Gilbert's system of connecting steel strips with bolts and nuts was very similar to the Meccano construction sets of the Englishman Frank Hornby (introduced in 1901 and exported to the United States in 1910). Gilbert's first erector sets of 1913 were distinguished mostly by their motors and gears and pinions. But Gilbert himself was as important to his success as was the design of his toy.[26]

In his autobiography Gilbert paints himself both as a businessman with integrity and as a perpetual boy. He was earnest and energetic, serious about machines and business but playful, loyal to lifelong employees yet always willing to try new things. Gilbert specialized in construction toys (taking over American Meccano in 1920), but he also manufactured real soldering irons (allowing boys to "mend as well as construct new things" like mother's pots and pans). His chemistry and other science experiment sets became staples in the 1920s. Gilbert manufactured amateur radio kits and even broadcasted from his own radio station to "his boys" in the early 1920s. In 1938 he bought American Flyer toy railroads. In 1950 he blazed new frontiers when he produced the "Gilbert Atom Energy Lab" (with government support because it showed the "constructive side" of atomic power). Even though it proved to cost more than it could be sold for and failed, it illustrated well Gilbert's commitment to introducing American youth to the technological future.[27]

The heart of Gilbert's enterprise was his own highly publicized personality. From 1914 Gilbert touted his background as an Olympian and big game hunter in expensive advertising campaigns in boy's magazines like *Youth's Companion, St. Nicholas,* and *American Boy.* In 1916 he boasted in *Playthings* that he had already spent $150,000 advertising erector sets. He kept his name in the public eye as a commentator on a radio sports program in the late 1920s (even interviewing Babe Ruth). In 1941 he opened in New York the "Gilbert Hall of Science" (a six-story salesroom and display). From the beginning he spoke directly to boys in his advertisements and catalogs. His hearty "Hello Boys" greeting introduced his "personal messages." Later he observed: "I was convinced that boys became interested and excited when a *person*, not a corporation, spoke to them . . . I built erector sets because I know what boys like." Gilbert also offered "degrees" from the "Gilbert Engineering Institute." His advertisements proclaimed: "Win fame while at play. Be a Gilbert Diploma Boy."

He built on this dream when he published *Erector Tips* in 1915. This periodic booklet included stories about college life and letters from boys describing new and exciting models to be built. Gilbert offered prizes for the best models (and sometimes used the models and pictures of the winners in catalogs). In 1933 the gifted boy who won the first prize had his choice of a trip to the Empire State Building, the Panama Canal, or Boulder Dam (each, of course, a feat of engineering genius). Whereas other companies stressed durability and fidelity to engineering principles, Gilbert offered an ethos of vitality and participation. He invited boys to dream. "Yes Sir! You can win degrees of merit and diplomas just as though you were in a big college like Yale or Harvard." He promised a leg up on a business or technical career: "Be an electrical engineer. Through an exact knowledge of electricity, you can command a good salary and a good position."[28]

The appeal was not mere fantasy. Gilbert took pride in how educational his toys were. In 1920 he hired scientists and engineers from Yale, Columbia, and General Electric to develop his line of science kits. Gilbert went beyond the common chemistry set to kits featuring experiments in hydraulic and pneumatic engineering, each including a detailed booklet explaining the scientific principles involved. His Books for Real Boys were juvenile versions of the "how to" articles that filled the pages of *Popular Science* and *Popular Mechanics*.[29]

Gilbert also appealed to the anxious parent in an advertisement in the *Literary Digest:* "our new educational idea which is the result of a study of child psychology, is developing a new angle of vision upon education . . . The element of fun and pleasure has a wonderful effect in stimulating the inventive faculties which lay dormant in the child. Why not develop them in a sort of subconscious way?" American toys built character, Gilbert insisted, and helped "visualize to the boy his future occupation." But even though he linked his products to new educational and childrearing theories, Gilbert discouraged schools from buying erector sets. He feared that "if kids saw our things in schools, they'd think they were just as deadly dull as the rest of school and would have nothing to do with them."[30]

Gilbert's advertising approach was flattered by much imitation. His early competitor, Frank Hornby, maker of the Meccano construction set, adopted a very similar appeal. In M. P. Gould's celebratory biography, Hornby was the "boy inventor." After having read Samuel Smiles's *Self Help,* Hornby dreamed of building a "perpetual motion machine." Then, as an adult in New York City, while working on the installation of a water pump he observed bridgework that inspired his Meccano toy. He hoped that it would make "it easier for boys all over the world to start building aeroplanes." Meccano even offered Gould's book to boys who sent in the names of five friends for Meccano's advertising list. Both Gilbert and Meccano tapped into the mystique of the individualist inventor and the energetic, optimistic ethos of Teddy Roosevelt.[31]

Porter Chemicals, maker of chemistry sets, may not have had a heroic founder. But it did encourage boys to become Chief Chemists by starting Chemcraft clubs in their neighborhoods. The club magazine combined serious chemical analysis with ideas for stunts that "will tell you how to have some real sport." Porter Chemicals tried to build brand loyalty around the social needs of boys from eight to eighteen years old.[32]

Model railroad companies also imitated Gilbert's approach. In the 1926 catalog Ives copied Gilbert's personal touch in a letter from Harry C. Ives signed, "Yours for lots of fun." Ives could also brag that for fifty-eight years American boys had "graduated from the fun of running an Ives Train to the manly love for mechanical and electric things which help the world do its work." But Ives noted that his toys had progressed from the "odd looking things" of Dad's day to the latest technology. Ives "invention Laboratory" proudly announced their latest innovation, the "Automatic Reverse Locomotive" and the "Push Button Control Switch." In imitation of the inventive factories of Edison and Bell Labs, Ives offered boys the dream of sharing in the real world of practical invention. He stressed that "regular electrical engineers design these sets" and "clever craftsmen fit them together." These advertisements read like publicity for industrial machinery. They invited boys to imagine themselves capitalists "investing" in capital goods and equipment.[33]

It is difficult to know what all this meant to boys of the 1910s and 1920s. But some clues may be found in the models shown in Meccano and Gilbert catalogs that boys could copy using their construction sets. Meccano catalogs featured representations of the railroad era: jib cranes, swing bridges, pile drivers, inclined delivery shoots, and coal tip cranes. Meccano produced miniature dog clutches, universal couplings, and cone pulleys in accessory packages. And, when we look at the prizewinning models that boys made themselves in Gilbert's contests, we find boys extraordinarily informed about contemporary machinery. They made boom derricks, mortising machines, industrial swing saws, along with a few ferris wheels and even a doll's carriage. On balance, these boys imitated, in detail, the practical industrial world. They either knew what a jib crane did or wanted to know.[34]

Still, if boys responded to the call of technological realism, they were also learning the ways of consumerism. All these toys stressed brand identity through contests, clubs, and even tradition. Being an "Ives," or a "Gilbert" boy meant something. Boys purchased the aura of self-made men and progressive innovators with roots in the past and assured futures. Manufacturers of construction and train sets arranged catalogs from the simplest to the most complex and expensive. The idea was not merely to provide consumers with a playset that fit every household budget but to encourage the association of growing up with bigger and better toys. Step by step the boy was to climb from the easiest and simplest construction set or train to the more difficult and complex. Meccano, for example, advised that boys "begin with Model No. 1" and follow "every model in turn." Gilbert manufactured a "Brik-tor" line, a "little brother to Erector" to get the very young started. Each of these thin steel blocks in bright colors had a single hole that could be interlocked with rods to be made into model castles, houses, and churches. As the boy's motor skills and hands grew, along with his understanding of "engineering," he could move up to the big-boy sets. In the 1920s the modern marketing ideas of adding on and moving up were exploited by Alfred Sloan of General Motors who pioneered the idea of a full line of cars at every price range. Like Sloan, Gilbert introduced annual changes, each promising to be bigger and better than last year's models. Toymakers integrated these ideas into the boy's dream of growing up and getting closer to the real world of technology and business.

An element of boys' toys today that was relatively rare in toys of the time was war play. Given the popularity of the Spanish-American War of 1898 and the impact of World War I, advances in military technology were surprisingly seldom reflected in toys. Toy weapons did exist. Cap guns appeared as early as 1859, pop guns had their debut in the early 1870s, and the Daisy Air Rifle (BB gun) began its long success in 1888. But Montgomery Ward sold the rubber-tipped arrow pistol in 1894 as a family parlor game, not as an invitation to war play. Ward featured brigade guns, but they appeared along with toy drums and ceremonial "captain's swords," appealing to make-believe military parading, not to combat. A few cowboy suits with holsters and revolvers appeared shortly before World War I. Battleships and even machine guns arrived during that conflict. But they were temporary appeals to bonding with older brothers and fathers at war. Advertisements for toy guns in Sears catalogs dropped off sharply after 1921. Milton Bradley offered a toy soldier line in 1926, but the advertising stressed the "appeal of pageantry with none of the suggestion of war." In any case, most toy soldiers were expensive and European-made until the mid-1930s. They were meant to teach the history of past wars more than preparation for future ones. The Butler Brothers catalog of 1930 had only one corner of its twenty-two pages of boys' toys devoted to metal soldiers. The excitement of trains, cars, commercial flight, and construction filled boys' play in the thirty years after 1900, and war play could not yet dominate boys' attention.[35]

These objects of childhood reflected and imitated an optimistic, expansive age that preceded the Depression of the 1930s. Although parents still bought the toys, manufacturers appealed to the child's imagination. The fantasy was not in war play or an unreal world of superheroes. It was in the dream of participating in the exciting world of machines and construction and of dynamic growth and invention. These toys represented the latest technology but also claimed to prepare boys for a future responsible role in society.

Father and son shared in the excitement of contemporary machines and the glorious future of technology. In and through the celebration of progress, both in keeping up-to-date and in growing up, the boy learned to want the "latest thing" and to "upgrade" his equipment. If a company could convince boys and their fathers to let Ives, Buddy "L," or Gilbert be their guide through the process, so much the better for these businesses.

Girls and Dolls

If, between 1900 and World War II, boys played with machines, girls played with dolls. Boys' toys were make-believe tools that young males used to fantasize their future roles as *Homo faber*, as participants in the wider world of work and business. Girls' play involved few tools and little speed and power. Instead, it focused on dolls and the imaginary world and relationships that surrounded them. Dolls became the girl's own babies, her companions, or even herself. Girls learned their expected gender roles by making their dolls into the protagonists of the domestic dramas of modern caregiving, conviviality, and consumption. They rehearsed the worlds of the caring mother, dear friends, and modern shoppers. The look of girls' dolls did not transform as dramatically as did boys' playthings, but the roles dolls were called upon to play did change after about 1900, reflecting new values and shifting gender identities.

In Victorian America dolls served as imaginary friends for young girls as they do today. But they were also learning tools in ways very different from the twentieth century. Before 1900 dolls commonly trained girls in the essential art of sewing. Catharine Beecher, a founder of modern home economics, claimed that a well-prepared girl "had not only learned before the age of twelve to make dolls of various sorts and sizes, but to cut and fit and sew every article that belongs to a doll's wardrobe." Indeed, in 1850 few dolls (except expensive French imports) were sold already dressed. Many were plain "sewing dolls," designed as miniature mannequins for modeling clothes sewn by young girls. It was uncommon for girls to grow up without knowledge of needle and thread. Sewing machines appeared only in 1846 and were widely available in homes only from the late 1860s, and even then they were very expensive. Ready-to-wear fashion was largely confined to men's clothing until the 1890s. As late as 1894 the Sears catalog included no women's clothing. Patterns that appeared after 1870 eased the task. But sewing was a vital duty that nearly every girl and woman needed to perform. As late as 1907 the Butterick company, which manufactured clothes patterns, advertised a rag doll to "teach the Future Mother to Dress the Future Child." These dolls meant work and the learning of a practical domestic skill at least as much as play.[36]

Also important in Victorian America were fashion dolls. They long predated the nineteenth century and played an important role in the history of female apparel and style. But especially from the 1860s through the 1890s, "lady dolls" with adult body dimensions and faces became a central part of the middle-class girl's life. They were clearly designed for families with money to spare. A doll's outfit could easily cost $30 in 1890, when the average laborer earned $486 annually. Newly affluent mothers increasingly encouraged their daughters to imitate the rituals of high society with their dolls. Here we find the origins of that Victorian innovation, the doll's tea party. Dolls instructed girls on the "proper" handling of objects and the exercise of self-control. The fashion doll taught daughters the social rituals of middle-class family life and provided skill at identifying quality fabric and fashion. These talents were very important in an age when middle-class women were expected to create a decorous home and become knowledgeable consumers.[37]

The doll's accessories provided the props for this training. The 1882 Erlich Brothers' catalog offered "The Improved Little Housekeeper" with "kitchen and table all set with Chloe the cook getting dinner ready." But this sort of preprogrammed play environment was rare. More often mothers gave girls generic miniature tea sets, tin kitchen stoves and cupboards, and doll furniture. Girls learned their play scripts through imitating pictures of tea parties and other social rituals—often from trade cards or stereograph images. They also acted out the stories in doll books and magazines. Children even imitated mourning rituals when they gave dolls funerals.[38]

Victorian girls mimicked adult social and work roles with their dolls, but until midcentury there were few dolls to train them for motherhood. Wax dolls in vaguely baby form had occasionally appeared from the seventeenth century. Papier-mâché infants were displayed in Germany in 1855 and French "bébés" produced by Jumeau and Steiner were a rage in the 1880s. But these dolls looked more like miniature adults than like babies: their faces seldom suggested an exuberant youthful personality, and their heads were small in proportion to their bodies, more like mature women than babies. Most dolls looked like adults with whom the child was to identify. They had straight, often unbending bodies, and "doll faces" of pursed lips and blank stares. Lady dolls, usually made of porcelain or bisque, were also easily broken, a far cry from the lifelike and cuddly baby dolls of the twentieth century. Such dolls represented neither infants to be mothered nor companions to serve as imaginary siblings.[39]

Most nineteenth-century girls did not need baby or sibling dolls because they had the real things in their houses. Birth rates dropped from 55 per 1,000 in 1800 to 38.3 to 1870. But that was still nearly double of the rate of 20.2 in 1930.[40] And there were few one-child families. Parents were less prone to concentrate their births in just a few years as became the case in the twentieth century. So a girl of six, or even ten was likely to have a baby sibling. The baby and "pal" doll appeared when the real infant and sister began to disappear. When mothers bore fewer children, they also tended to assume more of the nurturing responsibilities. These mothers preferred to have their young daughters play with baby dolls rather than risk letting them care for their baby siblings.

It is difficult to know just what girls thought of their dolls or how they used them in the generation before the changes of the early twentieth century. However, an oral history of doll play conducted at the Margaret Woodbury Strong Museum may shed some light on these elusive questions. Interviews with women born between 1890 and the early 1930s concerning their recollections of doll play show a profound change over these decades.

The comments of women who were children in the 1890s and 1900s illustrate the doll play of late-Victorian American girlhood. The most important factor was simply the rarity of dolls. One woman born in 1890 from upstate New York recalled having only one "clothespin doll," and claimed that she had no time for play after doing her farm chores. Another born in 1899 in rural Pennsylvania had only a stocking doll and made a playhouse out of an old corn crib. Several remembered plain dime-store "sewing dolls" with celluloid or china heads. Girls of this era sometimes also had "Frozen Charlottes," figurines with which they were allowed to play only on holidays or when relatives visited. Sometimes called "shelf dolls," these and other fragile lady dolls were more souvenirs than true playthings. Aunts often gave these dolls for special birthdays or Christmas. Other sources suggest that little girls in the late nineteenth century preferred rag dolls, especially black-skinned ones, to fashionable bisque or all-porcelain figures. But the ritual of giving girls shelf dolls was enjoyed by adult women even if girls sometimes favored cuddly dolls.[41]

Girls received few dolls, and they were often repaired rather than replaced. One woman born in 1913 recalled receiving a Schoenhut doll at the age of four but playing with it until she was twelve. After being given a doll these late-Victorian girls had to wait until the next Christmas before "Santa" repaired a broken doll or gave it a new head. Parents might cut the hair of an old doll or replace an old-fashioned dress with a new style rather than buy a new doll. This custom was more than an example of old-fashioned thrift. It represented a tradition of craft work that complemented the decision to purchase manufactured dolls. A major Christmas gift might be doll clothes, hand-sewn by mother or an aunt, to be worn by an old manufactured doll. This was merely a natural extension of the custom of hand-sewing the clothing of family members. A well-to-do mother of a girl born in 1913 actually hired an "Auntie Mit," a professional dressmaker, to make "dolly dresses" in their Brooklyn home. These gifts of handmade doll clothes were often as close as mothers got to their daughters' play.[42]

The image of girlhood in the Strong Museum oral history is probably conservative. It reflects the experience of small-town and rural upstate New York. But most Americans lived in such places in the 1890s and 1900s(These girls had childhoods very much like their nineteenth-century predecessors. Their dolls and accessories were few; often they were used to learn sewing; and handcraft traditions blended with a new acceptance of manufactured toys.[43])

But during the first decade of the twentieth century, girl's playthings were beginning to change. Technological advances affected girls' play as much as that of boys, but less dramatically and less directly. New machines of domesticity appeared in miniature in doll's houses, but they were less important to the play than were the new-style dolls that encouraged nurturing and affection. In some ways this change was a response to the obsolescence of women's crafts like sewing and the decline of the formal social conventions that ruled Victorian middle-class homes. As preparation for a future less burdened by domestic labors and time-consuming social rituals, girls' playthings encouraged the expression of personal relationships with children and friends.

The decades that produced automobiles and planes also introduced domestic electricity and a vast array of appliances. In the late 1890s alternate current spread across the land, electrifying half of American homes by 1920 and almost all urban homes by 1930. Rural dwellings mostly had to wait until the New Deal. Electricity mechanized almost all facets of housework. The electric iron appeared in 1893, followed quickly by the electric kettle, toaster, and waffle iron. Hoover introduced the first home vacuum cleaner in 1908; by the end of the 1920s almost half of wired households possessed a vacuum. In the 1930s electric stoves began to compete with gas. And in 1930, when the coolant freon was introduced, refrigerator sales took off. These years also saw the widespread introduction of indoor plumbing and the modern bathroom.[44]

Not surprisingly toy manufacturers offered miniatures of these revolutionary emblems of domestic modernity. In 1893 Ives sold a working model sewing machine. In the 1900s and 1910s miniature washing machines began to replace toy washboards and wringers. In the 1920s the Tappan Company produced toy gas stoves to advertise its new models. In 1929 Hubley sold toy refrigerators and a very up-to-date toy Maytag washing machine. Metal Ware's 1929 miniature stoves came in blue and green "that match the colors used on big modern ranges." As early as 1913 the old wood-toy company Morton Converse offered a "bungalow" dollhouse complete with garage and wooden car at a time when this new house style was becoming popular. By the 1920s architects designed dollhouses for major toy companies. Dolls carriages and beds similarly reflected changing fashions in baby furniture.[45]

New technology produced cheaper materials that introduced

more children to the upper-class traditions of dollhouses and tea sets. The McLoughlin Brothers, noted for their board games, offered a "folding dollhouse" in 1896 using lithographed paper on cardboard to affect the illusion of an elegant interior. Pewter tea sets gave way to tin and later aluminum at less than half the cost.[46]

Still, these copies of new domestic technology were secondary. Almost all girls' toy tools were accessories to doll play. In 1919 Sears featured paint sets and stringing beads for girls. But there were no career toys as there were for boys. The exception was an occasional nurse's outfit. Structo offered girls not construction toys but Artcraft looms for "home weaving." And Porter Chemicals presented a "dainty outfit for girls," the Sachet Craft set, a lesson in cosmetic chemistry. This should not be surprising. Girls' play reflected the expectations of middle-class white parents that their daughters would become "modern" housewives for whom technology was an aid in their nurturing roles, not an end in itself. In the 1890 census 95 percent of white married women were listed as homemakers. By 1930 that figure had dropped only to 89.3 percent. The career woman was still a small minority.[47]

Dollhouse appliances mirrored up-to-date domestic technology. But girls' playthings were definitely not wrapped in the aura of "scientific homemaking" as were boys' toys in an ethos of industrial progress. This was true even though home economics had become a respectable field in the 1900s. Christine Frederick with her *Household Engineering* (1920) attempted to make the modern kitchen the domestic equivalent of the scientific factory. She advised women in efficient food storage and effective use of new domestic machinery. But scarcely any of this seeped into the play culture of girls in the 1910s and 1920s. Sears catalogs throughout the 1920s featured enameled bathroom sets, but toy domestic appliances were relatively rare. The dollhouses were poorly detailed two-story pasteboard items. Only in 1931 did they feature a garage and come with an icebox.[48]

The appeal of domestic miniatures was less that they expressed technological progress than that they symbolized a new world of consumption. The Pet's Toy Grocery Store of 1909 gave little girls the thrill of make-believe shopping for doll-sized boxes of "Lifebuoy soap," "Argo Starch," "Uneeda Biscuits," and other goods packed by "the best known food product manufacturers in the country." These manufacturers willingly offered their names to Pet's Grocery Store in hopes of inducing future female consumers to associate soap or biscuits with their brand name. This toy taught that a central task of modern woman was to be an informed shopper.[49]

The girl's play also paralleled the mother's work. Pet's Toy Grocery Store, like miniature Bissel carpet sweepers and other girls' toys, did not invite mothers and daughters to join in play. If long-absent fathers wished to bond with their sons around model railroading, the ever-present and always busy mother at home had no such need or opportunity to play. If there was a sharing between mothers and daughters, it certainly was not in the technological optimism shown in boys' playthings. Rather, females of both generations were to share in an emotional intensity best expressed in the doll.

Instead of technology or even comforts, the marketing of girls' playthings stressed the building of warm interpersonal relationships and style. This was the meaning of progress for most women. By end of the 1920s dolls shared a "look" that exuded "personality" and vitality. They were to serve the child in role playing close friendships and mother-child bonding. At the same time they invited the girl to enjoy her own childhood, not just to dream of the adult world.

These changes began with the New Kid dolls of the 1900s. These dolls were portrayed as children instead of as "ladies." This style had diverse origins, and its representations ranged from the romantic to the ultra-realistic. But they all stressed a positive image of children that appealed to the parents of the era. The clean "Dutch boy" look of the Campbell Kids dolls (1905) with their dimpled, rosy cheeks and well-fed faces was typical. All the New Kid dolls exuded cheerfulness, energy, optimism, and "personality." They were usually made to look like real children and often wore new styles of informal children's clothing. Many New Kid dolls were sold through soap and other household-product companies. The sprite on the package of Fairy Soap inspired Horsman's Fairy Doll, and Dolly Strong was marketed through Naphtha Soap coupons. Perhaps the most popular were the Kewpie dolls of Rose O'Niell

(1909), the famous cherubic, slightly impish image of childhood that so attracted adults because it conformed so well with their new image of childhood. These new-style dolls invited girls especially to identify with the New Kid image. Girls were encouraged to be as cute and cuddly as their dolls.[50]

The New Kid dolls were made of soft and washable materials and sometimes had flexible joints. These were changes that encouraged cuddling and play. American toymakers also embraced the "unbreakable" composition material, especially for dolls' heads. In the 1910s doll companies introduced their own mass-produced versions of the old-fashioned hand-crafted rag doll. Perhaps the most famous was Raggedy Ann, along with her companion, Raggedy Andy. These cuddly characters, with freckled faces and sparkling eyes, were instantly recognized with their yarn hair. New Kid dolls often were simple, without mechanical gadgetry. Yet, unlike homemade rag or wooden dolls, they exuded "personality."[51]

In the 1910s doll companies like E. I. Horsman and Effanbee (Fleischaker and Baum) fully exploited these trends when they produced the companion doll. Faces featured dimples and rosy cheeks and eyes that sparkled. Some were modeled after real children and displayed mischievous or even pained looks. Horsman's Baby Bumps, modeled after a real baby, was enough of a hit in 1911 that a Negro Baby Bumps and imitators like Bobby Blake and Dolly Drake soon followed. Boy as well as girl images appeared, often in sister-and-brother pairs evoking impressions of the cute and impish.[52]

Catalogs placed these companion dolls in imaginative, grouped settings, inviting multiple purchases. In 1914 Horsman produced an Art Dolls line, each model complete with a "charming name" and personality: Miss Janet, "all spic and span" with her "white lawn frock," was paired with Robbie Reffer, a "spruce little fellow with a suit of snowy well-cut white duck." These personalities "every little girl will want in her doll family." The Babyland Rag doll collection of 1912 featured the American Maid Doll, "a little country lassie," and Aunty Dinah, "bright and clean and neat from her yellow turban to her slippered feet." There were many varieties of these pert dolls. Ideal's Flossie Flirt featured "those marvelous rolling eyes in the gayest most delightful childlike manner." Madame Hendren offered Soozie Smiles, American Beauty Dolls countered with Toodles, and Horsman presented Baby Dimples, all three sold through Sears in the 1920s.[53]

Some of the new dolls allowed for double personalities, with, for example, black and white heads on opposite ends of the doll's body. The Famlee line of Berwick Dolls improved on this concept by offering eighteen interchangeable heads on a single body. Susie Bumps could become Jap Boy with a little assembly work. The Famlee doll set offered the "same universal child appeal as paper dolls—but life-like," and provided an "ever changing playmate that multiplies the joy of every play hour." Girls were invited to skip from one fantasy friend to another, not, as were the boys, to construct a replica of adult life. Women in the Strong Museum survey who were born in the late 1910s and 1920s vividly recalled their little girl dolls and how the jointed legs and "real hair" made it possible to change their poses, positions, and apparently their personalities. They thought of their dolls as "confidants."[54]

Effanbee was a leader in the companion doll industry. Like many of the new toy companies, it had its roots in the novelty business. Its founders met in 1910 while operating adjoining stalls on the Atlantic City boardwalk. With the creative talents of women designers like Anna Edele and success in touting the "Buy American" slogan during World War I, Effanbee emerged as a major doll company in the 1920s. One of its most successful lines was headed by Patsy. When she first appeared in 1924, Patsy was a wardrobe doll. McCall and Butterick offered patterns sized for her. Patsy's fashions of sunshine suits, organdie frocks, and other "romp" clothes were similar to those worn by young middle-class children in the 1920s.[55]

But Patsy was far from the conventional generic sewing doll of the past. She was a child, not an adult. And adults rather than children made her clothes. Most important, she was a personality. She was hyped as "the doll of a million moods" and a "loveable Imp with tiltable head and moveable limbs" in the New Kids mold. By 1929 the Patsy concept was expanded into a merchandise line that included a "boy friend," the "Famous Mischievous Skippy"—an impish storybook and movie character. About 1933 even a Patsy Tinyette Doctor appeared, dressed in a surgeon's gown. In a 1931 catalog disguised as "My Doll's Magazine," Effanbee touted the

Patsy family of six doll sisters (twice the size of the typical American family of the period). These included Patsy Ann, Patsykin, Patsyette, Patsy Joan, Patsy Lou, and, of course, Patsy (in sizes ranging from 12 to 22$\frac{1}{2}$ inches). Patsy also had an infant sibling, Patsy Babykin: "She is so cunning and adorable you just want to hug her." Each doll came with the yellow heart label, signifying "authenticity."[56]

Effanbee had only a few stories about Patsy to tell girls how to play with her or to encourage multiple purchases of the Patsy line. But the company's image was clear: "The Effanbee spirit—always gay and ready for a romp." In 1930 Effanbee offered a doll pair—"A cunning Flapper and her Sheik [who] 'strut their stuff' to the latest jazz rhythm." This may sound like Mattel's Barbie and Ken until we note the five-year-old faces on these dolls. They only played at being part of the adult world (no doubt to the amusement of parents). These companion dolls celebrated childhood even while being up-to-date.[57]

In 1932 Effanbee introduced the Patsy Doll Club in a brochure with a letter from "Aunt Patsy." Like Gilbert and Ives clubs for boy enthusiasts of erector sets or electric trains, the Patsy club was a marketing tool to distribute sales brochures to likely buyers. The club had 270,000 members at its height. In the 1930s an Effanbee employee, Bea Orland, toured American department stores posing as "Aunt Patsy." Wearing a nurse's uniform, she gave demonstrations on proper doll care and promoted club membership. The Patsy Doll Club offered girls a social identity built around a line of manufactured goods. The difference from the boys' clubs was that the dolls, not the girls, were invited to be members.[58]

These dolls were more than tools for learning women's roles. They were designed to be children's companions. In a real sense they were replacements for siblings. Boys without brothers had their Buddy "L" trucks to occupy them (and to bring the neighbor kids around). But girls had their doll friends. And they could join these pals in the charmed world of the cute and current. These dolls ingeniously combined an invitation to the joys of a romantic childhood with an appeal to contemporary fashion. And they embodied an ideal of female progress that could be shared by mothers and daughters.

The baby doll complemented the companion doll. This rise of the infant image, of course, had roots much earlier than the 1920s. Martha Chase (1851–1925) and other female dollmakers in the 1890s turned the old craft of the stuffed cloth doll into a commercial enterprise. While male dollmakers stressed mechanical innovation, Chase emphasized dolls that felt like real babies and were made of safe and cleanable materials (especially stockinet). To heighten the naturalistic affect, Chase sculpted her baby dolls' hands in a natural cupped shape.[59]

The most notable of the new baby dolls was the Bye-Lo Baby of doll artist Grace Storey Putnam. This doll was modeled on a three-day-old baby, so that it "touches the cord of Mother love in every little girl's heart." The Bye-Lo Baby, introduced in 1923, was part of a trend toward baby care dolls that culminated in the late 1930s. Bubbles of Effanbee was "modeled after a real baby, a baby who laughed and cooed all day. No little girl can be cross or unhappy with this doll in her arms."[60]

Effanbee's Dy-Dee Baby of 1934 (followed shortly by Ideal's Betsy Wetsy) demanded a "mother's" care in feeding and diapering. When the Dy-Dee baby "nursed," water collected in a tube. It squirted out when the "mother" pressed the doll's stomach. A teacher from Brooklyn, Marie Wittam, invented this drink/wet doll. Despite early test marketing in England, where mothers found it vulgar, it became a big hit in the United States. A 1937 Effanbee catalog pretended to be a brochure similar to those published the government's Children's Bureau to teach women modern baby care. Entitled "What Every Young Doll Mother Should Know" and written by "Aunt Patsy," this pamphlet instructed the doll owner on diapering and feeding. Aunt Patsy warned that the young mother must be "ever watchful for the baby's comfort and happiness." The catalog also included a note to parents, much like similar messages to fathers in the Gilbert promotions. It stressed how Effanbee had helped replace the "stilted, stiff and unnatural dolls" of the mother's childhood with realistic and loveable line of Dy-Dee dolls. "Child psychologists all agree that the best training for a happy adult life is a realistic understanding developed during childhood" of mothercare.[61]

The same idea appeared in the Sears' catalog of 1931 in an editorial which reminded parents: "dolls influence children's characters developing sweetness and affection which they retain throughout their lives . . . Every 'little mother' loves to add new dolls to her 'family.' Dolls are a tender influence for little boys." The last sentence was a rare admission that boys too played with dolls. Still, few boy dolls were manufactured except when paired with girl models (indicating that they were designed for girls' gender play). More ominously, advertisements claimed that baby dolls were an "antidote to race suicide" and counteracted the threat of "one-child mothers." Indeed, from 1905, when President Theodore Roosevelt condemned the trend toward smaller families, critics blamed restricted births on the decline of mother love. Despite protests against the family planning movement that emerged in the 1910s, the birth rate continued to decline in the twentieth century (dropping from 32.1 per 1,000 Americans in 1900 to 18.4 by 1936). Baby dolls addressed parental anxieties that mother love was in decline in a time when parents were having fewer children.[62]

Whether appealing to companionship or motherhood, doll marketing was increasingly imaginative. Dollmakers attempted to copyright the emotionally charged facial expressions on their products. The more upscale dolls were linked with their artistic creators. Grace Corry, the sculptor of the Little Sister and Brother line, wrote a "letter" in a trade advertisement expressing appreciation for the "faithful rendering" of her creation by the manufacturer, Averill Dolls. These dolls were supposed to express the gentle genius of the female artist. In effect, doll companies claimed to have "captured" the new image of childhood in their products.

And for consumers to participate they had to buy more and more. Clothing dolls in the latest fashion encouraged repeated purchases. A company's line of goods was transformed into a doll family sharing the emblem of a "golden heart." The mail-order list became the doll club. The friendly "Aunt Patsy" put a maternal face on a company run by two men who had once worked on the Atlantic City boardwalk. Manufacturers cultivated the many-sided doll personality that wore a different mood with each change of clothes or even head. These gimmicks inevitably encouraged multiple purchases in order to have the complete joy of a well-equipped, full-size "doll family." What was Patsy without Skippy? Girls with the encouragement of their mothers joined the new culture of relationships and mothercare while they consumed.[63]

Of course, the women in the Strong Survey who had been girls in the 1920s did not see these dolls merely as commodities. Dolls shaped their childhood. This generation no longer had either the old sewing dolls or the shelf dolls. Instead they had pal and baby dolls. One women born in 1920 believed that her "dolls had personalities." She and her cousins took them everywhere and "made up stories or plays about them." This woman had Patsy dolls, and, unlike her predecessors, she had accumulated new dolls rather than reconditioned old ones. By the time she was eleven years old, she recalled, she had fifty dolls and even a dollhouse with electric lights and a piano.

This was an exceptional case. At the other extreme, a woman born in 1924 remembered her washable "Bubbles" baby doll by Effanbee. Here, an old custom survived: when Bubbles got "hurt" "Santa" repaired her for Christmas. But repairs were less necessary. For the 1930s generation of girls, baby dolls, especially those made of rubber, were very common. A woman born in 1930 who played with dolls until age twelve recalled with affection: "I had a baby doll and I wanted to do what real mothers did." Mothers less often sewed doll clothes. Instead the interviewees recalled their mothers' buying packaged doll dresses as the art of sewing began to decline.[64] Dolls no longer were aids in acquiring social graces or the skills of sewing; nor were they rare gifts embodying the crafts of parents and relatives. Rather these dolls engendered feelings of friendship and mothercare in a world of the store-bought.

Between 1900 and World War II toys mirrored the revolutions in the technologies of industry and the home. Manufacturers of boys' toys no longer catered merely to the parents of toddlers and young boys with "child quieters." They reached out to older youths by offering them dreams of success and power in an endless array of transport, construction, and science toys. Boys' playthings were no longer just miniatures of men's tools. They trained boys for manhood through the latest machines of men. Boys went from blocks to wagons, from pull to electric trains, and from Tinkertoys to erector sets. Boys played at being machine operators and builders, but not gunslingers or very often even soldiers, much less superheroes. Play meant anticipating the future. These boys' toys idealized technological change and let children take pleasure in the details of machines and how they worked. They were miniature tokens of progress, teaching the glories of an erected world, based on "exact scientific principles."

Girls' playthings went in almost an opposite direction. Companion and baby dolls replaced sewing and lady dolls. Play was transformed from practical training in crafts and etiquette to acting out personal relationships and keeping up with fashion trends. The new dolls reflected the future roles of doll owners. They taught a nurturing motherhood, an informal and active ideal of friendship, and, intermingled with it all, the fun of spending and being fashionable. Doll accessories followed the revolutions in domestic technology. But far more important in girls' playthings was putting on roles and learning to feel and to care. The emphasis was not on a future as "efficient" homemakers, much less participants in the rational world of science and business. In contrast with boys, girls had permission to retreat into childhood even as they were cajoled into being good future mothers and homemakers.

Of course, many girls and boys resisted or ignored these messages in toys. Many girls played with their brothers' Lincoln Logs and erector sets and preferred their dogs to their dolls. Only 25 percent of girls in an 1898 survey listed dolls as their favorite toy. And boys did play with dolls.[65] Still, despite the insistence of some adults today that more gender-neutral toys be offered older children, gender differences in playthings persist and have even grown more extreme. Surely the sharp division between boys' and girls' toys today has roots in the new toybox that emerged early in the twentieth century.

For many adults today, it is easy to prefer the erector sets and the baby dolls of the early twentieth century to the violent video games and Barbie fashion dolls that dominate play at the end of the century. It is hard to deny that these playthings exuded an attractive optimism and realism that seems to have disappeared. While these toys certainly reinforced sex-role stereotypes, they offered an attainable, if highly romantic, vision of the future. As important, they expressed values shared between parents and children. These training toys were part of a society that had a clear vision of the future and of sex roles. That confidence would be greatly undermined in the decades to come.

4 FREEING THE CHILD'S IMAGINATION

ADULTS TODAY often contrast the realistic and optimistic toys of their youth with the fantastic and sometimes violent playthings of the present. The incessant parade of TV-based superheroes, fashion dolls, and huggables bewilders grown-ups. But fantasy toys are not new. They originated in the same era that produced the erector set and the baby doll, roughly between 1900 and World War II. The teddy bear, now a beloved emblem of child-hood and innocence, in 1906 was just another silly fad. And the mostly forgotten space pistols inspired by the Buck Rogers radio show of the 1930s share much with today's action figures derived from Saturday morning television.

Fantasy toys embodied well-known personalities and/or stories, often of topical significance. Instead of training children for adult-hood, these playthings invited the young into a "secret garden" of imagination where they could be free from the constraints of the adult world. Fantasy toys drew upon rich traditions of folk and literary characters. But primarily they were the forever-changing products of an emerging American commodity culture supplied by the dream factories of the comics, films, and radio.

Although the fantasy toy reached its full significance only in the late 1970s with the orgy of licensed cartoon action figures and

Barbie fashion sets, it first appeared around the turn of the twentieth century. City shopping districts and the boardwalks of seaside resorts created eager crowds for the spread of toy fads. Mass-produced newspaper comics and illustrated books disseminated images of attractive characters and stories. Toymakers found that these characters evoked strong emotions in American parents and children and that these feelings sold toys. Fantasy playthings were closely linked with the emergence about 1900 of a national entertainment industry built around "stars" and celebrity.[1]

From the beginning of the twentieth century parents gave fantasy toys to preschool children. It was not the young who bought the first movie or comic-strip character dolls or teddy bears and Kewpie dolls. It was parents. These playthings reflected spunky but innocent images of childhood, and the young came to identify with them. But they appealed first to adults. These toys embodied parents' longings to give their children, and share with them, both an exciting future and a nostalgic, "timeless," past. They also reflected a growing parental acceptance of children's self-expression.

By the 1930s fantasy playthings began to mirror the actual aspirations of children, as the young took up their parents' offer of freedom. The key to the fantasy toy was that it embodied the story and image of a celebrity. By the 1930s the celebrities could be marketed directly to children through new media like comic books and radio. The child's imaginary character was detached from parents' values, representing instead the child's own world of fantasy and aspiration. Toys that had begun the century expressing parental images of a free childhood that adults shared with their offspring led to toys in which children's images of themselves predominated and parents had no substantial role.

Origins of Fantasy Toys

While nineteenth-century toymakers treated playthings as hardware sidelines, innovators gradually learned to sell imagination and novelty in toys. By the 1890s even vintage toymakers were giving their old locomotives colorful names like "Whistler" and "Grand Duke." At the same time, manufacturers dressed up their goods by associating them with current and historical events. The

Bliss Company sold "Uncle Sam's New Navy . . . in which American Citizens take so much pride" in a series of miniatures of the exciting new flotilla that the United States was building in the 1890s. Bliss also offered a simple toy based on rolling a marble down a chute that was made "charming" by its seemingly irrelevant lithographed scenes of the "landing of Columbus" in 1492. This slightly late (1895) commemoration of the four hundredth anniversary of the "discovery" of America was capped by an image of Columbus himself on the top holding an American flag. Most toys remained simply miniature trains, animals, guns, and tool chests. The cost of licensing, among other factors, discouraged many toymakers. But by 1900 not all toymakers simply stamped out toys like nuts and bolts. Some packaged them in fantasy.[2]

The aggressive consumer marketing of the 1900s made a new association of toys with fantasy images irrepressible. Generic toys and dolls became "name branded" at the same time as soups and soaps. Just as plain processed soup became part of Heinz' 57 Varieties, E. I. Horsman created a line of Babyland rag dolls. Makers of food and household products found that sales increased when buyers identified products with attractive "personalities," and these personalities in turn became the subjects of toys. A St. Louis flour company, for example, sought an image that could distinguish its brand of pancake flour from many others. Aunt Jemima, who looked like the stereotypical nurturing back Mammy famous for wholesome southern cooking, fit the bill. In 1905, as an advertising ploy, packages of Aunt Jemima pancake flour included coupons to be mailed in for printed cloth that could be sewn and stuffed to make an Aunt Jemima doll. This sales gimmick was so successful that doll companies turned character trademarks into dolls (for example, the Uneeda Biscuit Boy, Fairy Soap Girl, Cracker Jack Boy, and Sunny Jim).

These were New Kid images—children depicted as fresh, happy, and even impish, but essentially wholesome. The most famous were the Campbell Soup Kids. The image of the apple-cheeked "Kids" in their overalls graced an advertisement for Campbell's Soup in the *Ladies' Home Journal* in September 1905. The image conveyed health and vitality in an era of concern about food purity and good nutrition. The Kids immediately became the spokespeople for Campbell's soups on postcards and lapel buttons. By 1910 Horsman made a set of Campbell Kids dolls. This began a partnership between the soup and toy businesses that continued on and off into the 1970s.[3]

That Americans would purchase an advertisement, especially for their children, is astonishing until we realize that literary and commercial images flowed together. They shared a world of the exciting and new that many children and adults hardly distinguished. Commercial artists and storytellers created a flow of character images and narratives that crossed freely between magazines, comic strips, jar labels, and toys and dolls. Rose O'Neill's Kewpie is only the most famous of these. The Kewpie became a standard doll, but it also sold chocolate, china, soap, and Jell-O.[4] Artists, advertisers, and the consumer goods industry (including toys) interacted in mutually beneficial ways to sell their symbols of American fun and innovation.

But the argument that fantasy/novelty toys were merely a product of skillful merchandising begs the question as to why these characters were popular. It is not just that children and parents became immersed in a consumer society. Rather the appeal of character images reflected changing meanings and values attributed to childhood by parents. By 1900 American children were beginning to serve more the psychological than the economic needs of adults. Modern middle-class parenting rejected the older view that offspring were an appropriate source of family income. But children did not lose quantitative value: adults increasingly cherished them as emotional assets, bringing meaning, love, and vitality to the home. Babies that were "cute and cuddly" were increasingly desirable in adoptions, while demand for "productive" older orphans diminished. The lovable child was the ideal. And parents expressed their love in the number and cost of toys they gave their children. While children were no longer in the wage market, they were very much a part of the consumer market.[5]

At the same time, merchandisers were recognizing the sales potential of the new sentimentality toward children. *Playthings,* for example, stressed that giving toys made adults happy: "Real merchandising demands that the desire to become loved by little children be awakened where it will do practical good"—in filling homes with toys. The pitch concluded: "No home is a home without toys."[6] Toy manufacturers tapped into adults' desire to be "accepted" by children and to live through them. This thinking had roots in early-nineteenth-century romantic literature, but twentieth-century advertising exploited it fully for the marketing of playthings.

Toymakers grasped that parents sought in their offspring the lost innocence of their own childhoods at the same time that they saw the young as the promise of a better future. In an age of flux, children rooted adults in both the timeless past and beckoning future. Thus toymakers invested their products with both images of a timeless world of imagination and images of novelty that captured timely, up-to-date events and the appeal of topical celebrities.

Modern fantasy toys drew heavily upon the literary imagination of Victorian English writers and their appeal to a romantic and even nostalgic ideas about childhood. Lewis Carroll, Charles Kingsley, Rudyard Kipling, Beatrice Potter, and J. M. Barrie created the idea of a special world of children's fantasy. It began with Kingsley's *The Water Babies* (1862), a story of a runaway boy servant of a chimney sweep who plunges into a stream and magically becomes a water baby. In an environment inhabited entirely by humanlike sea animals, the boy enters a world of fantastic adventure. Carroll's *Alice in Wonderland* (1865) similarly abandons the dull realm of adults for the bizarre world of Unbirthday Parties and Queens of Hearts. A longing for escape from industrial society was projected onto a children's fantasy world in Kipling's *Jungle Book* (1894), a series of stories featuring a boy's adventures with humanlike animals of exotic India. Barrie's *Peter Pan* (1904) treats the Darling siblings to Never Never Land where nobody ever grows up and Peter Pan spares Wendy of the fate of having to vacate the nursery until she is finally ready. The children prevail over their father's obsession with order and over Captain Hook's vicious but ultimately pitiful attempt to best the perpetual boy, Peter Pan.[7]

As with the earlier fairy tales of Grimm, these authors offered characters who reflected the yearnings of children. Even more, the growing-up adventures of these make-believe girls and boys were free from parental interference. These children lived in an "imperishable world" where the supernatural became natural." And they found refuge and nurture in the magical worlds of talking animals who befriended them.[8]

These characters existed in a timeless world which children alone understood and from which adults were usually excluded. Yet it was parents who remembered these stories from their own childhood and brought them to their offspring. Adults patronized theatrical performances of *Peter Pan* at Christmastime for a generation after its appearance as a story. And the toy industry used the image of Peter in its failed attempt to promote a new mid-June holiday, "Children's Day," in the late 1920s.[9] Parents embraced timeless tales which they could enjoy in nostalgia through their children. Some of these late Victorian stories and personalities were transformed into toys in the 1930s with Walt Disney's help. But they expressed common formulas to be found in fantasy playthings that had emerged earlier.

Adults also sought to share with their children the excitement of participating in the here and now. This was achieved first with another kind of plaything, board and card games. By the 1880s Milton Bradley, McLoughlin Brothers, and Parker Brothers were skillfully using lithography to produce cheap and rapidly changing games based on current concerns and personalities. Many celebrated the contemporary world, and travel themes were very common. Parker produced many games like "Innocence Abroad" and "Across the Continent." "Around the World with Nellie Bly" (1887) drew on a contemporary fascination with global touring and the topical appeal of a famous young female journalist. It featured fine lithographic images of exotic places like Siam. Also up-to-date was "The World's Fair Game," advertised in 1892 on the eve of the Chicago fair as the "game of the season." And, in a celebration of the new automobile, Parker produced the "Motor Carriage Game" in 1899.[10]

Doll companies also tapped into the immediacy of the contemporary news event. In 1909 E. I. Horsman offered "Cook" and "Peary" dolls in lifelike replicas of the Arctic explorers. Others manufactured "Rough Rider" playsuits commemorating Teddy Roosevelt's celebrated military exploits. These products gave children an imaginative means of reenacting the heroic events of the day. At the same time, manufacturers extended the topical appeal of exotic adventure with a line of eskimo dolls and Indian playsuits and figures. *Playthings Magazine,* founded in 1903 to promote American toys, was as much a vehicle of the novelty trade. It advertised not only fad toys and games but also topical postcards and knickknacks. Often advertisements were unclear about the age of their target market. This ambivalence was part of the "magic" of manufactured novelties: these products slid easily from appealing to adults to amusing children. And they shifted without notice from commemorating documented events in the newspapers to sheer fantasy.[11]

The early twentieth century hardly invented the fad, but there certainly were an abundance of them in this period: ping pong appeared in 1903, ouija boards in 1908, Rook in 1910, pogo sticks in 1921, Mah Jong and crossword puzzles in 1924. Not all of these were designed for children. But when games like Rook had a successful run with adults, manufacturers reissued them for the young. Parker's bobbin-and-string plaything, the Diabolo, became a rage in 1908. Advertisements showed "Gibson girls," not children, playing with it. But a toymaker immediately marketed a doll "playing" with a miniature diabolo for children. All these games were novelties that celebrated the ever-changing excitement of that optimistic age of adventure.[12]

The idea of timeless childhood merged with the timely fad in toys. Good examples are the playthings that borrowed the image of the Brownies.[13] In 1883 Palmer Cox published an illustrated poem about the adventures of invisible elflike characters in Scottish folklore called Brownies. Between 1887 and 1918 Cox wrote thirteen children's books about these "humorous but wholesome" characters. At first the Brownies were animal-like, with wings, and had no distinct personalities. Gradually they took on human appearance and characteristics. In fact they grew into distinct contemporary social stereotypes—as the "Chinaman" (with pointed hat), "Irishman" (in the costume of an mid-nineteenth-century Irish immigrant), "Policeman," "Uncle Sam," "Indian" and the "Dude."

In both looks and behavior the Brownies were antecedents of modern character sets (the Smurfs and Teenage Ninja Mutant Turtles, for example). Their whimsical hats and costumes distinguished them from one another. But they shared large heads, potbellies, stick legs, and oversized googly eyes. And typically they were all boys. Although they represented people who in real life were often in conflict, the Brownies were pals. They symbolized American urban society in the 1890s in a mythically harmonious way. But they were also up-to-date adventurers, trying airplanes as early as 1904 and joining the Rough Riders. Their antics got them into trouble, but their good deeds always led to happy endings.

The Brownies charmed Americans of various ages and thus were natural for novelty items of every sort. In the 1890s Brownies appeared on cigar holders, egg cups, napkin rings, and school supplies. The popular characters helped to sell Armour's Mincemeat and Upton's Fish Glue in trade (that is, advertising) cards. Inevitably they invaded the toy industry. By 1894 the Brownies replaced clowns as stuffed figures and were featured in jigsaw puzzles. It was acceptable to knock down these characters in the shape of pins in toy bowling sets.[14]

The Brownies were the first of an endless flow of comic characters that became toys. In 1895 Richard Outcault's the "Yellow Kid," a comic strip for the *New York Sunday World,* was popular enough to win several toy licenses. The Yellow Kid was an ideal figure into which to cast a cap bomb that children threw on the ground, making a loud bang. This toy fit the image of this bald urchin with floppy ears, who wore a yellow flour-sack nightgown. The Yellow Kid lived in a world of independent, indeed parentless, children. But the comic strip was hardly directed toward children, with its allusions to the poverty and depravity of urban slums of the era. Moreover, the mischievous antics of this slum child had limited appeal to middle-class adults.

So, after two years, Outcault replaced the Yellow Kid with Buster Brown and his dog Tige. Buster was very much like the Campbell Kids with his bow tie, broad smile, and ever-so-slightly impish look. His antics took place in a bourgeois setting comforting to most readers of the comic strip. Buster Brown and Tige made attractive rag dolls, first manufactured in 1900. The image survived and was successfully marketed for Buster Brown Shoes. Other comic strip characters before World War I were also adapted to toys. Between 1897 and 1907 the Katzenjammer Kids, Happy Hooligan, Foxy

Grandpa, Little Nemo, Alphonse and Gaston, and Mutt and Jeff appeared in the major newspaper chains and their life as toys followed soon after. A second generation of comic characters, including Gasoline Alley, Barney Google, Moon Mullins, and Felix the Kat, emerged in the 1920s and followed the same path.[15]

Creators of popular comic strips (or the syndicates who owned them) were quick to license their characters to toymakers and dollmakers. In 1909 *Playthings* touted Baby Snookums, a comic-strip star created by the cartoonist George McMannus. This comical infant of America's "worst looking father and best looking mother" was to be the next character-toy fad. Guaranteed to "boom him further" were plans for a musical comedy based on the young couple's joys and frustrations with their first baby. McMannus sold licenses for Snookums dolls and bisque statuettes featuring Snookums's trademark smile revealing one baby tooth. But Snookums also appeared on the pins in bowling games and the targets of shooting galleries.

Bud Fisher, the creator of the popular comic strip Mutt and Jeff, attempted the same trick. In 1911 Fisher used advertising in the trade press to point out to potential licensees that his Mutt and Jeff characters appeared in seventy-one newspapers. A musical comedy featuring Mutt and Jeff and a movie were expected to further promote sales of licensed figures. One of Fisher's customers was the Mysto Manufacturing of A. C. Gilbert, which sold a line of card and magic tricks featuring Mutt and Jeff. As the manufacturer, Live Long Toys, pointed out, comic-strip dolls and toys "bring to life characters which have become national figures." These fantasy personalities promised yearlong sales, "for the newspaper season is an all-time season."[16]

Comic-strip characters made excellent adornments for a wide assortment of playthings and other goods because of their simple graphic design and cheerful and amusing demeanor. Comic-strip characters shared a similar look (oversized heads, strong whimsical facial features, and spindly legs). They were parentless or independent kids, frisky but basically decent (or as a variant, foolish adults). They were impish American versions of Peter Pan and Alice in Wonderland either living in an adult-free world or getting the better of adults. The Katzenjammer Kids endlessly played pranks on grown-ups even if they got thrashed for it. These were images of a gentle rebellion against adult authority, a rebellion tolerated by parents, even embraced in the innocence of playthings.[17]

Other character images came from Hollywood. Toymakers, often with roots in the broader novelty industry, were quick to copy the images of another sign of modernity—the movie star. Charlie Chaplin was probably the first movie star doll, appearing in 1914. By 1925 Chaplin's personality was captured in a lithographed windup figure that rocked at the waist (roughly approximating the Chaplin shuffle). Other Chaplin wind-ups had a spinning cane. In the 1920s American Colortype made paper dolls with lavish wardrobes in the likenesses of Chaplin and Mary Pickford. In 1926 George Borgfeldt distributed "Little Annie Rooney," a pigtailed child doll presumably in the likeness of "Mary Pickford in her recent most successful motion picture . . . representing the irresistible romping child spirit." The child movie star Jackie Coogan appeared in 1921 as a doll with special clothing for "the Kid." And Hal Roach's "Our Gang" characters were licensed to be dolls in the mid-1920s, years before the talkies made Roach's "rascals" famous for generations thereafter.[18]

Not all the celebrities turned into toys were movie stars or even lovable. As early as 1926 a group of eight artists offered their services to toymakers to create dolls from "characters which are known and loved the country over." Among their list of "Famous People and a Famous Line" was Red Grange, the football star. Babe Ruth authorized Milton Bradley to make a "Baseball Game" featuring his name and likeness. The advertisement claimed that "the girls like it too, and often their mothers." Even the irascible W. C. Fields allowed his image to be reproduced in a doll in 1929. Like the mythical comic-strip characters, these celebrities represented exciting new images that made an ordinary doll or mechanical figure more appealing.[19]

Characters in movies, comic strips, illustrated stories, and even advertising logos offered the child fun but wholesome innocence and the thrill of the new. But these toys were rarely sold directly to children. Instead they were bought by adults, usually for the very young and still dependent child. Most of the cartoon characters appeared on the toys of toddlers, especially rag, roly-poly, and wood dolls, windup figures, and pull toys. They were not used in wagons, bicycles, or toy guns for older children, who would have more influence on the purchase decision than would the very small child. These character toys said more about the imaginations of adults than those of children.

Billikens and Teddy Bears

The themes of early fantasy toys were drawn from diverse origins. But they all were part of a particularly modern social phenomenon, the commercial festival. In contrast to traditional festivals like Christmas, commercial festivals were not fixed by season and could occur any time novelty items so captured the public's imagination that consumers rushed to buy them. They were a peculiarly modern happening, dependent on mass means of communication. While toymakers promoted and tried to manage these early commercial festivals, they often did not start them and had little control over their duration. The intensity of interest was in part prompted by the desire to be a part of a community of fashionable consumers; but a novelty's success depended on its ability to touch the emotions and sensibilities of a particular historical period.

The crazes for teddy bears, Billikens, and Kewpie dolls between 1906 and 1912 are particularly good examples of this phenomenon. More than amusing novelties passed from parents to children, Billikens and Kewpie dolls mirrored the complex and positive feelings of adults toward the young. Whereas the Billiken was a figure with an oriental boy's face on a monkey's body, the Kewpie was a white youngster (usually female) with the appearance of a cherub. Portraying children as either urchins like the Billiken or angelic like the Kewpie was common in nineteenth-century painting and photography.[20] But the sweet Kewpie also had a roughish look with the eyes askance, and the animal-like Billiken appeared on a throne with the power to bring happiness. These images were more contradictory than the common representations of children in Victorian America. They suggested that the young could be both innocent and mischievous, uncivilized but also bringers of joy. The adults who bought these dolls recognized, tolerated, and even celebrated the complexity of children.

Even though Billiken and Kewpie dolls became expressions of the new ideal of childhood, they began their careers as adults' charms and novelties. The first Billiken was a "god" that was to bring "prosperity" in the wake of the recession of 1907–08. These good-luck charms appeared first in Chicago store-window displays as "trade producers" and then were sold or rather "borrowed" for a hundred years to bring good luck to their holders. This advertising jingle of November 1908 was hardly directed toward children:

> I am the God of Luckiness
> Observe my Twinkling eye;
> Success is sure to follow those
> Who keep me closely by;
> I make men fat and heal they
> Who were quarrelsome and thin;
> I am the God of Luckiness,
> My name is Billiken.

He became the patron saint of that new contraption—the car—and was fitted on radiator caps to ward off the dangers of the open road. Imitations inevitably followed, like the "Killiblue" doll of 1909. Unlike traditional amulets, the Billiken was ephemeral, rooted not in a legend of a saint but in the social dynamics of a commercial fad. But in another way the Billiken followed a traditional path—turning from an adult's magical charm to child's toy. The dollmaker E. I. Horsman licensed this novelty, selling 200,000 Billiken figures in the second half of 1909. Horsman adopted a new jingle for the Billiken doll in the spring of 1909, designed for children.

> If you would have me stay with you,
> And like to have me play with you,
> Be very sure that you are good,
> And always act just as you should;
> I love obedient girls and boys.
> I am the King of all the toys.

From a good luck charm for adults to a Santalike figure for children, the Billiken was a doll for all ages.[21]

The Kewpie doll was similar. First appearing in a story by Rose

Neill in the *Ladies' Home Journal* in December 1909, Kewpie became a popular doll in a licensing deal with the Georges Borgfeldt company late in 1912. In magazine stories Kewpie was an androgynous figure who came to the relief of slum dwellers and the exploited. She took on the character of a Progressivist reformer. But as a licensed image Kewpie abandoned her reforming spirit, and instead reflected popular images of gender. Kewpie took the form both of the bashful girl and of a comical boy, dressed as a policeman or soldier. The Kewpie was a fad in 1911 and 1912, but it remained a popular subject for dolls for many years. "See their plump bodies, roguish eyes, and smiling faces. Everybody loves a Kewpie," trumpeted a Sears advertisement in 1919. And everybody did. Billikens and Kewpies were neither children's playthings nor adult's novelties. They were both—and thus served as a bonding agent between adults and children. The Billiken and the Kewpie dolls were part of a commercial festival that celebrated novelty even as they expressed adults' deep longings feelings toward children.[22]

The teddy bear provides even a more revealing case study in the novelty toy as part of a commercial festival. Bears seldom appeared in nineteenth-century toy catalogs, and when they did they looked mean and were apparently designed to upset young children.[23] The teddy bear was a distinctly new concept, a brilliant merging of the fierce and frightening with the cute and cuddly. It probably originated with Morris Michtom, New York storekeeper (and later founder of Ideal Toys).[24] In 1902 he noticed a newspaper cartoon first published by Clifford Berryman in the *Washington Star* showing Teddy Roosevelt sparing a baby bear on a hunting trip. He promptly asked his wife to turn the bear into a doll. Having won the permission of Teddy Roosevelt (always the publicity seeker), Michtom labeled it "Teddy's bear" and sold handmade cloth bears from his New York candy store. In 1903 he sold his stock to a jobber, Butler Brothers.

A German producer of plush toy animals, Margarete Steiff, also claimed to have invented the stuffed bear. Her nephew Richard, according to an official history, designed a cuddly soft bear in 1903. This was a revolutionary concept, for the bear was squeezeable, not hard and stiff like the common wooden toy animals and characters of the time. Moreover, it had a plush furlike exterior, unlike the traditional rag doll. Steiff had already made a mark on the toy world by adapting new technology used for manufacturing upholstery to the making of soft toy animals. Her first effort was an elephant in 1880 (doubling as a pincushion). Steiff shifted production from cottage craftspeople to a modern factory in 1905. This was shortly after she gained access to an international network of buyers and perfected her design of a jointed plush doll.

So successful was Steiff's bear that other toymakers quickly copied it. In an effort to create an emblem of "authenticity," Steiff sewed a "button in the ear" of each of its plush bears, thus creating a distinctive trademark. By early 1906 the American jobber G. Borgfeldt was marketing Steiff bears at the New York toy fair and advertising them. During the summer of 1906 the bear market surged when toy bears, sold as zoo souvenirs, attracted crowds of little boys and their parents along boardwalks at the seaside resorts of the Jersey Shore. The emergence of this fad at a seaside resort is hardly surprising. The boardwalk, even more than the new downtown shopping district, was an ideal place for novelty toys. Here a crowd appeared, eager to stand out and to blend in, a perfect setting for the frenzy of playful innovation and imitation.

The teddy bear swept the "civilized" world in 1906–07. In September of 1906 the bear was definitely linked with the name "Teddy" in *Playthings* advertising. One advertisement warned that any child without a teddy "now-a-days is quite out of fashion."[25] The teddy was a doll that was acceptable for boys because it was "masculine." Because it was cute and cuddly, taking the form of a character doll, it was also embraced by girls. Like the Billiken, the bear was not only for children. During the recession of 1907 Columbia Teddy Bear Manufacturers produced a doll with Roosevelt's trademark smile and gritting teeth that laughed "at tight money, hard times, and pessimists."

The bear quickly took on new meanings when it entered the world of adult fashion. The boys' doll was picked up by women, who dressed it like a New Kid in a sweater or overalls. Specialized bear "fashions" were sold separately by 1907. Even magazines like the *Ladies' Home Journal* offered patterns for teddy bear clothes. These included pajamas, Rough Rider, fireman, sailor, and clown suits. Other teddy bear accessories were up-to-date auto goggles and scarf pins. Teddy bears were all the "rage in the cities." "Women were seen carrying them when they went out for a walk or ride or in the theater." They had become a fashion accessory.[26]

The teddy bear character soon had his own narratives separate from the image of Roosevelt. Beginning in September of 1906 Seymour Eaton published a series of Teddy Bear story books. Songs inevitably followed, including the "Teddy Bear's Lullaby" and "Teddy Bear's Picnic," both published in 1907. Later teddy was adapted to less childlike musical forms as well: "Teddy the Hunter March and Two-Step" (1909); "The Teddy Bear Blues" (1922). Thomas Edison's film studio, not about to be left out of the craze, produced a "Teddy Bear" movie in 1907. Teddy even appeared with the British black doll the Golliwog on postcards in 1907. The practice of photographing children holding teddies also appeared as early as 1906.[27]

In 1907 the teddy was sold in a wide assortment of playthings. He became a pull toy on a wheeled platform, a mechanical bank, and a member of a Schoenhut playset, the Roosevelt Bear Menagerie. Ideal Toys manufactured a teddy bear target game (with rubber arrows) in 1910. Teddy was also sold in games. Butler Brothers featured "Home from the Jungle" and "Teddy Finds the North Pole" in 1910.[28]

In June 1908 *Playthings* announced that the teddy bear fad had ended except in the west "and in all localities where Roosevelt is greatly admired." But "the wonderful run of the bear" had sold manufacturers on the permanence of novelty. The *Playthings* author was putting his money on rabbits as the next fad. Others tried to re-create the linkage of the presidential with the cute and cuddly. In 1909, following President William Howard Taft's "memorable" ordering of possum and "taters" at a dinner in Atlanta, toymakers dashed out to market "Billy Possums" in plush. This crude attempt to create a fad around Roosevelt's successor failed and proved that fads could not be forced on the public. They emerged from the unpredictable brew of public mood and manufacturers' grasp of timing and consumer appeal.[29]

The identification of toddlers (and older girls) with plush animals has continued to the present, with many fads in between. Robert Peary's arctic exploration touched off a minor craze for polar bears in plush in 1909. In the Montgomery Ward catalog of 1923 teddy bears remained both children's companions and amulets: they were advertised as "real pals" that will "scare all gloom away." The bear theme was revived in 1930 when A. A. Milne's Winnie the Pooh character was incarnated in a plush doll. And in 1937 the arrival of a Panda at the London zoo sparked a new fad of panda bears in plush. The teddy bear became that rarity, a fad that turned into a standard.[30]

To a great extent, the teddy craze was a successful merchandising gimmick. It was a new way to dress up tired lines of dolls, games, and even savings banks.[31] It worked, and the question of why remains. Teddies embossed the old children's "tools" with a tangible and happy personality—a "pal" and a protector to young children. They offered both security and strength, a reassuring combination for the very young. But the teddies succeeded because they attracted parents—serving for a time as good luck charms and as substitute pets or even as babies in much the same way that Cabbage Patch Kids did in the early 1980s. More important, the teddy bear gave adults special feelings about their children. Parents had photographs taken of their children hugging teddy bears because this made them see their offspring as lovable like the bears.

Racist Images and Fantasy Toys

Fantasy toys often took their cue from the social and political currents and concerns of their era. It is not surprising then that the racial prejudices and divisions which solidified in the post–Civil War decades should have given rise to racist images. Many of the cast-iron and mechanical banks and wind-up figures of the 1870s and 1880s had racist themes. The Automatic Toy Works advertised its "Old Uncle Tom, the Colored Fiddler," as "comically quaint" and as "fiddl[ing] in an ecstasy of enjoyment. Funny as it is, there is something almost pathetic in it, too." Other mechanical toys from this company included the "Celebrated Negro Preacher," whose "face and dress alone provoke irresistible laughter." Not all the images were disdainful. Others were patronizing. "Old Aunt Chloe, the Negro Washerwoman," was "faithful at her toil," while the "Negro Nurse" with a child was "as natural as life." But more common were toys like the "Jolly Nigger" mechanical savings bank, where the mouth moved and eyes rolled in an "amusing" manner.

Another racist image, the Golliwog, became a common doll, especially in Britain, from 1900. It was derived from a child's short story of 1885, "Adventures of Two Dutch Dolls and a Golliwog." The Golliwog was a version of the black dandy and minstrel dressed in blue swallowtailed coat and red bow tie—but with paws instead of feet and hands, and with exaggerated eyes and lips. These racist stereotypes were not restricted to blacks. Stevens and Brown produced a mechanical bank called the "Reclining Chinaman." It featured a stereotype of a devious oriental whose hands revealed four aces when a coin tripped a lever. The "Paddy and the Pig" of 1882 showed an Irish man wolfing down a pig—playing on a stereotype of the Irish as uncivilized.[32]

Racist images of blacks persisted and found form in toys of all kinds during the 1890s and 1900s. This was the height of Jim Crow legislation that denied blacks the right to vote and legalized racial segregation in schools. Even the black rag doll was made to be "humorous." The *Ladies' Home Journal* in 1914 offered for Christmas a doll pattern for a pair of "Pickaninny Twins" who, when stuffed, were to hang from an elastic cord and be "made to dance a jig to a ragtime tune."[33]

Many racial toys seemed to give permission to treat minorities abusively. The mechanical bank called "Always did 'Spise a Mule" involved a mule kicking a grossly caricatured black man off its back. A similar idea was expressed toward the Chinese when the saying "The Chinese Must Go" was inscribed on a novelty pop gun in 1879. When a child pulled the trigger, a figure of a Chinese man was kicked in the pants. By the 1890s, with the increased popularity of target games, black images became the thing to hit. Ives sold a "Pickaninny Toy Target" featuring three black children who fell into the mouth of an alligator when the target was struck: "Three little darkies, what a jolly crew. An alligator swallowed one then there was two." In "Jim Crow Ten Pins" and "Sambo Five Pins" children were supposed to use a bowling ball to knock down wooden pins in the shape of blacks. As with other fantasy toys, the object of play was not merely shooting a pop gun or bowling. The character image shaped the meaning of the toy. While other fantasy toys were intended to evoke positive feelings about the character or event they portrayed, these racist playthings were designed to prompt negative emotions, feelings of power at abusing an outcast character, who was pictured as uncivilized, insignificant, and foolish.[34]

These toys surely passed on racist stereotypes to children through mockery and demeaning poses and situations. But they were also emblems of the exotic and unknown. In this way they were an anticipation of the character toy. Repeatedly advertisements introduced racist play objects as "grotesque" and "amusing," the same words used for marketing teddy bears and other fantasy characters. Game companies like McLoughlin Brothers sold "Chopped Up Niggers" (a jigsaw puzzle) in 1887. But they also offered "Chopped Up Animals." The theme again was the exotic and comical. Racist dolls were grouped with character dolls. In 1911 Horsman's Art Dolls included a line of twenty characters such as Pocahontas and Cotton Joe (a "Plantation Coon" in red shirt and overalls) as well as the Campbell Kids and Little Nemo. The Sears catalog of 1912 introduced comic-strip toys but also featured the Negro Dude. And in 1919 it offered a Charlie Chaplin Walker "just like he does in the movies" on the same page as black "coons" dancing the jig.[35]

The same mix of the racist stereotype and the character image appeared in play costumes. An Indian playsuit was advertised in 1908 for boys aged four to fourteen. By 1910 the On On Daga Indian Wigwam Company presented thirteen Indian playsuits beside a Teddy Roosevelt African safari costume. In 1912 Sears introduced Halloween products, offering both "Negro makeup" and the "Famous Mutt and Jeff" in masks. Others sold penny masks of Negroes, Indians, and Chinese along with clowns and devils. The invitation to the exotic and the race stereotype were joined.[36]

While character dolls and racist images in toys had common traits, the comical figure of the black person persisted through the 1920s. In 1921 the young Louis Marx made the "Alabama Coon Jigger" into a standard item in Sears catalogs, ultimately selling 8 million. This was an updated version of the dancing blacks in the iron mechanical toys of the 1880s. When wound up, the Jigger did "an old fashioned plantation break down." Marx also manufactured "dandy" variations, including "Dapper Dan," "Jazzbo Jim," and the "Spic Coon Drummer," which portrayed popular music ensembles of the era, but in particularly mocking terms: the "over-dressed" dandy made music and danced in an exotic manner that no white person would ever imitate. Children were supposed to be amused by Marx's mechanical toy "Hey Hey the Chicken Snatcher" (1926); when wound up, a dog bit the pants of a black chicken thief. One of the most famous of Marx's creations, introduced in 1928, was the "Amos 'n' Andy Fresh Air Cab," one in a very long line of "crazy cars" (which ran erratically when wound up). This toy featured images of a famous pair of black men (played ironically by two white men) on a popular radio comedy that began airing in 1928. In 1930 Ward sold the "Trick Trio," a wind-up featuring a "circus Dog and two happy Coons. The big Coon 'Charlestons' as the little one fiddles." All these toys offered the same racist images of grotesque, "amusing," and harmless blacks.[37]

Gradually, however, cartoon characters replaced these racist caricatures in toys. In the 1930s the Coon Jiggers and Amos 'n' Andy gave way to dancing Mickey Mouses and the ventriloquist's dummy Charlie McCarthy driving a "crazy car." The images of the Golliwog and the sambo survived well past World War II in stories and children's rhymes. But the transition from "coon" to character toy was relatively seamless and irrevocable. Both reflected an image of the exotic and comical, an image to which one can show disdain and hurt, and over which one can feel superior. As the United States moved away from overt racism and institutionalized segregation, the racist images of the Jim Crow era gave way to the new "fools" of the comic strip and movies.[38]

More Fantasy in the 1930s

During the 1930s fantasy toys underwent a subtle but important change. While the teddy bears and comic character toys of the 1900s through 1920s celebrated the special charms of early childhood, the Shirley Temple dolls and Buck Rogers pistols of the 1930s gave older children the means to voice longings for self-expression. The growing empathy of adults for the strivings and feelings of youth led to children's assumption of the right to self-expression. But the economic depression of the 1930s accelerated this trend. The Depression destroyed many established toy companies as sales languished. It forced enterprising firms to try to sell not only playful objects but a celebrity culture. New vehicles of communication, including sound movies, radio, and comic books, created a heroic fantasy world specifically for the young, largely bypassing adults. In the process the appeal of toys began to shift from parents to children themselves, and this shift gave fantasymakers greater control over fads.

"It's the heart strings against the purse strings this Christmas," noted a *New York Times* article in November 1931. Drastic decline in family income inevitably meant a sacrifice of "extras" like Christmas toys. The number of jobless in the United States rose from 1.55 million in 1929 (3.2 percent of the workforce) to over 12.8 million by 1933 (24.9 percent). Unemployment never dropped below 7.7 million (14.3 percent) in the 1930s. The toy market reflected the economic crisis as the estimated personal consumption of toys (together with sport supplies) dropped from $336 million in 1929 to $181 million in 1933. Despite price cutting, at least 96 toymakers disappeared between 1929 and 1931. Among the most prominent were old manufacturers like Ives and Schoenhut, whose expensive products were priced out of the market. Survivors worried not only about the diminished disposable income of American families but also about cheap Japanese imports and price-cutting competitors.[39]

Nevertheless, despite uncertain and reduced incomes, Americans clung to their "luxuries." They kept their cars and actually increased their consumption of cigarettes by 22 percent between 1929 and 1936. They even bought new gadgets like refrigerators and radios. The same was true of toys. Parents had a pronounced tendency to sacrifice "necessities" in order to give children tokens of affection and representations of innocence.[40]

But hard times did force toymakers to find new ways of selling playthings. In fact companies that adapted to the Depression economy did well. A good example is Louis Marx. He succeeded with cost-cutting manufacturing and marketing. Marx's rural factories provided low-cost seasonal labor, and his Japanese subsidiary, Lin-Mar, had even smaller wage bills. Cheap materials (even recycled tin cans) kept his toys inexpensive. Many toy companies improved packaging (using oversized boxes and color), lowered prices, and sought new retail outlets (such as drugstores). Meccano broke from tradition by offering new construction sets for boys of five or under that used no bolts, thus making play "faster" and "less tedious." These innovations were the beginnings of a long-term trend toward cheaper, flashier, and less demanding toys aimed at a broader, downscale market. This meant that not only lower-income parents but also children themselves increasingly found toys in their price range.[41]

Despite these "improvements," it was hard to sell toys as merely playthings in the Depression. A more promising avenue was to add the licensed character image to the ordinary toy. The selling of a personality or a famous media story was a way to make toys more than objects of play. Consumers purchased the fantasy worlds of Mickey Mouse, Charlie McCarthy, Shirley Temple, and Superman along with the toys that embodied their images. These toys invited children to participate in the stories and images of their heroes. This was not new to the 1930s, but the pace increased and the direction changed. In particular, licensed characters reached far beyond the infant and toddler toys of the days of the Brownies and Foxy Grandpa. The new generation of fantasy toys did not always draw upon parental ideas about what childhood meant, nor did they always offer a cross-generational appeal which parents could share and understand. Character toys entered into the imaginative worlds of older children, encouraging a more independent youth through fantasy.

A shift from parental tutelage accelerated in the 1930s. The joblessness of many men may have contributed to this trend insofar as fathers lost power over their offspring, especially older children, when they had less pocket money to give them. In many households ten- or twelve-year-old boys earned money at part-time jobs. With reduced family income, toymakers in the 1930s, anxious for sales, reached out to the child market by packaging playthings at prices affordable to the young. They also began to appeal directly to children with toys featuring their, rather than adults', celebrities.[42]

Perhaps most important in the trend toward child celebrity toys was the media. When movies got voices and radio, a mass audience, it became possible to reach children directly with fantasy entertainment. The big change began in 1926 when sound came to films and when network radio broadcasts were first heard. Weekly movie ticket sales rose almost 55 percent between 1926 and 1929, in disproportionate numbers to the young. The movies distributed novelty on a national, even global, scale and did much to create the modern celebrity. In the 1930s the movies made children want to own objects that made them feel connected to this fantasy world. This desire did not have to wait for the imitative crowd on the boardwalk in the summer or for department store window displays during the holidays. It was whetted weekly at the movie theater or at home listening to the radio in the living room. These were worlds available to most children, and often without much parental involvement. The celebrities did not even have to be real people. Cartoon characters like Mickey Mouse and Donald Duck as well as young celebrities like Jackie Coogan and Shirley Temple appealed to children.[43]

Toymakers and retailers had long understood the selling power of movie characters. But a toy buyer for Gimbel's department stores claimed the movie tie-in was an alternative to price cutting in the Depression. The store with character toys could sell at full markup "without worrying about selling merchandise for less than the fellow across the street." "Hitch your product to a star," trumpeted The Famous Artist Syndicate when it offered manufacturers licensed images of John Wayne, Clyde Beatty, and Mickey Rooney.[44]

The year 1926 not only brought voice to the movies but also saw the formation of the National Broadcasting Corporation and the beginning of network radio. In the 1930s dramatically lower prices brought radios into most American homes: in 1932 about 17 million American households had them. A survey in 1938 found that 40 percent of American households on a typical winter evening had the radio turned on. Most early network radio programs for children were presented as a public service without commercials, and radio producers were reluctant to annoy parents with violent programming designed to attract the attention of the young and impressionable. But by 1930 advertisers learned that children were extremely attentive and loyal listeners. Thus they were excellent targets for commercial messages. The radio reached everyone and did so throughout the year. It was a far more effective means of creating a community of youthful consumers than were the Sunday comics (dependent on reading skill) or the shopping and seaside crowds.[45]

Doubtless Walt Disney had the greatest impact through films on children's playthings. He learned very early in his career the potential for turning a cartoon image into a marketable personality. With the artist Ub Iwerks, Disney produced a silent Mickey Mouse cartoon in April 1928. But the real breakthrough came when, in November of that year, they made "Steamboat Willie" with sound. This added an irreplaceable element to the animation. Still Disney, like other cartoonmakers, faced a financial crunch. Costs for making movie cartoons rose with the coming of sound and the need for more realistic backgrounds, smoother, more lifelike animation, and more sophisticated story lines. At the same time, exhibitors offered Disney very low prices for these cartoons, and their rates scarcely rose in the Depression despite increased cost. Disney recognized the need to find ways of subsidizing his art.[46]

The solution was to exploit the nation's love affair with Mickey. Walt and his brother Roy hired Charlotte Clark to design a Mickey Mouse doll in January 1930 and soon thereafter hired Georges Borgfeldt Inc. to distribute Mickey Mouse dolls and novelties.[47] Disappointed by the quality of Mickey dolls produced abroad under Borgfeldt auspices, Disney hired a former Kansas City hat salesman, Herman Kay Kamen, in July of 1932 to represent Disney in merchandise licensing. Kamen proved to be a genius in the growing image business. He synchronized exposure with newspaper advertising and window displays. Beginning in 1934 he issued a total of seven Campaign Catalogs to help local merchants and theater owners coordinate their marketing efforts of Disney products. In 1935 Kamen and Roy Disney drummed up licensing deals in a well-publicized tour of Europe, winning fifty British and eighty-one continental European licenses. Kamen was a tireless promoter of the Disney image at annual toy fairs and advertised lavishly for licenses in the trade press. In the 1930s and 1940s he was an apostle of novelty. "The Walt Disney Studios have their ear to the ground continually" listening for the drum beat of change, he bragged in 1940.[48]

Many Disney licensees were not toys. In the 1930s Kamen saturated the market with Mickey Mouse's image on blankets, watches, toothbrushes, lampshades, radios, breakfast bowls, alarm clocks, Christmas tree lights, ties, and clothing of all kinds. These products, in effect, advertised for one another and for the Disney image. Kamen insisted that the Disney name appear on all licensed goods. He strictly limited the number of manufacturers producing similar items, thus winning royalty fees of up to 10 percent. And he was careful to associate the Disney name only with high-quality and appropriate products, rejecting, for example, a request for a Mickey Mouse ash tray. Kamen was quick to exploit the publicity of new characters like the Three Little Pigs (1933) and Donald Duck (1934). Major department stores featured the three pigs in their window displays during the Christmas season of 1933, putting the sentimental image of Santa in the shadow.[49]

Mickey became a kind of universal symbol, appealing to all from Soviets to patrons of the Metropolitan Museum of Art to South Sea "head hunters" (to whom Douglas Fairbanks showed Mickey cartoons). Yet he also became the all-American boy. Indeed, his cartoon behavior became more constrained, less anarchistic, over time. In 1934 Donald Duck and from 1937 Bugs Bunny, Daffy Duck, and other Warner Brothers cartoon characters took up the violent and defiant themes that Mickey had abandoned (appealing to older children with a message of freedom from the constraints of family and authority). But Mickey's shift from bad boy to choirboy made him a good role model in the eyes of parents. Mickey was still adventurous, and boys as well as girls could see him as a fun-loving child. He had joyful times with his pet dog, Pluto; and, unlike the admiring children who watched his cartoons, he did not have to go home when his mother called. With this cross-generational appeal, Mickey Mouse was the inheritor of the tradition established by the Brownies, a tamed rebel, embraced by children but also tolerated by parents who, within limits, accepted of the freedom of their children.[50]

Mickey appeared on many infant and toddler toys chosen by parents. The fledgling toymakers Fisher-Price and Ohio Art got their big boosts with rolling chimes, tea and housekeeping sets, and sand pails featuring Mickey, Minnie, and the Three Little Pigs. The older Lionel company also supplanted sagging sales of its expensive electric train sets with the Mickey Mouse windup "Hand car," selling a quarter of a million in 1934. Even the educational blocks by Halsam featured Mickey Mouse. Disney emblazoned every imaginable toy from toy carpet sweepers to printing kits with his characters.[51]

Other moviemakers attempted to join in the feast, but none was nearly as successful. Paramount teamed with Gimbel's Department Store in promoting an "Alice in Wonderland" film and Alice dolls in December 1933. Columbia Pictures pushed the image of a dog named Scrappy from a children's cartoon in 1935. Terry Tunes offered Kiko the Kangaroo for toy licensing in 1936. And Paramount hoped to sell licenses for its cartoon production of *Gulliver's Travels* in 1939. But the big winner was Disney, who pioneered the licensing arrangements that now are commonplace.[52]

Mickey Mouse dolls and toys appeared after the character had already become a "friend" of American children. But by 1937 Disney had grown more daring. He licensed the image of Snow White and the Seven Dwarfs before the public had even seen them in the movie. Ideal Toys and Madame Alexander Dolls announced Snow White dolls months before the release of Disney's first feature-length cartoon on December 21, 1937. Even though the film had reached only a tenth of the American market by April 1938, the merchandising frenzy was well under way. The Disney name was enough to sell licenses to Fisher-Price, Halsam, Ideal, Lincoln Logs, and Lionel. And department stores ran Snow White window displays in cross-advertising schemes with movie theaters when the movie was in town. The toy trade was effusive in its praise of Disney for creating a special gift-giving season by marketing *Snow White* after Christmas: "Through this magnificent creation, Walt Disney has made possible the manufacture and sale of merchandise which has given employment to thousands, has increased sales and profits for wholesalers and retailers, and has brought unbounded joy to many children."[53]

In the midst of the Snow White frenzy, Disney announced plans to issue full-length cartoon features annually. By the summer of 1939 Pinocchio toys and dolls were in production for the February 1940 release of the movie. By the late 1930s Disney had already developed a marketing strategy that now dominates children's culture: he coordinated the appearance of licensed goods and movie fantasy, creating a commercial festival during which Americans were pulled into a craze for owning Snow White merchandise. Disney had taken the commercial festival to a new level by effectively managing it. Only in the 1970s would this pattern become standard operating procedure in toy marketing, but the simultaneous push of movie story and toy began with Snow White.[54]

Radio was another venue for the growth of the character toy. Those hours after school and before dinner became the children's time to control the radio dial. Radio advertisers used the heroes of their programs in premiums to increase sales. Jack Armstrong, Tom Mix, Buck Rogers, Charlie McCarthy, and Little Orphan Annie won loyal audiences and sold malt drinks, breakfast foods, and coffee when children collected labels and box tops to "earn" compasses, pedometers, decoder rings, and even pocket knives with their favorite hero's picture on them. These premiums initiated children into the licensed fantasy market in ways similar to the role played today by McDonald's Happy Meal toys.[55]

But the radio was more than a conduit for licensed products. It shaped the toy culture by introducing play narratives that were designed specifically for children and that required toys to serve as props for the reenactment of radio story lines. Radio serials gave voices and sound effects to the images in the daily comic strips. Chester Gould's Dick Tracy (a comic strip introduced in 1931) featured strong images and colors, manly personalities, and striking situations that were easily converted into boys' toys. A radio program made Tracy come alive. The Dick Tracy Jr. Click Pistol (with "Oh Boy! It's just like Dick Tracy" on the box) was a typical toy generated by the radio program. When children heard Tracy's police car screech down the street and his gun fire as he chased crooks, they wanted official Dick Tracy police cars and pistols.[56]

One of the biggest radio celebrities was Charlie McCarthy, the wooden puppet of the ventriloquist Edgar Bergen. In 1937 Bergen won an audience of 20 million listeners for his Sunday evening program even though radio deprived the audience of witnessing his skill at throwing his voice. The fun was in Bergen's playing the straight man to Charlie. This was a live performance of a well-established comic-strip genre—the child in Charlie getting the better of the fatherly Edgar Bergen. Again, their act attracted parents adapting to a more democratic, child-centered family. But the show also directly appealed to the young with its premiums. When children mailed in four labels from cans of Chase and Sandborn Coffee, Bergen's sponsor, they received a cardboard Charlie McCarthy. Bergen also licensed Charlie's image to an amazing variety of toys and novelties. Charlie was sold on everything from bingo games, vitamin bottles, and pencil sharpeners to ventriloquist instruction manuals. Of course, Charlie was a natural as a wind-up toy and doll. In an unusually creative effort at cross-over marketing, there was even a child's book, *Charlie McCarthy Meets Snow White.* The intensity and speed of the radio-induced Charlie craze left many stores with shortages of Charlie merchandise in the weeks before Christmas of 1937.[57]

Character toys from the movies and radio added an extra licensing expense to the manufacturer and, because of this cost, often reduced retailers' profit margins But they did help overcome some common frustrations in the business. General advertising for generic toys was of uncertain value because unadvertised substitutes were so easily found at stores and thus no particular brand could be certain of benefitting from advertising. Manufacturers understood this and so they promoted their wares to jobbers and retailers through trade magazines and traveling sales staffs rather than directly to the consumer. Manufacturers had to win access to sales shelves from retailers before they could reach children.

However, character licensing changed everything. The media personality put a "child's friend" on an ordinary sand pail or pull toy. These toys stood out from the generic version and in effect sold themselves. Retailers then had an incentive to seek a specific line of goods featuring Mickey or Popeye. This gave manufacturers who used licensed characters leverage over store owners. These celebrity images also helped increase retail sales. Disney-licensed products freed the retailer from expensive promotions because Disney provided attractive displays. Character toys rationalized selling, or, at least, reduced the need for trained sales staff and in-house promotions. Ultimately, licensing changed the nature of the toy. As one toy insider noted in 1936, Mickey Mouse "toys and games do not need to be so complex as formerly." A simple pull toy with Mickey on it would sell as well as a clever windup.[58]

The sale came not so much from the utility, function, or even quality of the licensed plaything. Customers would often recognize these attributes only if a costly sales staff pointed them out. Rather what sold the toy or doll was the image of Mickey or Shirley. Consumers bought more than a plaything with their purchase. They won entry into a special community of the initiated and of fantasy as embodied in the celebrity image. A McCarthy doll gave the radio listener possession of a celebrated voice even if the doll could not talk. And passive viewers of movie cartoons won three-dimensional action with a Mickey Mouse hand car. In both cases the toy made the owner a player in the world of the character. These playthings often gave the owner something that the star had—the gun, rocket, decoder, hair bow, or just the "look" of the personality. By possessing a celebrity toy the child owned a bit of the spunk, charm, power, or even good luck of the character. These toys retained the mark of the good luck charm embodied in the Billiken. And, like the novelties of the 1900s, they arose not from a folk culture but in the ephemeral world of the commercial fad.

Many of these playthings of the 1930s continued to appeal to both adults and small children. They shared with earlier character toys a complex image of children as charming if impish, innocent if daring. Mickey Mouse and Donald Duck may have been childlike, but they were not children. Charlie McCarthy was impudent, but everyone understood that he was really the voice of a fatherly ventriloquist. These toys were a celebration of a more tolerant child rearing. But the parent was always present.

A Separate World of Child's Fantasy

Other toys of the 1930s represented a sharper break from the past. These reflected not adults' fantasies about children but children's fantasies about themselves as interpreted by the profit-seeking imagemakers. Fantasy became equated with freedom. A key to this change was the marketing of character toys directly to school-aged children. These playthings appealed to a youth's quest for autonomy and were almost always directed specifically to either boys or (much less often) girls.

The boys' toybox changed subtly in the 1930s. The hero began to replace the machine as the central prop of play. While the construction set of the 1910s and 1920s called the boy to imitate men and to imagine his future role in an orderly world of economic and technological progress, the new male fantasy toys beckoned the youth to a far away realm where conflict dominated. Rather than inviting the boy to identify with the father, the new toys evoked an image of strong men, but free from the bonds of family. The cowboy star, the tough detective, the boxer, the spaceman, and the superhero became father substitutes. In the 1930s Tom Mix, Dick Tracy, Popeye, Buck Rogers, and Superman offered boys a wide variety of fantasies based on courageous, powerful individualists who defended right against wrong. They all shared a penchant for conflict, not construction, for control, not achievement. And they all lived in a world free from families, where a boy could forget that he was a child and that he might have had an unheroic father without a steady job.

A toy industry eager for sales in the Depression appealed to youth through celebrity playthings. But these personalities did far more than endorse toys. Their heroism became an integral part of the toy itself when the boy was invited to take the role of the hero in fighting the bad guys. Of course, mock battle and the fantasies of heroism had roots long before the new character toys of the 1930s. And the imitative play of the 1920s as embodied in the erector set long survived the Depression. But the origins of the modern action figure are in the 1930s. In order to understand how these figures departed from earlier toys of conflict, it is necessary to look at the earlier history of military toys and how they changed in the Depression.

The standard boy's arsenal—cap, pop, spring, and air guns—all had roots in the thirty years before 1890. The Ives catalog of 1894 included six pages showing nineteen guns, including a self-cocking "Wild West" pistol. Despite advertisers' claims that these toys were harmless, many guns and cannons used "bullets" of wooden sticks or balls that doubtless caused many injuries and restricted sales to older boys. After 1900 the trend was toward safer toy weapons with the introduction of elastic tip projectiles and repeating cap pistols. In any case, toy guns were still relatively rare before World War I and no advertisers encouraged mock combat between children.

Many were sold in target games, designed for family fun in the parlor or yard.[59]

Shortly before and during World War I, toy guns became more prominent as the nation prepared itself for war.[60] Toymakers tried to associate these guns, not with violence, but with training for manhood and patriotic imitation of the men at the front. Advertisements show that these play weapons were still sold to parents rather than children. In 1913 the toy firm of Kilgore produced the Boy Scout Machine Gun, complete with hollow rubber balls and toy soldiers to shoot. This toy rather brazenly identified itself with that respectable organization, founded in 1910, which promised to make men of boys. This may have helped disguise from parents the toy's real purpose—shooting toy soldiers.

Liberty Toys introduced a playset called Modern Trench Warfare in July 1917 that claimed to be built on the "recommendation of the world's best war correspondents and authorities." It came with a grenade thrower, barricade bags, trench shovel, periscope, and semaphore flags, and sword. Interestingly, however, it did not include the deadly machine gun. C. R. Williams Toys offered a miniature of the Springfield rifle as "recently adopted by the USA" without appealing to war play in its advertisements. Hoping to exploit patriotism, Milton Bradley produced a Black Jack Machine Gun in 1920 in honor of General John Pershing. An advertisement noted the advantageous timing of the toy: "just now big brothers are coming home and little fellows are saturated with the spirit of hero worship." This toy machine gun commemorated the recent military victory, not the emotional intensity of combat. And imitation of real war quickly faded in the 1920s.

A more lasting selling point was the association of toy weapons with training for manhood. Again the appeal was to parents (or children trying to please parents). The Daisy Air Rifle, manufactured in Plymouth Michigan since 1888, gradually became a training toy for the manly art of shooting.[61] As advertising bragged in 1919, the Daisy was a "plaything that grew into a National Sport." By that year "old boys [were] buying Daisys for their sons." The air rifle was "an education for the American boy" and provided vital "lessons of manliness, self reliance, keenness of eye, and steadiness of hand and nerve that will reinforce [the boy] for the battle of life in later years." Daisy advertisements recalled the "countless generations of American marksmen" and noted "your boy's natural craving for the New Daisy" in appeals to fathers.

Daisy's sale pitch was similar to Gilbert's or Ives's for erector sets and electric trains. They all claimed to bridge the generations and to make boys into practical and effective men. Daisy's training for the "battle of life" was the struggle for success, not military victory, much less fantasy combat. Throughout the 1930s Daisy promotions in *American Boy* and similar magazines continued to appeal to manhood training. Advertising even aided boys seeking to win reluctant parents to invest in this initiation rite of American youth. Daisy offered printed "reminders" that boys could place under mother's milk bottles or in father's newspaper.

Children used these toy guns and military playsets to reenact battle and war. But manufacturers tried to mask this fact with appeals to father-son bonding, patriotism, and history. Manufacturers set these toys in a social context that connected them to adults and noble values, not just a child's world of make-believe combat.

But toy guns began to change in the 1930s in ways that allowed the self-expression of youth through fantasy role playing. Toy gunmakers dressed up their plain weapons with the romance of media heros. For Christmas of 1934 Daisy offered a rifle endorsed by the movie cowboy Buck Jones for boys wanting to play Daniel Boone. Hubley presented the "Winner" to "kids who idolize the G-men" and the "Dandy" to the "youngster who still swears by America's hard-riding, sure-shootin' western heroes." Gone were the appeals to mundane adult values and concerns. These were toys sold to boys.[62]

The combination of more aggressive marketing of toy guns and general anxiety about crime in the gangster-ridden 1930s produced a negative public reaction. In 1934 and 1935 Rose Simone, a militant opponent of weapon toys, organized a bonfire into which guns gathered from children in sixty Chicago-area schools were thrown. One Chicago judge endorsed this gesture with the comment: "When [the boy] gets used to pulling the trigger of a toy gun, it's not a long step toward pulling the trigger of a real one." In a similar vein, Nelson Crawford wrote that military toys "not only encourage aggressive instincts but tend to make the child think of war as a normal event."[63]

The trade magazine *Toys and Novelties* responded with an editorial and its opposing pop psychology: to ban toy guns would fuel boys' desire for their dads' real guns. Blaming toy weapons for crime was the "same as saying baby dolls promote illegitimacy." The toy gun was a "natural article of childish enjoyment." The makers of Daisy air rifles insisted that there was nothing wrong with guns, real or for play, because they built "comradeship" between fathers and sons. Guns taught boys how to protect property and loved ones. This was a debate that would be repeated in the decades to come.[64]

The militarization of boy's play was not restricted to toy weapons. There was a decided growth in the quantity and variety of toy soldiers from about 1934. While American companies had made lead soldiers from 1890, most toy soldiers were imported until World War I. They were usually sold to parents in expensive sets and retained the aura of privilege befitting their aristocratic origins. The upsurge of the 1930s came with cheaper metals, introduced especially by Barclay Manufacturing. The Manoil company began producing toy soldiers only in 1935, soon innovating in plastic. These soldiers were not only cheap but were sold as individual figures and accessories in neighborhood dime stores. For the first time, ordinary boys could purchase toy armies, one soldier at a time, with their own money. Rapaport Brothers offered an even cheaper route, in their popular Junior Caster set, which allowed boys to cast their own toy soldiers in special molds. In the 1930s boys' age-old habit of collecting began to shift from shells or bottle caps to the constantly expanding number of military figures.[65]

War play in the 1930s retained its traditional associations with history rather than with combat for its own sake. The Greycraft Iron Man series of 1940, for example, was an invitation to reenact a real war—in this case the boy's fathers' experience as doughboys. However, Greycraft hedged its bets on the new military fashion. Included with this popular line of toy soldiers were miniature clowns, Boy Scouts, and even Red Cross nurses. This was a long way from the modern action figure. But it was a step in that direction.[66]

Boys' war play was first given "cosmic" significance with Buck Rogers. When the tale of Buck Rogers in the adult magazine *Amazing Stories* was turned into a comic strip in 1929, space fantasy became available to children. This science fiction hero became even more the property of the young when Buck spoke on a radio show in 1932 and was seen in a movie serial in 1939 during Saturday matinees. According to the basic story line, Anthony Rogers, a lieutenant in the U.S. Air Corps, accidently fell into a "radio active coma" in 1927 and awoke in the twenty-fifth century. There he found an America divided into forest-dwelling gangs who were lorded over by Mongolian conquerors, the Han. These Asiatic tyrants had become decadent with the technological comforts of their glassed-in cities. This became the setting for an endless run of adventures with Buck, his twenty-fifth-century girlfriend Wilma Deering, and Dr. Bill Huer, an older inventor of space gadgets. Together they battled Killer Kane and the female co-villain, Ardala. Buck Rogers lived in a world of technological imagination and heroic individualism. His story tapped into the same romance of gadgetry that made erector sets appealing to boys in the 1920s. But Rogers's technology was pure make-believe and had no relationship to the world of the boys' fathers.[67]

Buck Rogers was easily converted from a fantasy story to a toy. The premiums offered by Cream of Wheat cereal and the well-timed extension of exposure made Buck Rogers an excellent property for toy licensing. Another major advantage was the sheer gadgetry of the series. Each year new weapons, vehicles, and characters were added, contributing to the fun of children and the profit of toymakers. In contrast, Tarzan, another comic-strip figure that moved to radio in 1934, had none of the licensing success of Buck because of the primitive setting and lack of gadgetry.

In 1934 Daisy Air Rifles offered a Buck Rogers Rocket Pistol for fifty cents. Compared with the BB gun at two to five dollars, this pistol was within the economic reach of many boys. After the price was reduced to a quarter, 3 million were sold. Daisy even offered a Space Helmet to make the fantasy more playable. The follow-up was the Buck Rogers Disintegrator Pistol, "able" to destroy buildings with an electronic charge. Buck Rogers toys covered the range. Sackman Brothers sold Buck Rogers costumes. Junior Caster sets

featured molds for figures of Buck, Wilma, and Killer Kane. Tootsietoy offered complete Buck Rogers playsets with figures. Manufacturers did not fail to remind retailers that 25 million Americans
heard Buck on radio or read his comic strip.[68]

The tying of the Buck Rogers story to toys reflected a subtle
change in boys' play. Daisy's foray into licensed fantasy weapons
illustrates a shift from the training toys of the 1910s and 1920s to
the play props of a parentless and ahistoric world of the imagination. Buck Rogers hardly invented war play. But radio fantasy legitimized it and gave it new significance. While imitating Buck
Rogers, boys ceased to reenact the battles of their fathers or even to
re-create the clashes of historic wars. They played out their own
heroic roles in a fantasy world.

Superman followed in Buck's wake. Unlike Buck Rogers and his
imitators like Flash Gordon, Superman's success began not in the
comic strips but comic books. The difference was significant: The
comic book was specifically designed for children, not for family
reading. Collections of Sunday newspaper comic strips in booklet
form appeared in 1934. By 1936 six companies produced "picture
stories" featuring detectives, cowboys, and other adventures. But
the full potential of the fantasy/graphic story arrived only in June
1938 with the first issue of *Action Comics* which featured the story
of Superman. This is an excellent example of the trend toward
autonomous children's fantasy. By 1940 up to 1.35 million Superman comic books were sold per issue, a movie series was already
in the making, and Superman had a radio series three days a week.[69]

That same year, Marx, ever quick to pick up on a trend, produced
a tin-lithographed wind-up called "Superman Fighting the Airplane." Mechanical toys increasingly featured fighting rather than
dancing. Popeye, a comic-strip figure from 1929, boxed with Bluto
in a wind-up of the mid-1930s. The comic strips and cartoons offered an endlessly repeated theme of individual combat that easily
translated into toys.[70]

The appeal of boys' fantasy play was surely complex. The space
theme may well have expressed the common expectation of a high
technological future and helped the young adapt to rapid change.
These toys were liberating—freeing children from the constraints of
memorializing the past and allowing the unimpeded flow of the

imagination about the future. The boy could choose his own forms of fantasy, not merely accept his parents' nostalgic vision of play. Even the stress on individual combat play was geared to the child's imagination and expression. It vented aggression and prized ingenuity rather than attempt to teach military tactics and team play as did the older toy soldier sets.

These boys' fantasy toys also escaped from the world of economic instability in the 1930s—of technology that took away jobs and seemed to betray the older promise of exciting careers as "railroad superintendents" and engineers. And the cowboy and war play of the Depression years was no longer connected to the reality of future careers or the experience of fathers. The advertisements in magazines like *The American Boy* or *Child's Life* featured construction toys and electric trains in the 1920s. Boys and their fathers at play was a common theme. In the 1930s, however, these were partly replaced by guns and space age gadgetry. The dreams of business success receded; in their place emerged fantasies of interplanetary combat. The fathers' role in play faded while Buck Jones and Buck Rogers replaced them. The boy's need to identify with adults remained, but it was often displaced onto imaginary characters. In the Depression these timeless heroes had more appeal than the sometimes jobless dads, who reminded all of a future difficult to predict.

These were toys unlike any recalled by parents, and yet few parents objected. Increasingly each age group and gender had its own fantasy figures—be they living or historic heroes, cartoon characters or movie stars. Adults and children, men and women had their own spaces on the store shelves where they could find props of play and dreams. Celebrity worship permeated the culture in the 1930s, and boys' fantasy toys reflected this phenomenon.

More subdued in their appeal to fantasy and autonomy were character toys designed for girls. The Shirley Temple doll offered a subtle shift in girls' mothering, clothing, and friendship play. Ideal Toys introduced a doll in the likeness of this child movie star for Christmas of 1934. Although she was really only a companion doll, serving as a friend for little girls, the Shirley Temple doll commanded a price of $4.49 in 1935, while Sears sold a similar nonlicensed companion doll for $1.48. Even so, the Shirley Temple doll accounted for almost a third of all doll sales in that year.[71]

What made this doll different was her association with Shirley Temple movies. Indeed, marketing by Ideal and other manufacturers of her image was linked to the appearance of her films. The coincidence of Shirley's birthday with the appearance of the movie *Captain January* in April 1936 prompted a publicity binge that would have made the merchandisers of *Star Wars* forty-one years later proud. Department stores ran Shirley look-alike contests and advertised the movie in their toy departments while theaters set up Shirley Temple doll displays in their lobbies. Meanwhile, merchants featured Shirley Temple songbooks, handbags, sewing cards, paper dolls, coloring books, soap, and other novelties. Ideal Toys bragged that this was to be the "biggest non-Christmas toy event in history."[72]

Temple's hairstyle and hair bow became a craze with mothers. Adults bought the doll (which looked like Shirley down to her hazel eyes and fifty-two curls in her hair) to share with their daughters. Nevertheless, the doll appealed to girls for their own reasons. In the Strong Museum oral history of women and their dolls, women who had been children in the 1930s recalled how important it was to own a "real" Shirley Temple doll. Participation in the fad made them part of a nationwide community of consumers. When *Child Life* offered girls a Shirley doll for selling subscriptions, the magazine also included an "autographed" photo of Shirley. American girls were invited to imitate the celebrity worship of their mothers and older sisters with a star of their own.[73]

The Shirley Temple craze followed a pattern similar to the teddy bear and Kewpie fads. It brought together adults and children in a collective fantasy of the adoring and the adored, a celebration of playful parenting and a childhood full of play. Parents shared with their daughters the fun of participating in the craze and of shopping for and purchasing the doll that "everybody" else wanted. The Shirley Temple marketing phenomenon originated in the cross-generational medium of the movies. And the character was a real girl, one other girls could fantasize as a companion. At the same time, this fad of the 1930s was different from its predecessors.

Shirley was not merely a pal doll like Patsy. She was bigger than life on the movie screen and lived out charming stories of a spunky child surmounting adversity. The doll gave girls access to Shirley's world and, in so doing, took the girls out of their narrow life of home and family and into the broader world of excitement and challenge.

Shirley Temple had the disadvantage of growing up. By the late 1930s she lost that adorable look, and parents were not quite ready to give a teenage doll version of Shirley to their young daughters. Other child celebrity dolls inevitably followed (Jane Withers, Margaret O'Brien, Judy Garland, and Deanna Durbin especially). The Dionne quintuplets, born on May 28, 1934, became instant celebrities for nothing more than the novelty of their number. Their likenesses were exploited on postcards, spoons, calendars, and especially toys and dolls. The Madame Alexander Doll Company obtained an exclusive license in 1935 and marketed quint dolls the next year with the help of a movie, *The Country Doctor,* featuring their story. But none of these child celebrities had the impact of Shirley.[74]

Little Orphan Annie represented a somewhat different image of girlhood in the 1930s. As a comic-strip character with poker-chip eyes, Annie would never grow up or change her personality. A victim of the Depression, Annie was saved by the rich war profiteer Daddy Warbucks. Children were attracted to her story because it featured a child like themselves, but also a hero, prevailing over the poverty and insecurity that many children of the Depression knew all too well. Annie's radio program encouraged children to identity with her by touting memberships in a "secret society" and promoting decoder rings and other "special" premiums. Like her more numerous male counterparts, Annie's image was a major licensing success in the mid-1930s. She appeared not only as a doll and on clothing but in and on coloring books, paint sets, playing cards, knitting sets, tea sets, moccasins, cash register banks, ball-and-jacks sets, wall pockets, bubble pipes, travel games, skipping ropes, and toy electric ranges. Her image was on virtually anything a parent might buy for a daughter or a girl might buy for herself. Annie became practically a trademark of the girls' consumer culture in the 1930s.[75]

Glimmers of a more independent girl were reflected in Annie on craft kits and even toy fire engines. These playthings told girls that they could be creative and do the same things boys did. Indeed, by the end of the 1930s the marketing expert E. Knowles noted that the old market for companion dolls was saturated. She thought the next success might be a teenage doll appealing to a more mature and less dependent girl. The fulfillment of that prediction would have to wait another twenty years until Barbie appeared. Annie remained a little girl just like her owners. She did not invite girls to imagine themselves superwomen. But she did endorse an expanding world of female-oriented goods and identify consumption with the freedom that came with growing up. In this way, at least, she anticipated Barbie.[76]

Still, media character dolls and toys for girls in the 1930s were a far less dramatic break with the past than the space and war playthings of boys. They were mostly a new breed of companion dolls. Shirley Temple was a New Kid doll in the flesh, a perfect image of the cute and cuddly, that was turned back into still another New Kid doll. Like that of Buck Rogers, her celebrity status was a creation of the media and its ability to tell a story. But Shirley and Annie remained tethered to a world of caring adults. They were spunky but cute, as much a reflection of parents' fantasies of "perfect children" as children's idealizations of themselves. Boys' toys went further. Boys had a fantasy world free of families. Theirs was the realm of heroic men. Girls could join (and maybe even identify with Wilma Deering). But they had to participate on the boys' terms. And there were no Wilma guns.

A new age of the fantasy plaything had emerged in the 1930s. And it was a commercial success. Estimated personal consumption of toys (including sporting supplies) rose from $181 million in 1933 to $285 million in 1939 (though this was still below the $336 million of 1929). The impact of fantasy toys is impossible to measure. But toymakers surely believed that Mickey, Buck, and Annie had helped save them during the Depression.[77]

The fantasy toy appeared about 1900, at a time when aggressive marketing and revolutionary media interacted with an increasingly child-centered, child-indulgent family. Manufacturers did not merely manipulate nostalgic and insecure parents, nor exploit naive children. Rather, fantasy toys met the changing needs of a new family as it evolved in the first forty years of the century. The first generation of fantasy/fad toys responded to parents' desire for playthings that expressed their growing empathy for the complex emotional and social lives of children. These toys represented children both as priceless innocents needing protection from a world of calculation and as harbingers of the new and the future expressed through an expanding and exciting consumer culture. They embodied complex meanings that could be embraced by both children and adults. The American toy industry, newly skilled in the arts of advertising and marketing, responded with familiar characters that subtly represented these complex feelings.

A second phase emerged in the 1930s. The message that parents had expressed through toys for thirty years—that children had the right of self-expression—was taken up by children themselves in fantasy playthings. In an effort to revive markets in a time of grim economic and social realities, toymakers collaborated with a new breed of mythmakers in appealing more directly to children through movies, radio, and comic books. Ironically, those teddy bears and kewpie dolls that expressed parents' empathy for the young and desire to share in the joys of childhood led to the Buck Rogers and Orphan Annie toys that gave voice to the child's imagination and left adults out of the picture. The impact of this change would haunt parents thereafter.

Among the few toys of early American children was the Noah's Ark, a playset first made by German woodworkers in the sixteenth century, given by pious parents to children for uplifting play on the Sabbath.

This German doll by Simon and Halbig from the 1890s instructed
daughters of the middle class in the latest fashions and the proper care
of delicate objects.

Miniature kitchens acquainted girls in the 1890s with their future household tools.

Boys were introduced to the wider world through transportation toys like this 1895 cast-iron horse and fire wagon made by Wilkins.

Other playthings were as much for the amusement
of parents as for children. In this famous mechanical
savings bank called the Jolly Nigger, the racist stereotype of white adults was confirmed when the black
figure was made to put a coin in his mouth and to
roll his eyes. This toy was widely sold in the 1880s
but it and many other toys depicting grossly racist
themes were reproduced into the 1920s, as seen in
this British copy by Starkie.

Early signs of change can be seen in this set of playful acrobats patented in 1867 by Charles Crandall. This construction toy was supposed to teach the child, but it also celebrated innocence and delight in play.

Unlike the traditional Noah's Ark, Albert Schoenhut's Humpty Dumpty Circus of the 1900s changed yearly, enticing children with the promise of novelty and unfettered fantasy.

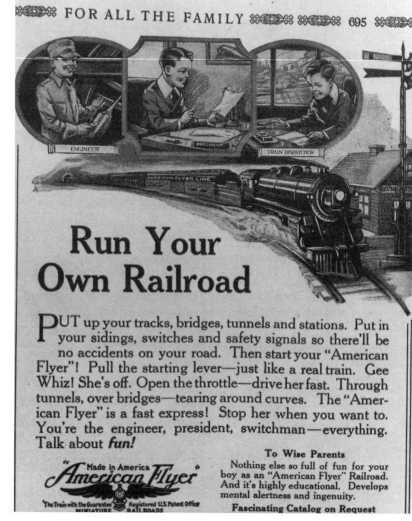

In the first decade of the twentieth century automobiles and trucks replaced the horse in boys' play just as in the real lives of their parents. Even more important were electric train sets, like this one from Lionel in 1919, which helped middle-class boys imagine their futures in a real world of work and technology.

FRANK
MURCH

He Holds the Key to Wonderful Days

WONDERFUL days, and wonderful joys, the whole year through. For this is more than a catalog of toys—it's brimful, from cover to cover, of "American Industry in Miniature." It describes dozens of toys the American boy has never before had the opportunity to own. The great motors and generators, you've seen and read about—and the machinery they run—all are here, modeled in miniature. With

KNAPP ELECTRIC TOYS

you can set up a Lilliputian factory in your room or workshop. Motors use either lighting current or batteries. Everything—motors, generators, gears, transmissions and machinery—is made to work and to last.

Knapp Electric Toys are sold at Toy, Depart-ment, Electric and Hardware Stores everywhere. Your dealer will gladly show you the catalog, or we will send it to you for 6c postage. Write us or see your dealer now, in order to have plenty of time to make your selection of Knapp Electric Toys before Christmas.

oymakers also offered sophisticated construction and scientific playthings that in-
roduced boys to the latest technology and to an ethos of scientific progress. Accord-
ng to this ad, Knapp's Electric Toys were really "American Industry in Miniature."

This Butterick Rag Doll, designed to teach the girl the necessary art of sewing clothes, was still common in 1907 but became far less so by the 1920s, when dolls with distinct "personalities" came with ready-made dresses.

Patsy by Effanbee (first made in 1924) was a character doll, intended to be a girl's companion, not a miniature mannequin. In contrast to the Victorian "lady" dolls, Patsy and her little sister Patsy Ann had childlike faces.

The baby doll became far more common as the number of real babies
in families declined. This Bye-Lo Baby, first introduced in 1923 by Grace
Storey Putnam, was supposedly modeled after a three-day-old infant.
It was advertised regularly in women's magazines as a doll that would
encourage the maternal instinct in girls.

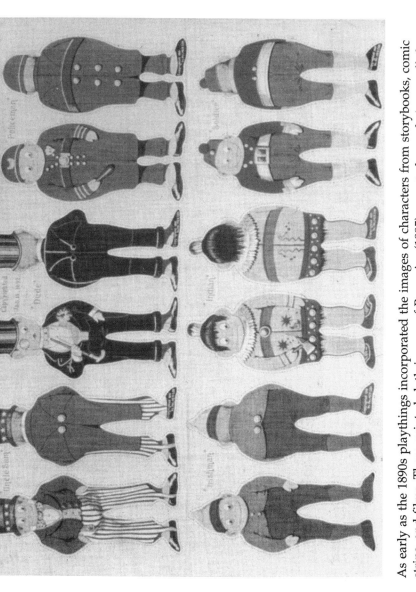

As early as the 1890s playthings incorporated the images of characters from storybooks, comic strips, and films. These printed cloth images of Brownies (1895) were to be made into stuffed dolls. The Brownies encouraged an image of childhood as a celebration of youth and play more than as a time of preparation for adult roles.

The Billiken doll, a commercial craze in 1907 and 1908, like its near contemporaries the teddy bear and the Kewpie doll, was enjoyed by parents as well as children.

While comic-strip characters appeared occasionally in toys and dolls from the 1900s, only with the movie cartoons in the 1930s did they have a major impact on playthings. During the Depression years toys based on Disney characters, like this Mickey Mouse Hand Car by Lionel (1936), attracted scarce toy dollars.

Help Your Boy Grow

Different Daisy models range in price from $1.00 to $5.00, and in size to suit the younger as well as the older boys. Ask any hardware or sporting goods dealer.

When your boy asks for an air rifle remember that it is the strong, upstanding American man in him asking for a chance to grow.

Millions of clean-cut, alert American boys, now grown, had their first training in manly sport with a Daisy Air Rifle. Mothers, as well as fathers, now generally recognize that this training makes for character and manliness.

Give your boy a chance to develop character while he's having the time of his life in harmless fun.

DAISY MANUFACTURING COMPANY
Plymouth, Michigan, U. S. A.

"The Happy Daisy Boy"

DAISY
AIR RIFLES

Many toys served to pass values from parent to child. That certainly was the theme of this ad for the Daisy air rifle of 1922.

Brand New!

A GENUINE,

Official

BUCK ROGERS
ROCKET PISTOL
that retails for **20**¢

THINK THIS OVER!!

★ A brand new *genuine* Buck Rogers Rocket Pistol . . . 7½ inches long.
★ Has *every* feature found on the original Rocket Pistol—the toy sensation of 1934.
★ Packed in the same famous display carton that pulled such tremendous sales for the original Rocket Pistol.
★ New low price opens up a huge NEW market for you!
★ Nationally advertised—naturally—like everything DAISY builds—your guarantee of *100% SALABILITY.*

Ready for delivery about February 1st. All orders will be filled in the order they're received. We will gladly furnish you additional information and prices.

and of course

IT'S
A
DAISY

DAISY MANUFACTURING COMPANY, PLYMOUTH, MICHIGAN

When writing to Daisy Manufacturing Company. will you please mention PLAYTHINGS?

By the 1930s imaginary radio and movie characters began to replace the father as role models and fantasy gun play began to supplant realistic toy weapons, as illustrated by this 1935 Buck Rogers Rocket Pistol by Daisy.

The Shirley Temple doll illustrates the transformation of the character doll into a celebrity figure in the mid-1930s.

The birth of the Canadian Dionne quintuplets in 1935 was a celebrated event captured by these German-made quints.

The Build-At-Will Doll House and Playskool, The Home Kindergarten, are two Playskool Products which provide many happy play hours for children of kindergarten and primary age.

See Them At Leading Stores

DEPARTMENT stores and other alert retailers are well aware of the tendency toward educational playthings, and are featuring the products of Playskool Institute in their holiday displays.

Hammer-Nail .. Makes the child's desire to pound, a constructive pastime. A popular number.

They will be glad to show you the complete Playskool line, and to suggest the proper items for the good little boys and girls you want to remember this Christmas.

We, too, will be glad to help you with your shopping by sending you the colorful new folder describing Playskool Products, together with an interesting booklet entitled "Pre-school Training in The Home". Just send the attached coupon and enclose Ten Cents to cover mailing cost of booklet.

Cart-Block Peggy — a colorful collection of large sized pegs and blocks, and a fascinating pull-toy, too.

PLAYSKOOL INSTITUTE
594 COMMERCE ST.   MILWAUKEE, WIS.

Playskool Peggy Box .. Pegs, blocks and peg-board in sturdy wood container.

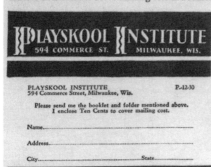

Playskool Parquetry Blocks — stimulate a sense of color and design. In various assortments and sizes.

By the late 1920s new specialty companies like the Playskool Institute offered home kindergartens and Built-at-Will Dollhouses to parents hoping to stimulate creativity and competence in their preschoolers in preparation for a competitive world.

A Child at Play today...

a responsible citizen tomorrow

Learning while Playing

PLAYSKOOL TOYS

PLAYSKOOL educational toys are designed in co-operation with child psychologists. They direct the play instincts into channels that build muscular control, eye-hand coordination, color and shape perception. There are special PLAYSKOOL toys for each stage of child development — from three months to eight years. Laboratory tested to assure complete safety — with rounded corners and harmless colors.

Playskool claimed the authority of child psychologists, as in this ad in *Parents' Magazine* in 1946.

After World War II Lionel and other toymakers offered fathers the opportunity to renew emotional ties with their sons by joining them at play with electric trains.

For girls the link to the mother was more often a toy that imitated mothers' work, such as Topper's Suzy Homemaker Oven (1966).

Boys' play in the 1950s and early 1960s was shaped by romantic ideas about the Old West, as seen in Louis Marx's popular Fort Apache playset.

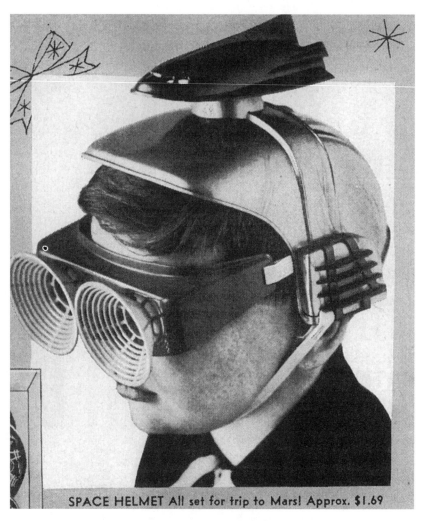

SPACE HELMET All set for trip to Mars! Approx. $1.69

Other boys' toys of the 1950s and early 1960s focused on adventure in outer space, as did this Banner space helmet.

Mothers brought up on Patsy or Shirley Temple dolls gave companion or baby dolls to their daughters after the war. Ginny (second from left), popular in the early 1950s, still looked like a child. While Ginny had a teenage sister, Jill (left), the older doll was secondary to Ginny. However, the later Barbie (second from right), introduced in 1959, upstaged her younger sister, Skipper (right). While Ginny left the girl in the play world of the child, Barbie invited her to look forward to carefree spending for fashion that presumably came with young womanhood.

previews

ROBOT COMMANDO™

U.S. PAT. PEND.
©IDEAL TOY CORP.

Already being billed as Ideal's best commercial ever, the scene opens on a replica of a deserted city. Suddenly, Robot Commando dramatically appears on the horizon, moving steadily down the streets. Tanks and airplanes attack him, but he swings his arms to hurl grenades, and rockets fly from his head, downing the tanks and aircraft. A little boy is seen directing all of Robot Commando's actions with the voice-control microphone. He alone commands his friend, the robot, to fire grenades or rockets. The announcer states that Ideal's Robot Commando is "here to help, and takes orders only from you!"

From the mid-1950s television began to shape toys by giving children stories to animate their play. This frame from a TV ad for Ideal's Robot Commando seen in 1961 provided an exciting, even frightening, story to reenact in play.

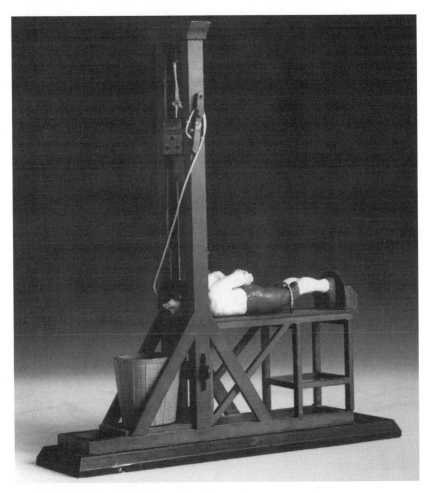

By the mid-1960s boys' toys began to break from the parent-pleasing objects of the past. This toy guillotine by Aurora Plastics (1964) showed a trend toward recognizing children's fascination with the grotesque.

In the mid-1980s appeared the Garbage Pail Kids, a line of sickening images of children blowing their brains out or squashed by a truck. The Garbage Pail Kids, featured on trading cards like this image of Valerie Vomit, mocked the sweetness of the Cabbage Patch Kids, and appealed especially to boys as they moved from the innocence of soft animals to tough-guy action figures.

From the late 1970s many toy lines were closely related to movies and TV cartoons directed toward children. An example is He-Man, the leader of a boys' action figure line that appeared in 1983. The muscular hero (left) attacks the evil Skeletor (center) and his fortress, Snake Mountain.

Another toy line related to movies and cartoons was Strawberry Shortcake, designed for little girls (this set from 1985).

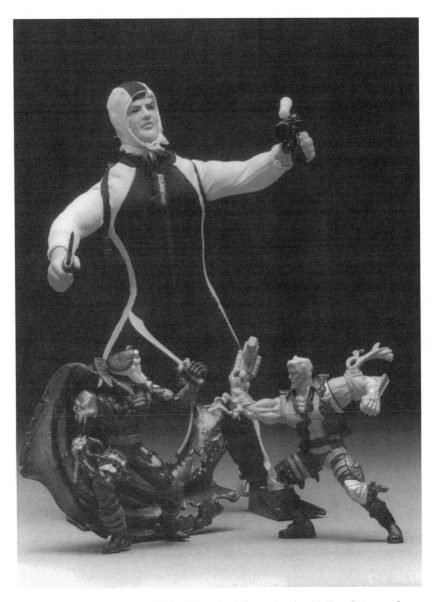

The large G.I. Joe was a doll with which boys in the 1960s play-acted the duties of real navy frogmen. In 1982 G.I. Joe became a constantly changing line of action figures. Pictured here is a 1995 version, G.I. Joe Extreme, a pair of fantastic figures designed for combat.

In 1986 Hasbro challenged Mattel's Barbie with Jem, a rock star at night with her own band, who was transformed by day into Jerrica, a successful businesswoman.

In 1988 Tyco took the action figure to new flights of fantasy with its Dino-Riders, a line of space warriors mounted on prehistoric dinosaurs. This Tyrannosaurus rex was equipped with missiles. Despite manufacturers' hopes, many children found Jem and Dino-Riders too complex for their play.

By the end of the 1980s the action figure was beginning to lose out to video games. One exception was the Teenage Mutant Ninja Turtles, which dominated the boy's toy aisle from 1988 to 1994, partly as a parody of the grim fighting action figures of the past.

Some parents demanded toys that reflected their values. Attempting to meet this call was Special Blessings, an uplifting line of dolls at prayer (1988).

Toys no longer are gifts presented mostly on special occasions but have become as common as hamburgers and fries. And toys have increasingly captured in plastic figures the images of characters appearing in the latest animated movies. Combining both trends are these figures offered by Burger King with packaged children's meals and licensed by Disney to promote the 1992 film *Aladdin*.

5 BUILDING BLOCKS OF CHARACTER

NOT ALL PARENTS in the 1930s bought their children Mickey Mouse hand cars and Shirley Temple dolls. While toymakers were selling Brownies and Kewpies, psychologists and teachers were promoting plain wooden blocks and pegboards as early learning tools. Advocates of educational toys appealed to parents concerned about their children's development and ability to compete with others. They frowned on toys that offered children little opportunity for creativity and skill development. As one critic put it, "Toys are made to attract the eye; durability, use and need from the child's point of view are rarely considered."[1]

Advocates of educational playthings also asserted the right of those parents who embraced the pedagogical vision of reformers to shape the play of their children. These parents refused to cede children's play to the noveltymakers and the mass media. Toys, they believed, should be parents' gifts of rationality to their offspring. These playthings would teach children scientific principles they would need to meet the challenges of the future.

Those who favored plain building blocks and chalkboards for home use believed that the purpose of school had to be brought into the playroom. They were in favor of play as an outlet for children's self-expression. But their vision of play was radically different from that of toymakers like Louis Marx and E. I. Horsman. Far from seeing play as a chance for the young to relax and indulge themselves, proponents of educational toys perceived it as a chance for children to learn skills and information and to develop good character. Play was the child's work, not diversion. Toys were to direct play to learning, rather than mere fun. They were not ends in themselves but rather instruments of education. As one expert noted, "Toys are the tools of play."[2]

The Century of Children's Play

In a provocative book of 1909, Ellen Key declared that the twentieth century would be the century of the child. "Through our posterity, which we ourselves create, we can in a certain measure . . . determine the future destiny of the human race." Key was a widely read Swedish advocate of a mother's wage, eugenics, and other controversial progressive policies. But she was not the first or the last to believe that only the careful raising of children would guarantee progress. The academic study of childhood and the publication of childrearing manuals increased dramatically in the 1890 and 1900s. This literature stressed the character and needs of children apart from the desires and convenience of self-centered parents. It rejected the traditional view of childhood as a time of "correction."[3]

Victorian thinking about the proper raising of children had evolved over the course of the nineteenth century. From the 1830s to the 1860s childrearing manuals told parents that the child was a plastic creature that could and should be trained to religious uprightness. The admonition to break the child's will with strict discipline and religious indoctrination gave way by midcentury to the beliefs of reformers like Horace Bushnell, who held that the same objectives could be reached in a nurturing family that communicated values by example. By the 1860s the more secular goals of success and happiness began to replace the older ideal of spiritual salvation in childrearing manuals. The emphasis remained upon parental control of the means to these ends. Authorities like Jacob Abbott argued that parents should understand children's needs and abilities in order to shape the children and to win their obedience. Harsh words and punishment were largely ineffective. Those enlightened parents who followed Abbott's advice did not practice permissive childrearing, but they did try to adapt their parenting techniques to the personality of the child.[4]

It was to the mother that most of this responsibility fell. Reformers like Ellen Key proposed that through constant attention to the upbringing of children women could produce a race of "supermen"—fearless, competent, and happy. As early as 1888 the Child Study Association organized small groups to help mothers become competent participants in the mission of improved childrearing. Beginning in the 1890s popular magazines like *Women's Home Companion, Good Housekeeping,* and the *Ladies' Home Journal* featured the latest in childrearing advice. Finally, in 1926, a group of child development professionals founded *Parents' Magazine,* which quickly became an important popular source of information about new methods of raising children.[5]

Scientific motherhood raised the status and authority of women—but only those who followed the guidance of the child experts. The English psychologist Susan Isaacs put the point bluntly: "Mothers and nurses have begun to turn away from mere customs and blind tradition to science. Hearsay and habit are now no longer enough." Children required more than a mother's affection. They needed a well-informed parent in those critical years before school when "some of the most important things that ever happen to them are already in the past." Some experts, like the behavioral psychologist John Watson, advised against too much mother love, insisting that mothers should treat their children "as though they were young adults." Watson may have been extreme, but he shared with other professionals the conviction that mothers should abandon emotion and custom for a purely rational approach to childrearing.[6]

Most experts, however, adapted their advice to compromise with mothers' desire to enjoy and be affectionate toward their children. The broad trend by the mid-1920s was toward more permissive child training—replacing the old doctrine that mothers should ignore crying babies and adhere to fixed feeding schedules with advice that they should hold fussy infants and feed them on demand. When the first edition of the government bulletin for mothers, *Infant Care,* appeared in 1914, it declared: "Much of the play that is indulged in is more or less harmful." But by the 1929 edition play was a beneficial exploratory activity. According to the new way of thinking, children transcended their infantile pleasures only after they had first engaged in them. Arnold Gesell of Yale was a key popularizer of these views. His most famous student was Benjamin Spock. Gesell's books recorded "typical" behavior for children at different ages, thus reassuring parents that their children were merely "going through a stage" when they did something upsetting to grown-ups.[7]

By the 1920s these views reached many American parents.[8] In their famous study of "Middletown" (Muncie, Indiana), Robert Lynd and Helen Lynd observed: "One cannot talk with Middletown mothers without being continually impressed by the eagerness of many to lay hold of every available resource for help in training their children." In a national survey of American parents in the early 1930s, 90 percent of mothers in the professional class read works by childrearing experts and 35 percent of lower-working-class mothers did so (for an average of 73 percent). A surprising 65 percent of professional men claimed to read articles on child care (while 12 percent of unskilled laboring fathers and 37 percent of all fathers reported the same). The child-improvement ethos had a wide appeal by the 1920s, particularly but by no means only in the educated middle class.[9]

Parents influenced by the new childrearing theories understood that play shaped youthful character and behavior as well as learning. As late-nineteenth-century society mechanized and prosperity increased, and as parents had less need for children to work, reformers recognized a need to turn the child's play time to productive use.

With this in mind, a small group of urban philanthropists and professional men led a movement for directed recreation. From the 1870s reformers advocated adult-managed play as a safety valve for young people's potentially disruptive energy. But by the 1900s play was also endowed with vital civilizing functions. The German Karl Groos considered play an "instinctual" need that prepared children for the mental, physical, and social skills they would need later in life. Groos argued that, unlike animals, humans needed long periods of play precisely because they had complex skills and social roles to learn. In this light, doll play "pre-exercised" the nurturing instinct necessary for civilization.[10]

By contrast, the American G. Stanley Hall claimed that in play "we rehearse the activities of our ancestors." Hall argued that children's play in gangs harkened back to a primitive evolutionary stage of humanity and was a necessary prerequisite for more advanced development of social and physical skills. Civilization required that children run through the instinctual history of humanity in play in order to achieve rational and mature adulthood. Luther Gulick, who helped found both the Playground Association in 1906 and the Camp Fire Girls in 1914, popularized Hall's argument. Gulick was far from advocating a crude return to nature. Rather play was to channel energy and create the self-discipline necessary to wisely manage the power and wealth of modern society.[11]

In the end, it mattered little whether play pre-exercised skills needed for a better future or salvaged a primitive "instinctual" past that could help revitalize civilization. Both sides agreed that play was natural and should be "free" and warned that, if suppressed, humanity's past and future would be denied. These views were popular and sparked a great deal of research into the play and opinions of children. But they were not based on rigorous investigation and science. They tell us more about the cultural concerns of elite professional men who theorized about play in the lives of children than about children's actual recreation.[12]

For Gulick and Hall play was a solution to the "Boy Problem," the task of creating self-motivated men out of boys who no longer faced the economic and physical adversity of an earlier time. The problem was to enliven and yet channel the vitality of youth that was threatened by a "soft" culture of the office and domestic comforts. Despite a gradual shift toward the cultivation of social or "democratic" values in recreation, an overriding "rugged individualism" prevailed, and with it a hostility to the popular culture of affluence, comfort, and change. Boys had to be strong and aggressive but in socially constructive ways. Play could help.[13]

Another boost for play as instrumental in child development came in the nineteenth-century movement for preschool and parent education. The German Friedrich Froebel, who founded the first kindergarten in 1837, denounced rote memorization and advocated that play become a central part of early learning: "The plays of childhood are the germinal leaves of all later life." His disciple Heinrich Hoffman insisted that child's play was not the adult's "fruitless pastimes." It was serious work. Adults should not try to drive the "instinct" for play out of children. The young "cannot yet do our work, they must qualify themselves for it by doing their own."[14]

According to these reformers, play was the young child's way of learning. But it should not be left to chance. Froebel had a detailed program of play that prescribed the child's activities, step by step. While later generations of kindergarten teachers abandoned Froebel's elaborate philosophy and rigid program, they stuck to the idea of managed play and insisted that parents adopt it too. In 1933 the American kindergarten advocate Josephine Foster noted that despite children's often-superior imaginations, they still had to be "taught how to play." Even spontaneous "frolics" required an educator. And "learning" play from an older playmate was "practically never . . . the most desirable training."[15]

For Patty Smith Hill, a leader of early childhood education, the problem of play was rooted in the conflict between parents' and children's needs: "Because parents inevitably sought to protect their possessions . . . the child's creative instinct is constantly thwarted by prohibitions with little or no provision for a legitimate and worth-while outlet for his constructive powers. He is left to drift into habits of idleness and destruction or into forms of play and work which are, due to poor play equipment or lack of guidance, unproductive." The solution was for parents to provide proper space and appropriate "play equipment" and to accept expert guidance. The professional would serve the child's needs in both preschool and home by defining the setting, tools, and methods of managed play. The kindergarten was also an opportunity for women to establish a professional expertise that supplemented home-based childrearing.[16]

The kindergarten movement inevitably drew on contemporary ideas in child psychology, especially those of Jean Piaget. By the 1920s the childrearing expert Edith Kawin understood play as the proper path to a "well-integrated personality" able to "adjust to an ever changing world." The exaggerated claims of G. Stanley Hall were abandoned for the more modest assertion of Josephine Foster: "The successful adult is, nine times out of ten, the person who was a successful child." Such a person not only prepared for adult life in childhood play but learned how to put the "most into the life of the present." Childhood play made for happy adults.[17]

Unlike the male advocates of urban recreation, the kindergarten movement was less insistent on sex-role differences and less biased toward boys' play. Leaders did not encourage early sex-divided play. Girls as well as boys should play at a workbench. Kindergarten leaders often endorsed boys' doll play. And instead of encouraging the "fighting" instinct they favored role-playing.[18]

Proponents of recreation and of kindergarten shared the belief that properly administered play fostered "normal" child development. Adults were to divide play activities by age cohort that grouped physical and psychological stages. Recreation and the use of the imagination would help children become rational and adaptable adults. As they matured, children who had proceeded through these carefully controlled stages would need less time for play. Play was essential only for children as they learned to become efficient workers.[19]

In a broader sense, play was seen not as the opposite of work but as another form of it. Maude Nash argued that children needed "beneficial occupations" if they were to learn "confidence and self reliance." The child had an "instinctive interest" in housekeeping. But such activity should be made into play to teach the child the "true joy of work." And, Hill declared, "Creative work and creative play are so akin that it is difficult to tell where one leaves off and the other begins." Josephine Kenyon, director of the Health and Happiness Club, insisted that parents (especially fathers) "must enter into the child's play life at home if they expect to be real guides to him later on." Such sentiments were appropriate in a society still wedded to a Victorian work ethic but clearly opening up to a "psychology of relaxation." Play was work; but work should also be playful.[20]

An essential difference between play and work remained, however. Parents were to isolate play physically as well as mentally from adult cares and labor. Mary Read insisted that concerned families have home playgrounds with protected sandboxes, swings, and playhouses. Parents should provide their children with play-rooms with bare floors and cheerful colors (yellow, not violet, for example). The emphasis on the proper space for play may have been best expressed in the report of the White House Conference on Child Health and Protection (1930). It legitimized the idea of the child-centered home as the key to a future society of well-adjusted individuals. Specific recommendations included a playroom or, at least, a corner of a bedroom for play with shelves and drawers set at heights reachable by children. The well-equipped home should also include a "workshop in which the men and boys of the house can putter." Playrooms should contain child-sized furniture, smooth, cheerful walls, and pictures which children helped to choose. Furnishings should include books, games, and at least one musical instrument. All this was vital to a well-ordered home and would help children "develop a wholesome attitude toward home life and prepare for their own future home-making."[21]

Children with such playrooms and plenty of good toys would not want to play in the street or to stray from a happy future of suburban living. Advice magazines were filled with recommendations for children's playhouses and backyard playground equipment. By the early 1930s, 46 percent of professional parents had backyard swings (as compared to nearly a quarter of lower-work-ing-class parents), while 58 percent of the professionals and 17 percent of the manual laborers had sandboxes.[22]

Not every child had the blessings of sheltered home play. Nash warned that some young people lacked the "right environment" for proper play: "Those unfortunate street urchins whose environment presents nothing refining to imitate . . . act out sordid happenings that lower their outlook on life." A partial solution proposed was the public nursery school or kindergarten. Parent education might also expose such children to the "finer things of life." Kindergarten reformers may not have been able to introduce all children to those finer things. But they thought they knew what those things were.[23]

Play was to be isolated in time and place; it was to be "free"; and yet it was to prepare the young for work. These complex require-ments reflected the social and cultural concerns of middle-class parents. These ideas about play rationalized their desire for protec-tion from lower-class culture and for the security of their own. The ideas reflected their confidence in their notions of "right" environments for their children. And these notions about recreation expressed a long-standing tension within the American middle class between work and play. Directed recreation was a way for children to learn about adult life without its constraints. Play had become the "work" of children. And work required tools.

Educational Toys

In 1812 the English author Maria Edgworth wrote: "A boy who has use of his limbs and whose mind is untainted with prejudice would in all probability prefer a substantial cart . . . to the finest frail coach and six that ever came out of a toy shop."[24] Generations of serious childrearers have equated the plain with the creative. Toys were not to be novelties, miniatures of aristocratic whimsy, mechanical curiosity, or commercial dazzle. For Edgworth and her audience, toys had to be unchanging, sturdy, useful, and craftlike. The twentieth-century educational toy is firmly anchored in a middle-class culture of self-improvement with deep roots in the historical aspirations and ascent of the bourgeoisie.

The classic educational plaything was the unadorned building block. Since the days of John Locke in the late seventeenth century, enlightened parents had believed block play prepared children for rational thinking. In the nineteenth century building blocks became a must in middle-class American nurseries, giving boys endless hours of constructive activity in stacking wooden pieces into the shapes of "useful" houses, churches, and bridges. In 1858 S. C. Hill was manufacturing blocks to meet that market. If parents largely reserved blocks for boys, by the 1880s they gave girls sewing cards. Girls were supposed to benefit from the practical lesson of sewing yarn through prepunched holes while learning the moral truths expressed in designs like "Waste Not, Want Not." Blocks and sewing cards shared a common character. They had to be "worked on" and were substitutes for manual training and laboring alongside a parent.[25]

A similar ethos produced the notion that children should construct their own playthings. Ebenezer Landells's *Boy's Own Toy-Maker* was typical. This mid-Victorian English primer on the construction of "useful things for the pleasant time of play hours" combined "instruction with the amusement of the juvenile circle." Only with the learning of "common things early in life" could parents hope that their child might become a "great inventor" and contribute to progress. But craft instruction had a romantic, backward-looking element as well. It would lend "dignity to the crafts" (in decline during that heyday of mechanization) and even make the uneducated toymaker a "helper to the schoolmaster." Landells offered detailed guidance in the making of kites ("better than store bought"), bows and arrows, and cardboard foxhunting scenes.[26]

With his daughter Alice, Landells offered a second volume, *Girl's Own Toy Maker and Book of Recreation*. Homemade cutouts of dancing dolls and paper bookmarks would teach girls the "habit of preserving." These toys were suitable as presents for friends or as gifts to "some charitable institution." Landells's manuals reflected the gendered culture of the mid-nineteenth century—junior engineering projects for boys and domestic crafts and benevolence for girls. Yet both required the child's participation and imagination. Twentieth-century toymaking books continued to advocate an ethic of ingenuity and creativity. Effort, common household materials, and self-discovery were the interlocking themes of the craft-toy tradition.[27]

Friedrich Froebel gave a particular cast to these Victorian principles when he introduced playthings to his kindergarten. Unlike the baubles of the toy shops, his play objects were "gifts" (ultimately from God) through which children were to fulfill their innermost potential. Froebel believed that "the still unthinking mind of the child can be awakened and taught only through symbols," and these symbols were embodied in his "gifts." These playthings were contained in six boxes kept by the teacher under lock and key. Only as the child progressed in self-understanding would each succeeding box be opened, introducing the child to more complex objects. Gift Box I, for example, was filled with colored balls of worsted yarn; Gift Box II contained a cube, cylinder, and ball; while the most advanced Gift Box VI held a "3 inch cube, divided to form 27 solid oblongs, of which three are divided into halves to form four sided prisms, and six into halves to form square half-cubes." Fourteen "occupations" or skills prescribed proper use of the gifts: These included paper folding, drawing, sewing, paper weaving, stringing peas, and clay modeling. Through Froebel's toys the inner worlds of children were to develop as they learned how the complex contents of Box VI and the simple balls of Box I were linked in a God-given cosmos.[28]

As early as 1873 the National Educational Association endorsed Froebel's system of kindergarten "gifts" and "occupations." Similar were the practices of the Italian Maria Montessori, who used a variety of objects with varying color and texture to teach small children how to distinguish and count. Other activities fostered competence in household chores. Early childhood educators made ordinary household objects rather than abstract verbal lessons the center of their pedagogy. They stressed the adult's control over the toybox and its uses while at the same time preaching "freedom" and self-discovery.[29]

But Froebel's methods were challenged as early education moved in an increasingly child-centered direction. At a meeting of the National Educational Association in 1890, Anna Bryan criticized Froebel's gift boxes for frustrating the child's self-expression. Bryan advocated that children's actual play patterns be observed and incorporated in the design of play objects.[30]

Ten years later the educator and philosopher John Dewey joined the attack on Froebel's system. The symbolic meanings that Froebel assigned to the balls and string, Dewey asserted, only encouraged mechanistic responses and "insincerity" in the children and teachers. Dewey mocked the idea that playthings should be as artificial as possible in order to stimulate the imagination. The use of cut paper to represent a tea party was "mere superstition." The more realistic the play objects the better, for such toys would conjure up more details for imaginative play. Far from unfolding an inner truth, play helped resolve inner conflicts and reduce tensions caused by the child's sense of impotence. Dewey attempted to root playthings in contemporary reality rather than an "eternal" world and to relate them to psychological needs rather than religious ideals. Yet he accepted Froebel's essential premise, that toys must lead the child to become a self-directed personality, not a participant in a culture of novelty. Toys must "carry the child on to a higher plane of consciousness and action, instead of merely exciting him, and then leaving him just where he was before, plus a certain amount of nervous exhaustion and appetite for more excitation in the future."[31]

From 1905 to 1935 Patty Smith Hill applied these reform principles at Columbia University's kindergarten laboratory school. Hill organized a progressive wing of the kindergarten movement in 1895 with G. S. Hall, Anna Bryan, and others. Her stress on the relatively free use of educational toys soon dominated teacher training. In contrast to Froebel's highly idealistic "theory of education," Hill claimed to base her kindergarten on "the nature and needs of children." She designed blocks large enough to develop motor skills and to encourage cooperation between children while they constructed "houses" and "wagons." She supplemented blocks with clay, cloth, and yarn (for sewing and weaving). Instead of Froebel's insistence that children make abstract geometric drawings, Hill stressed "gay crayons, large brushes and pails of bright-colored paint" for children to express "their own conceptions of the world."[32]

Hill's contemporaries included Luella Palmer (New York City public schools), Mary Read (the Mothercraft School of Boston), Charlotte Garrison (Columbia University), Ethel Kawin (Laboratory School of the University of Chicago), and Josephine Foster (University of Minnesota). This dedicated group of female advocates of kindergartens, along with the men of the playground movement, placed a heavy burden on the toy and its use. For them the plaything was no longer a mere amusement but "scientific apparatus." Research revealed that even the simple baby rattle helped children discern color, shapes, sounds, and surfaces. The objective must always be to improve and aid the child's development, not to amuse or even to celebrate a stage in life.[33]

Luther Gulick agreed when he defined toys as the "pegs on the wall of the mind on which to hang instinct feelings." Like Hill, Gulick rejected novelty. He recalled having had three hundred blocks made for his children (all the same size and shaped like ordinary bricks). These blocks occupied the majority of their indoor playtime for six years, as the children progressed from "simply piling up the blocks and knocking them down" to building houses complete with doors and windows in symmetrical design. Gulick insisted that his children discover the potential of these plain blocks on their own.[34]

G. Stanley Hall expressed this view in "A Story of a Sand Pile," an essay in *Scribner's Magazine* in 1888. Hall described how the two sons of a prosperous Boston family spent their summers building a play village in a sand pile provided by their parents. Using scrap wood rather than manufactured toys, they whittled figures and constructed model buildings. This play helped the boys "to realize their conceptions of adult life," and taught them self-control and cooperation as they brought neighbor boys into their play. But the sand pile also allowed parents to "indirectly control the associations of their boys" and to observe them without imposing undue restrictions. Each summer this play, Hall believed, was worth the equivalent of a school year in learning. It sustained the interest of boys between the ages of six and fourteen as the play village became progressively larger and more sophisticated. Hall's model of ideal play was an elegant reconciliation of opposites—initiated by children but contained by adults, simple in apparatus but encouraging complex development and learning. His model greatly influenced the construction- and vehicle-toy industry in the early twentieth century, although in Hall's sand pile the boys made their own toys.[35]

Perhaps few parents were willing to follow the rigors of Gulick's or Hall's sophisticated theories, but their principles were supported by most professional opinion. Ethel Kawin argued that a doll had to be sturdy enough to serve a child as the child passed from one developmental stage to another. The same doll should be dressed by four-year-olds, serve as a prop in the dramatic play of five- to eight-year-olds, and ultimately help nine-year-olds learn to sew. Such playthings taught the deep meaning of simple and well-made toys that could last a childhood. These ideas directly challenged the precepts of commercial dollmakers with their attempt to sell a doll for every age and mood.[36]

The skills learned in the play that these experts advocated were not directly useful in adult life. Indeed, they were not supposed to be. Educational play aimed to prepare the child for adulthood by building character, not by training for future occupations. Wisely conceived and chosen toys would encourage children to respect property, develop perseverance, and work well with others. Above all, these toys were supposed to arouse the child to act upon them in innovative ways. The educational toy did not seek to adapt the child to the group or to the consumer culture of suburban America. Rather it aimed to pass on to the next generation the traits of the individualist and the innovator which had been so prized in nineteenth-century America.[37]

Similarly, most of these child-development experts valued the virtues of fewer rather than many toys, quality rather than quantity. An influential English authority, Beatrix Tudor-Hart, insisted that parents should not "give more dolls or animals when the child is happy with those he has." She argued that the rag doll or teddy bear from which the child could not be separated fostered imagination and depth of feeling. An excess of toys impeded strong attachments. Another American expert warned that if children were given too many toys "their precious ability for enjoying the little things of life may be taken from them and a life of discontent is likely to follow."[38]

Hill insisted that parents should not shower children with toys at Christmas. Rather they should dole out playthings to meet changing developmental needs throughout the year. Overindulgence at holidays would arouse "a desire for unnecessary things." "Character dolls of a comic nature are not to be taken seriously." They were merely a "passing fad," which could never replace a realistic doll with which a child could identify and role play. Blocks and durable dolls represented none of the throw-away mentality or faddism of the Kewpie-doll culture. They and other educational playthings were intended to perpetuate Victorian values by developing the child's character and intelligence.[39]

This was a formidable task. It required that adults take charge at a time when parental authority was being challenged by a growing consumer culture and mass media that beckoned children to want novelty and their own fantasy worlds. To many middle-class parents that consumer culture seemed to express the narcissism and quest for immediate gratification that bourgeois Americans identified with the lower class. And it threatened to engulf their children as they went to the movies and ached for those flashy toys offered by Louis Marx. The ideals of self-directed play with objects of simple design had nothing to do with the appeal of character toys. Educational playthings represented, to middle-class parents, a bulwark against the tide of commercialism and its threat to undermine parental authority and Victorian values.

Educational toys were supposed to reinforce parental authority but also to affirm a child-centered culture. These seemingly contradictory objectives could be achieved if parents carefully planned toy purchases. Mary Read advised: "Choose [your child's] toys wisely and then leave him alone with them." After "careful observation," Patty Smith Hill advised, adults could introduce appropriate toys when the child was ready for them. Parents should "intervene to encourage sharing," and "monitor the number and variety of toys to assure self-discovery rather than overstimulation or boredom." The selected toy then embodied the indirect authority of parents. At the same time, the child enjoyed the semblance of autonomy or freedom within limits set by adults. The interaction of the child with the wisely chosen plaything was to do the work of childrearing.[40]

Educational toys were supposed to appeal to children's imaginations, not to amuse adults. Repeatedly the manuals warned against fathers' playing with toy trains (despite the fact that toy advertising recognized this paternal desire and encouraged parental participation). Some professionals went even further and expressed disapproval of bonding play between parent and child.[41] They attacked "unscientific" parenting centered on emotion and indulgence rather than on the experts' reason. Those mothers and fathers who mistrusted their own instincts and rejected the "irrational" methods of their own parents were attracted to the experts' promise of educational toys.

This obsession with the wise choice of toys reflected the broader dilemma of authority and expertise in a democratic society. Early in the twentieth century American business was learning how to substitute assembly lines and machines for authoritarian and arbitrary management. The discipline of machines partially replaced the confrontation between the boss and the individual worker. In a similar way educational toys replaced the problematic face-to-face relationship between parent and child.

The female-dominated child development and home economics

movements recommended that reforms in the home be modeled upon innovation in industry. Again listen to Hill: "While we recognize that productive work requires good material and tools, do we not realize the waste in play that comes from poor equipment?" At a time when "efficiency" was the watchword in American industry and up-to-date machinery was a common panacea, child development professionals saw that effective training through play required well-selected equipment. With the proper toy tools, "thought and feeling are transformed into desirable behavior." With such playthings guiding the future generation of leaders, Hill concluded, "a 'Great Society' may not be a dream but a prophecy based on a reasonable hope." The educational toy was part of a great progressive project to transform society into a new order ruled by rationality and appropriate tools.[42]

The educational toy offered parents a surrogate authority to teach skills. It also presented an alternative to the flashy and flimsy novelty toys fostered by the consumer culture. It inculcated a rational and realistic rather than fantastic and escapist approach to life. As Hill saw it, plain wooden blocks taught the child the "fact that [toys] cannot be cajoled or swayed by his whims, his moods, his passions." The educational toy was the first lesson in becoming a rational person—learning the "inevitableness of nature and her laws." Toys were not meant to induce dreams. The experts were not hostile to dramatic play (with dolls or dress-up costumes, for example). Indeed, most accepted that children went through a developmental stage dominated by make-believe. But they agreed with Hill that the dramas were merely "rehearsals" of "domestic and industrial" life.[43]

The psychologist Susan Isaacs noted that older preschool girls engaged in "unsophisticated family play" whereas boys played at some "heroic activity—policeman, soldier, engine-driver, bus-driver, or 'father in his office'—remote from merely domestic affairs." Toys were expected to teach adult sex roles and to inculcate realistic expectations. Fantasy play was acceptable when it prompted "actual discovery or verbal judgment and reasoning." Gradually, however, children should learn to test their own fantasies against reality and eventually limit them "to imaginative art and literature." Make-believe toys were acceptable only if they helped children assume adult roles and acquire adult skills. The point was to outgrow fantasy, not to celebrate it.[44]

Educational playthings not only were an antidote to the hedonism of the consumer society but could help children improve the world in the future. Kawin believed these toys would make children into a "better personality type," one which had a maturity absent in irrational adults who succumbed to an ephemeral culture of fast cars, spectator sports, and radio soap operas. Such views reflected an extraordinary optimism about the power of educational playthings to shape child development. For the expert, children were malleable and directed play could shape them into ideal citizens.[45]

Educational toys, however, also represented a "do-it-yourself" movement on behalf of children that rose in reaction to the instant gratification of manufactured goods. The marketplace seemed to diminish women's work when cake mixes replaced well-executed recipes and off-the-rack fashions made skilled use of the sewing machine superfluous. Automobiles and domestic appliances became so complex and mysterious that men lost mastery over their workings and repair.[46]

As sophisticated technology distanced adults from everyday objects, it is hardly surprising that professionals began to stress crafts for children's play and that parents embraced this idea. In 1916 the kindergarten advocate Luella Palmer insisted that toys not "do for the child what he should do for himself . . . Every child should have a few well-made toys which he cannot make for himself and also tools and play materials with which he may be helped to make toys . . . As good tools may provoke good work, so good toys and play material may stimulate good play . . . The tendency of the mechanical toy is toward 'You touch the button and I do the rest.'" This last allusion is significant. It paraphrases the slogan used to mass market the Kodak camera that became popular in the 1890s, and it aptly expresses Palmer's disgust with the prepackaged commodity culture.[47]

It was from the 1890s that the Arts and Crafts movement appeared. This group of intellectuals and their well-to-do friends rejected manufactured goods while promoting handmade "objets d'art" and traditional building materials. A similar impetus was behind Palmer's nostalgia for toys that "call forth real play." Her list included "balls, dolls, rocking-horses, wagons, drums, ropes, blocks, trains, . . . doll's houses and furniture, dustpans and brooms, scales, small animals, tops, marbles, jackstones." Palmer admitted that these were "old-fashioned indoor toys used by our great grand-ancestors." But they were all that was needed to meet the child's real needs. Whenever possible they should not be purchased at toy shops. Real dustpans were preferable to poorly made toy replicas. In any case, homemade was best. Dolls and animals should be made from corn husks, clothespins, or potatoes. Palmer also advised that children make their own picture puzzles (colored pictures pasted on basswood and cut with a jigsaw). Children also needed tools—including a miniature printing press, a typewriter "with large-sized visible type," rubber stamps, and musical instruments. Important too were compasses, scales, thermometers, magnifying glasses, magnets, and even a Japanese garden for the playful work of scientific discovery. Palmer and others heralded the lost arts of spool knitting, basketmaking, paper cutting, and whittling. As Susan Isaacs saw it, the best toys were "ordinary things in house and garden."[48]

Gulick shared Palmer's affection for crafts. He claimed that the child would soon lose interest in his electric train and prefer a simple knife to express his creativity, curiosity, and energy. "To a large extent independence, power, mastery over the material world comes from using old things in new ways rather than from having the tool or the implement that is perfectly adapted to the present condition." Gulick reflected a common anxiety that in that in an era of packaged goods and encased machines people no longer understood, much less mastered, their material world. The only way humans could recover control over the world around them was by preserving manual skill and familiarity with old technologies and work materials. The traditionalist ethos of the solitary craftsperson was to be passed on to children in their play through educational toys.[49]

These attitudes toward play reflected the concerns and prejudices of middle-class parents. Playthings were to teach investment in and responsibility for property, and the value of well-constructed objects. The "right kind" of toys set progressive, rational parents apart from the less "scientific" masses who were assumed to succumb easily to the excesses of the consumer culture. Child-study magazines appealed to parental anxiety about their children's future—whether they would rise from or even remain in their parents' social class: "The early home life of your school boy or girl lays the foundation for success or failure in school life." Learning to "read" alphabet blocks was critical for getting a head start and getting ahead.[50]

The educational toy was the perfect symbol of the status-conscious middle-class family. Through these playthings parents trained children for life. The mother protected her offspring from a hedonistic popular culture of novelty by sheltering the playtime of her children. Middle-class parents convinced themselves that their extraordinarily intelligent children required "special" playthings as the experts advised. After a description of how she introduced children to "real world" objects (including a bunsen burner) at her private preschool, Susan Isaacs speculated: "It may well be that this active interest in the real world is one of the distinguishing marks of the intelligent child." Presumably ordinary children were more prone to escapist fantasy and less capable of grasping the "real" world in play. With the aid of the educational toy, along with child-study groups, enclosed backyards, home playrooms, and summer camps, parents protected and perpetuated their middle-class standards even as these same toys encouraged creativity and autonomy among children.[51]

The Legacy of the Educational Toy

The ideals of Hill and Gulick survive today in enlightened homes and kindergartens, but despite their goal of creating an alternative form of play, these experts did not effectively challenge the commercial playthings industry. Indeed, they were not nearly so hostile to the industry as their words might imply. Early on they tried to interest toymakers in their messages and ideas. The toy trade in turn was open to new products and markets which promised profits.

Child experts and the toy industry had joined forces at the very beginning of the educational-toy movement. Milton Bradley, a lithographer turned gamemaker, gained a near monopoly in the manufacture of indoor play equipment for kindergartens and schools. In 1869 he agreed to manufacture Froebel's "gifts" in collaboration with the kindergarten advocate Elizabeth Peabody. A competitor, the Embossing Company, also offered "toys that teach." This manufacturer featured lithographed alphabet blocks from 1870 and distributed Harbutt's Plasticine modeling clay (from England) from 1907—products that were widely used in preschools and "progressive" homes. Numerous companies also produced home blackboards and spelling boards that promised to give children an advantage in school by preparing them early.[52]

The alliance between reformers and the toy industry continued. In 1910 Schoenhut manufactured Hill Floor Blocks. In the 1920s Toddler Toys produced a line based on Arnold Gesell's psychological work on preschoolers. In the 1930s the Holgate Company offered unadorned block-and-peg sets "approved by school leaders" for home use. Most successful, however, was Playskool. When this company was founded in 1928, it was called the Playskool Institute to indicate its educational as well as manufacturing purpose. Its first success was the Home Kindergarten, a child's desk equipped with an assortment of pegboards, blocks, and art materials. It retailed at a pricey $16.50 and was advertised regularly in *Parents' Magazine*. Playskool's commitment to educationally sound toys was evident when the Playskool Institute offered an "extension course" in modern childrearing to members (that is, purchasers of Playskool products). Advertising stressed "learning while playing" in a complete line of pegs, blocks, and "Build-at-Will Doll Houses."[53]

Toy companies adapted the themes of reformers in their products and promotions to the broader market without abandoning commercial appeals. From the 1870s the Charles Crandall Company offered building blocks and wooden play sets with whimsy and flash that obscured their educational value. In its heavily advertised "Can't Break Em" dolls, Schoenhut copied the naive folk styles and wooden materials favored by reformers. But this company went on to hire foreign doll designers and exploited its success commercially by creating a line of Schoenhut dolls that changed yearly. And Martha Chase's stockinet dolls crossed the boundary between the educational and the commercial. Her dolls were adopted by schools to demonstrate infant care, and she advertised her products as "built for all times, not just for the moment." But she also appealed to the snobbery of consumers when she claimed that her dolls had become a "tradition among discriminating American families."[54]

The Fisher-Price company began in 1930 by making lithographed wooden toys and blocks that appealed to parents. This company offered more economical versions of Albert Schoenhut's elegant wooden toys. And, like Schoenhut, Fisher-Price rejected the didacticism of the plain block for "shape, expression, and color" to "capture the child's attention." This company did not hesitate to join the crowd seeking Disney licenses in the 1930s and to cash in on their celebrity. Halsam Products followed a similar path when they offered colorful embossed blocks designed to be "unconsciously educational." Like Fisher-Price, Halsam eschewed the austerity of the kindergarten purists and joined the Mickey Mouse club by licensing Disney images for their blocks in the 1930s.[55]

From 1926 *Parents' Magazine* became an important advertising outlet for educational toys. The magazine guaranteed the accuracy of advertising claims and featured the expected array of Holgate Bricks, home blackboards, and doorway gyms. But it also found advertising space for Effanbee's Bubbles doll and the common line of Arcade, Dayton, and Strombecker toy cars, trucks, and even warships. From 1931 the magazine offered a "Playthings in Review" column featuring toys that were durable and educational. Even so, at Christmas of 1932 the writers endorsed a "Robotoy" by Buddy "L," a very early remote-controlled dump truck (at a hefty price of $12.50). Inevitably, the economic logic of romancing the market and appealing to the taste for flashy and amusing novelties prevailed over the ideal of encouraging the intellect and imagination with plain wooden blocks.[56]

The link between the toy industry and the educational-toy tradition took still other forms. In the 1920s a group called the Better Play for Childhood League of New York promoted a "Children's Day" in collaboration with the toy industry in the hopes of furthering awareness of the importance of play in children's lives. From the mid-1920s department stores began to hire buyers from the kindergarten movement to market educational toys.[57]

Edith Boehm, a lecturer at the Child Welfare Studies Association in New York, became a buyer of toddler toys for F. A. O. Schwarz and other stores. In 1930 she produced "The Five Year Plan for Toys," an age-graded guide for toy selection. Boehm asserted that, because of the popularization of the preschool movement, mothers realized the need for well-ordered play and that this required the necessary tools. Toymakers could provide these tool-toys if they realized that playthings were no longer merely in a "class of destructive seasonal holiday merchandise" but were "useful worthwhile necessities of the child's development." Thus, the promotion of educational toys was employed as a sales strategy in the Depression. If the fantasy plaything encouraged impulse buying, the educational toy philosophy promoted sales of distinct items for each developmental stage of childhood from birth to six years. At a time of declining births, the idea of selling a long list of improving toys had an understandable appeal to both manufacturers and retailers.[58]

Educators and child welfare advocates often welcomed collaboration with those toymakers willing to manufacture and market "constructive" playthings. Companies like Holgate, Embossing, Playskool, and later Creative Playthings were loyal supporters of their ideas and aims. Their enemy was the cynical toymaker who was only interested in products for profit and gave no thought to their effects on children. In time, however, the educational toy became another specialized line of merchandise, a sideline of huge conglomerates like Mattel and Hasbro. It had not triumphed over other toys but had found a secure place among them.

Childrearing experts played a vital role in the modern history of toys and child's play. They drew attention to the educational possibilities of play as an alternative to formal instruction, children's chores, and traditional apprenticeships. Their research into child development brought forth interesting patterns of play that had previously been ignored. They popularized the now universally recognized idea that play, especially in early childhood, is an effective way of shaping lifelong attitudes to learning and the world. They brought playthings into the arena of child education and management. In so doing, they helped to legitimize toys and the child-centered parenting they represented.

Educational toys embodied the confidence in science and progress that characterized the late Victorian middle classes. They had many duties to perform. They had to be linked to the child's developmental stage, encourage confidence, and create competence, and yet they could not obviously or directly impose the adult's will. If properly selected, educational playthings would provide enduring lessons of self-motivation and reliance.

But the educational toy movement also produced some ironies and failures. Despite the promotion of child-centered play, the childrearing experts encouraged a trend in the opposite direction. They helped turn an informal carefree activity, often controlled by children themselves, into serious "work" designed by trained adults. The child-centered ethos of the experts matched the toy to a specific level of mental and physical development and designed the toy to teach appropriate skills. That perspective largely obscured the fact that such skills met traditional parent-centered objectives. The professionals promoted an ideal of child development that conformed to a Victorian notion of "good character" rather than to the particular needs of the individual child.

The authorities who promoted education toys had important platforms for disseminating their ideas. They were based in preschools, kindergartens, and public recreation centers. They spread their message through childrearing manuals and magazine articles. But this could not compare to the access of the Louis Marxes with their attractive store displays, links to the mass media, and general message of fun. Over time the educational plaything became little more than a fixture of progressive preschools and kindergartens, the emblem of a cult of "good parenting" in an educated sector of the American middle class. The movement failed to reach beyond this social sector into the working class, where limited time and money and different cultural values often precluded such playthings.

The childrearing experts also ignored or simply underestimated the growing importance of popular culture in children's lives. Garrison, Kawin, and Palmer may have abhorred the pushbutton age of mechanized toys, but children inevitably wished to participate in it. The experts' rationalist approach to child development precluded most make-believe play and toys other than those used to act out parental roles as mothers and workers.

Occasionally these experts recognized the desire of children to play cowboys and Indians. Some encouraged such play as a way of working out aggression.[59] But they did not understand why children liked to role-play celebrities of popular commercial culture. None said anything serious about Buck Rogers pistols or Patsy dolls. This is partly because they wrote before the full onslaught of the fantasy/fad toy in the last quarter of this century. But they were oblivious to early signs. For them the toy was merely a tool, an instrument for the acquisition of skills and attitudes. They underestimated the social meanings of playthings, especially children's desire to share in a peer culture of what was current, fantasyful, and fun.

The experts may have attributed more importance to toys than they deserved. Unrealistic expectations abounded: Mary Read insisted that "international peace will begin in the nursery, in the training in ideals of activity and heroism that are constructive and helpful, not destructive."[60]

More subtly, educational toys were supposed to remove the contradiction between the adult's desire for control and the child's quest for independence. The experts had a professional interest in mediating the child-parent relationship. They saw mostly indulgence when adults gave themselves to their children through "fun" toys and play. The educational toy was a way to reduce that exchange. Toymakers like A. C. Gilbert and Effanbee understood, far better than did the experts, the longing of parent and child to share toys together. They actively promoted both parents' and children's desires and promised a play world for both.

Josephine Foster understood toys as mere things—"stable, constant, and inevitable"—unlike people, who were constantly changing and uncontrollable.[61] The idea that children's things should be immutable in a world of constant change in all other manufactured goods was extraordinarily naive. It suggests the desire to impose on children the longing for continuity and stability that adults were unwilling to impose on themselves. Children, like adults, wanted their goods to have personalities and thus to be changing, and wanted to have emotional ties with them. While the consumer industry understood this, the educational toy movement did not. It is no surprise that few toy collectors seek out educational toys. Their lack of personality and connection to a specific time made them uninteresting.

Child experts did have an impact with their forceful and imaginative attacks on many aspects of the commercial toy industry. But they and their messages were commonly co-opted by that industry. Commercial toymakers easily reduced them to irrelevance or even to absurdity. Louis Marx expressed the perspective of a lifelong manufacturer of novelty playthings when he said in 1955, "I don't go along with psychologists who want to sneak up on [children] and jam education into them through toys."[62] But this view was held also by many Americans who believed that children should sometimes just have fun.

Toymakers also absorbed the slogans of the experts without their program and melded these messages with fantasy themes. Fisher-Price offered products that promised to develop toddlers' motor skills with push toys made in the shape of Disney characters. Gilbert used the language of learning development to encourage the step-by-step acquisition of increasingly expensive erector sets. Advertising reminded parents of the diverse educational needs of children while pushing them to fill the toybox to the brim. And the promise of social status in overpriced Margaret Chase dolls was a constant commercial theme.

As part of the do-it-yourself movement, educational toys claimed to be the tools of play even though the child's toy corner was not to be the place of real work. It was more important that the child make a wooden boat with his or her own hands than that the finished product be usable. The same ethic guided the home-improving adult. Yet, despite this shared goal of doing it yourself and finding an alternative to endless consumption of new products, both had to have the "right tools" and called upon the expert to identify them and manufacturers to provide them. The idea of emancipating oneself from the market was inevitably an illusion.

More fundamentally still, the educational toy represented only one part of parents' desires for their offspring. It promised to train the child for success at work. But it ignored a growing arena of American life—the world of leisure with its ever-changing lures of fantasies and personalities delivered by the media and represented in playthings. Parents, even those with aspirations for "improving" their children, shared in this world of fun and indulged themselves and their children by buying the newest novelty. This the experts never understood, and so their alternatives failed to meet the needs of children and parents or to supplant fantasy playthings.

6 THE BOOMERS' BOX OF TOYS

THE GENERATION born after World War II was the largest in American history. More than 55.77 million children were under fifteen years old in 1960 compared to only 32.97 million in 1940.[1] At the end of the war G.I.s returning home and the young women in the war factories were eager to start or resume family life. The U.S. was also entering an unprecedented period of prosperity, allowing the parents of the baby boom generation to spend far more on playthings than their parents had. Affluence opened purse strings to the wishes of the young for the novelties of play. But that prosperity did not diminish parents' insistence that toys express the messages they wanted to send their offspring.

Toymakers understood this and returned to manufacturing the toys that had dominated American childhood since the early years of the twentieth century. They produced miniatures of modern technologies, novelties appealing to parents and children alike, and improving "tools of play." These were parents' gifts of the future, of imagination, and of rationality, each in different ways affirming parental authority while granting children a measure of autonomy.

These diverse playthings did not always sit comfortably in the toy box. The fantasy toys evolved from being parent-centered in the early twentieth century to being at least partly child-centered by the 1930s, freeing the imaginations of the young. And the advocates of educational playthings challenged parents who purchased fantasy toys.

But in the 1950s these tensions were subdued when toymakers went to great lengths to reassure parents that they were in charge. The knowing and pleased look of Mom or Dad served as a telling background to many a toy advertisement. Erector sets and Dy-Dee dolls were not of ancient vintage; but parents or even grandparents could have played with them in their own childhoods. Building blocks found a prominent place on the store shelves, attracting the attention of well-educated parents of preschoolers. And even the novelties—the hula hoops and Davy Crockett coonskin caps and rifles—were shared with adults or introduced by real grown-up heroes whom parents trusted. The toy industry continued, as it had since 1900, to appeal to parents as well as to children.

But the postwar generation of children also experienced radical change. The child's world of the near and familiar was passing just as Americans were glorifying it in common images of familial bliss. In the popular media of the 1950s America was experiencing a golden era of parent-child bonding, but the *Father Knows Best* family was not really the norm. By the middle of the 1950s television assumed the role that radio had played earlier in shaping a constantly evolving culture of consumption. TV accelerated a trend begun with movies and radio by creating a separate culture of children. Through network TV advertising that spoke directly to children, toys with which parents were unfamiliar made their way into living rooms across the country. The near, familiar, and harmonious was giving way to the distant, constantly changing, and divisive.[2]

The same forces that created annual model changes in cars also led to a quickening pace of innovation in toys. The marketing techniques that were used to promote the accumulation of goods among adults also cultivated the children's market.[3] As television programming shifted into high gear with exciting new children's shows, fewer children played in local street games and more watched national television shows and their advertisements. The tradition of children passing on neighborhood lore and play from one brief generation to the other was being replaced by a passive viewing of national entertainment programs and an embrace of Mickey Mouse guitars, Fanner 50 guns, and endless reincarnations of Barbie. Toys that trained for the future and promoted learning survived, but fantasy playthings, increasingly appealing directly to children, became dominant.

While parents enjoyed sharing novelty with their children, change in many ways frustrated them. Adults increasingly lost control over and even understanding of the play of their children when television and advertisers targeted their messages to the young. While television and the new marketing did not inevitably lead to this change, by the 1970s toys no longer served the needs of parents as they often had during the first half of the century.

The First Decade of Baby Boomer Toys

In some ways World War II put the toy industry on hold. Metal and stamping machines formerly devoted to making toy cars and erector sets were converted into manufacturing munitions and other military equipment. War themes were common, but animals in plush and wooden pull toys for preschoolers filled the ads of *Playthings*. With the coming of peace in 1945, toymakers looked eagerly to new opportunities for sales with the expected bumper crop of babies. Shortages at Christmas in 1945 and 1946 were reported in the press. Many new companies appeared to replace or compete with the old, often introducing new synthetic materials developed during wartime and lower prices. Still, given the certain market for toys, little real innovation was required.[4]

The old standard, the Weeden toy steam engine, was still advertised in 1948. Ten years later the Uncle Sam Dime Savings Bank, manufactured for nearly sixty years, was still sold. Daisy Air Rifles continued its effort to make the BB gun the measure of growing up for American boys. And Lionel and other manufacturers of electric trains came back with ever flashier catalogs. A new generation of mechanical toys soon appeared, and even though many of them were made in Japan they looked like the old American windups. Marx's Milton Berle car (based on a popular TV comedian) was merely the latest resurrection of the "eccentric" toy cars of the late 1920s. These were playthings that parents could share with their children because they remembered toys very much like them from their own youth.[5]

As in the past, almost all toys were advertised and sold to parents. Even those which appealed directly to children stressed the advantage of making the parent a "partner." Gilbert's American Flyer catalog of 1949 could still preach that in selecting a pal for play, "A boy's Dad is always a fine choice because operating a railroad together is a sure-fire way to get close to Dad." In 1953, for Father's Day, the model airplane manufacturer Revell suggested that boys should "give Dad more than a gift. Give him a hobby." Sons and fathers were supposed to share serious fun in building a train set and models of the latest aeronautic technology.[6]

The conservatism of the toy industry in part reflected the continued dominance of older toy manufacturers like A. C. Gilbert. After the war, Gilbert returned to his endless line of erector sets, American Flyer trains, and science experiment kits. The *New York Times* celebrated Gilbert's seventieth birthday with a recollection of his boyhood dreams of invention. Benjamin Michtom's Ideal Toys returned from the war with a full line of baby dolls. As a major publicity coup in 1953, Michtom won exclusive rights from the U.S. Forest Service to manufacture a Smokey the Bear doll as part of the government's campaign against forest fires. Ideal enlisted Teddy Roosevelt's granddaughter in the promotion to help commemorate an earlier Michtom's alleged "invention" of "Teddy's Bear" fifty years before. The younger Michtom even talked President Eisenhower into appearing with the doll.[7]

However, the biggest name among the old guard of toymakers was Louis Marx. Because he controlled from 10 to 16 percent of the American toy industry in the 1940s and early 1950s, Marx was repeatedly celebrated in *Time* and *Fortune* as the "toy king."[8] This fun-loving, if cynical, businessman insisted that only "spinster aunts and spinster uncles and hermetically sealed parents who wash their children 1,000 times a day" gave educational toys. He continued to sell his whimsical, brightly colored, tin-plated windups and cheaply but sturdily constructed playsets. Marx was a friend of President Eisenhower's and a benefactor of other World War II generals (to whom he offered nearly free stock in his company). This old noveltymaker was riding a wave of success and respectability in the 1950s.

Marx had been in the business since 1910. But his longevity did not come from his toy inventions. As he joked in a 1955 interview: "When they [other toy companies] copy you, it's piracy . . . When you copy them, it's competition." He continuously reused dies and molds, even keeping a "morgue" of old toys for later resurrection. There was something of the junk dealer about Marx. He was not even innovative in manufacturing techniques—introducing modern assembly lines and lithograph machinery only in 1936. He was a follower in the introduction of plastics. But he did recognize how to sell toys to the chain and department stores that were emerging as toy outlets in the 1920s. By 1924 he had won over Sears with promises of tailor-making toys for this growing retailing giant. Thus Marx avoided almost all advertising costs until the late 1950s. He was a master of the chain store age and was content that the toy business stay the way it was.

Many new and successful firms emerged in this period, specializing in a narrow range of products. A big hit in 1945 was Richard James's slinky. Inspired by a spring used on naval ships during James's wartime service, it created a sensation at a demonstration at the Philadelphia Gimbel's store. A nursery school teacher, who wanted a malleable clay that would not dry out, invented Play Doh. In 1955 it was mass marketed by Rainbow Crafts. In 1960 Ohio Arts, a picture-frame manufacturer with a side business in sand pails, made a killing by purchasing a French invention, Etch-a-Sketch, a plastic frame that looked like a TV set with knobs that etched lines in a screen when they were turned.[9]

Later giants had humble beginnings. In 1950 the founder of Aurora Plastics converted a plastic coat hanger into a bow-and-arrow set on the idle suggestion of a friend. This started what became a major model business. The Kenner company opened its first factory in 1947 to manufacture soap and soft-drink dispensers. As a sideline it made miniature toy versions. Hassenfeld Brothers, who began in 1923 in textile remnants and who shifted to pencil boxes in the 1930s, made their mark in the toy business with Mr. Potato Head in 1951.[10]

Of this group of new manufacturers, Mattel was surely the most innovative. This southern California company began in 1945. Eliot Handler, who had a small business in plastic jewelry and picture frames, talked his friend Harold Matson into a joint investment in plastic doll furniture (thus Matt-el from their names). Soon Eliot and his wife Ruth were on their own. They exploited a cheap but durable invention of a Hollywood music arranger—a rubber belt with knobs that twanged wires to make a tune when turned by a crank. The Handlers placed this device in a variety of plastic musical toys, especially guitars and ukeleles. But Mattel also made various bird-call novelties. Mattel identified itself as "Music Makers to his Majesty the Kid" at the Toy Fair in 1952. Three years later it was still offering a familiar grab bag of novelty products: a smattering of old musical toys, a Royal Knight figure with a jeweled sword, and a Bubble-O Bill Bubble Hat. All of these toys stayed within well-established conventions that reassured parents.[11]

The retailing of toys also changed little in the generation after the war. It remained a seasonal business. Trade leaders continued to push for a midsummer "Toy Week," but in 1948 a buyer from F. A. O. Schwarz admitted that a year-round toy business was "almost impossible." The focal point of toy promotions remained the downtown department store. Hobby stores continued to promote model train clubs. The trade press still provided homey features spotlighting Mom-and-Pop toy shops and advised prudent storekeepers to know their merchandise and even to talk parents out of expensive products in favor of the toys the child really wanted. The owner of Surprise Inc. Toy Shops of suburban Chicago hired former schoolteachers as sales staff to create the proper tone. Most advertising remained seasonal and directed to women's and general adult magazines. It was the parents who needed to be sold, not the children.[12]

This is not to say that the toy industry was stagnant. It was extremely competitive—even though an estimated 75 percent of American toy companies were headquartered within five hundred feet of the intersection of Fifth and Broadway in New York City. Most toys, even the successful ones, were ephemeral, disappearing within three years. There were very few toys that lasted from generation to generation. And, though many companies specialized in a single line, the largest like Marx and Ideal diversified. The wholesale value of toys rose from $86.7 million in 1939 to $608.2 million in 1953. The avant-garde of the advertising and retail industry promoted new strategies to increase sales. Stores should discard costly sales staff and replace them with self-service and open displays of colorfully packaged goods to encourage impulse buying. One expert insisted that nationally advertised goods were an inevitable store "traffic" builder.[13]

But most of the advertising was still in adult-oriented magazines like *Life, Saturday Evening Post,* and *Parents' Magazine.* Typical were the promotional efforts of the Toy Guidance Council. Since 1938 its director, Melvin Freund, had asked manufacturers to submit their "best" toys to a panel of educators, retailers, and women's club officials. This council then selected a list of "Educator Approved Prestige Toys" which won automatic orders from major wholesalers. Freund tried to further legitimize his Council's seal of approval by making Emma D. Sheehy, a noted child-development expert from Columbia University, the chair. The "preferred" toys remained conventional American-made baby dolls, pedal cars, paint sets, beauty kits, and farm and airport sets.[14]

Despite continuity, toys did change. New materials, especially plastics, found their way on to toy shelves. Injection molding machines appeared as early as 1934, forcing liquified plastic into standardized forms. Injection molding was fast and cheap compared to die-cut wood, pressed steel, and tin plate. And without sharp edges, plastic toys were relatively safe for the toddler. With improvements in the 1940s plastics begin to take over the industry. After the war hard plastics and "magic skin" latex ended the long reign of the composition doll's head. Toymakers converted a process for making vinyl balloons (used during the war to hold water for pilots shot down over the ocean) into soft inflatable balls. One of the great successes of vinyl was the Doughboy punch bag figures (perhaps best remembered by baby boomers in the form of Bobo the Clown, which with its weighted bottom always popped back up after the child knocked it down).[15]

Nevertheless, throughout the 1950s, plastic toys could not compete with lithographed tinplate for detail and color in toy cars, rockets, and garage sets. Many plastic toys were crude and appeared in garish shades of red, green, yellow, or purple. The Cootie game, featuring an insect's body with attachable legs and antennae, fit this description. Early plastic toys had a bad reputation for melting in hot weather or breaking with light use. Toy vehicles made of die-cast zinc nickel were more durable than plastic and offered manufacturers a cheaper and lighter alternative to pressed steel or cast iron. Only after 1960 would metal be pushed aside by improved plastics.[16]

There were many economic and even technological reasons for postwar toys to remain traditional. But these playthings were conservative mostly because American parents and grandparents in the 1950s wanted toys similar to those they remembered from their own youth. They wanted playthings that trained children and allowed parents to share children's fun and games. As in the 1910s and 1920s, many boys' toys were miniatures of contemporary technology. They invited boys to imitate a familiar adult world of work and technology. A. C. Gilbert could still say in 1946 that children "like to work" and want the "utmost realism" in their toys. Gilbert's Atomic Energy Set was a commercial failure (because of costs), but it was an extravagant example of the toy as promoter of progress. Chemcraft also claimed that its new science sets drew on wartime discoveries in plastics, wonder drugs, and atomic energy to inspire a new generation of children to be inventors. The new technology of jet propulsion stimulated a young model-airplane industry led by Revell. The appeal was not to war but to science and its industrial applications in the future.[17]

Only in the mid-1950s did many toys celebrate World War II combat, and then as a historical event commemorated along with other past heroics. Sears featured playsets that allowed children to reenact Civil War dramas, Robin Hood's adventures, and General Custer's demise along with World War II battles. Revell's "Victory at Sea Battle Ship" models were to give boys a way to relate to their veteran fathers. Bags of cheap hard plastic soldiers, two or three inches tall, were a common toy to early baby boomer boys, allowing them to restage World War II battles. Some boys required no props at all, playing war with sticks as rifles and dirt clods as grenades in undeveloped suburban lots.[18]

But most of this celebration of men's deeds and technology in boys' toys was more pacific and prosaic. For example, in 1946 an old industrial toolmaker, Doepke Manufacturing, launched a side business in high-quality toy roadmaking equipment copied from blueprints of real trucks and bulldozers. Fred Ertl of Dubuque, Iowa, used surplus aluminum (originally made for the Air Force) to make exact replicas of tractors. Mound Metalcraft's Tonka Trucks were perhaps the most successful of these vehicles in miniature. In the tradition of Buddy "L" in the 1920s, Tonka advertised realism and cultivated the idea of boys' sharing the world of men's work. An advertisement from 1959 displayed an amazing variety of pickup and service trucks and featured a boy saying "When I'm a man, there'll be roads to build and land to clear and lakes to be filled."[19]

Toys for playing grown up roles were everywhere. In 1953, Pressman even offered a Play Dentist set complete with chair, buzzing drill, dentures, "gold filling material," and Ipana tooth paste. This toy was three years in the making and promised to "eliminate the child's fear" of the dentist. More popular were Transogram's doctor (and nurse) kits. Gilbert continued his commitment to junior versions of adult technology with a medical laboratory and even crime detection kits.[20]

Boys' toys also celebrated a fantasy world of the future. Science fiction films and comics inspired a curious run of space toys in the early 1950s from diverse small companies. The "overwhelming demand for the streamlined, futuristic toys" of the "Atomic Age" prompted Norton-Honer to offer a Strato-Gun as Earth's only "interplanetary automatic zinc metal" weapon. Banner Plastics featured space helmets with "radar goggles," "designed to kindle the imagination." The entrepreneur Jerry Scanton made his stab at the space craze with a Space Scout Spud Gun that shot "harmless little plugs of raw potato up to 50 feet." Inland Manufacturing and others turned the conventional farm tractor toy into a rocket-ship pedal car. Sears sold Robert the Robot, a wired remote-controlled battery toy. Among the more curious of these playthings were Japanese-made space ships which looked like slightly modified military tanks or planes. A spiral eggbeater was placed on the front of one space truck, and a ping-pong ball fit in a cup on top. Most were made by ephemeral companies with little money to license Flash

Gordon or Space Cadet images. These toys surely appealed to the humor of parents and the naivete of children.[21]

By 1957 bigger companies had begun to imitate the space craze. The launching of the Soviet Sputnik satellite prompted a fury of space-related toys. The New York Gimbel's department store dressed sales staff in space suits and played recordings of Sputnik beeps from space to draw crowds to see Ideal's Satellite Launcher. In 1958 a new fad was inspired by the success of U.S. Intercontinental Ballistic Missiles. Kenner's replicas of the Titan Regular II and Bomarc missiles were "scaled from official blueprints" but launched from a blow tube. Monogram also introduced model kits of the U.S. missile arsenal of 1958. They were "endorsed by space expert Willy Ley," who, in the tradition of Gilbert, wrote a thirty-two-page pamphlet that went with the toy. This item presumably appealed to the science-minded of the era who saw Monogram ads in *Popular Mechanics.* Children were not exactly invited to reenact thermonuclear war, of course, but would-be buyers were reminded that this toy was as "timely as Sputnik." The idea was to share in the great national obsession with the gadgets of the arms race. They may have stilled young children's fears of nuclear war just as the Play Dentist was to overcome anxiety of the drill, but they mostly symbolized the power of a technological future.[22]

Curiously paralleling these futuristic toys was the western fad, a romantic extension of heroism into the past. The miracle of plastic encouraged the making of miniature frontier towns, ranches, and especially forts. Marx's Fort Apache playset was among the most successful. Plastic figures of soldiers and Indians animated a metal frontier stockade, inviting endless reenactments of Indian wars. Marx offered a slight modification, Davy Crockett at the Alamo, in 1955, shortly after Disney introduced Fess Parker's movie rendition of "The King of the Wild Frontier." Radio and movie cowboys, including Hopalong Cassidy, Roy Rogers, the Cisco Kid, and the Lone Ranger, graced the toy shelves of the late 1940s and early 1950s. But the rise of prime-time westerns in the five years after 1955 swelled the ranks of western toys. These westerns attracted fathers as much as sons. The 1958 Sears catalog offered cowboy gun sets featuring the heroes of *Gunsmoke, Maverick, Zorro,* and *Have Gun Will Travel.* Tomorrowland and Frontierland were central sections of Disneyland, which opened in 1955. They were, in effect, full-scale mock-ups of the playsets of American boys in the 1950s. These romantic settings of space travel and western heroes were imaginative worlds shared by fathers and sons.[23]

Just as boys were receiving "authentic" toy tractors, doctor's kits, missiles, and cowboy suits, girls were receiving miniatures of mother's work. In the seven years after its founding in 1949, Amsco rose to the top ten of toy companies with the philosophy: "A little girl wants to do what her mother does, and she wants the real thing too." In the tradition of Pet's Toy Grocery Store of 1909, Amsco manufactured a miniature linen closet with tiny boxes of "Shinola Shoe Polish" and other well-known household supplies. Children early learned that the "real" thing meant brand-name goods. Home-product companies relished the publicity on the theory that the daughter "tells her mother what to buy." Amsco did tie-ins with Johnson and Johnson, who supplied mini-bandages for Amsco's Kidd-e-nurse sets in the early 1950s. Ideal Toys linked up with Betty Crocker to produce a child's bake set. Other companies made their own miniatures: Revere Ware and Singer, for example, manufactured toy pans and sewing machines featuring their company's logos. These playthings gave girls a taste for their future roles as homemakers and educated them to buy "quality" name-brand products when they grew up.[24]

Dolls remained the central toy for girls. One notable change was the marketing of black dolls. While as early as 1908 black organizations had called for black dolls for African-American girls, Pickaninny rag dolls or brown-colored dolls with Caucasian features had long prevailed. However, the impact of World War II on race relations and the nascent civil rights movement encouraged several small companies in 1948 to begin producing dolls with realistic black features. *Ebony* magazine heralded the Patti-Jo, Saralee, and Amosandra dolls for their "delicate features, lighter skin and modish clothes," replacing the "ridiculous, calico-garmented handkerchief-headed servant" of old. Nearly 2 million Amosandras (the name taken from the Amos 'n' Andy radio show) sold between 1949 and 1951. Still major doll companies lagged behind and did not take up the black doll until the mid-1960s.[25]

Like girls' household toys, a large quantity of postwar dolls advertised women's products. Between 1949 and 1955 Ideal Toys teamed up with Revlon, producer of the Toni home permanent, to manufacture the Toni doll. Little girls could give their dolls' nylon hair a "permanent" just as Mother did to her own hair. *McCall's Magazine* joined with American Character Dolls to produce the Betsy McCall doll. Her "Pretty Pac" offered "good grooming fun" complete with lipstick, Camay Soap, and emery board. *McCall's* owned the license, offered paper-doll versions in its pages, and generally used the doll to promote children's fashions. Vogue Dolls marketed Ginny, a doll line that was sold from 1948 to 1982. With Ginny dolls and accessories, girls could "make dates for the football game [and] . . . the record hop." Most curious was the 49-cent Lingerie Lou, sold for a decade after 1949. Despite her girlish face and body, Lou assumed a very different image in her removable plastic lingerie.[26]

These dolls may seem like prototypes for Barbie with their emphasis on clothing, accessories, cosmetics, hair, and dress-up play. But unlike Barbie, they had the appearance of children. Ginny's "Bridal Trousseau" seemed out of place on the childlike body. But parents expected dolls to look like their daughters. Even if some of the fashion dolls of the mid-1950s (Cissy of Madame Alexander, for example) suggested women's breasts, their general shape remained chunky and childlike. Their faces were round and their eyes big and naive. Ginny had a teenage sister in Jill, but the leading figure was the child, not the older girl. Ideal and others were still very much in the business of making baby dolls. Betsy Wetsy had a big comeback for a generation after the war, and Tiny Tears dolls (which cried out for the little mother's care) were a major hit in the 1950s. These remained in the tradition of the dolls of the 1920s and 1930s that parents in the 1950s had known as children. And even as they made little girls aware of cosmetics and household products, they also taught them to envision their future as housewives and mothers.

Given the wave of licensed and fantasy toys in the 1930s, it is surprising how seldom parents were offered this category of toy in the ten years after the World War II. None of the ninety-six toys featured in *Life* at Christmas of 1953, for example, employed character licensing. Disney's character merchandising was still relatively limited. His studios produced a spate of major cartoon movies, including *Cinderella* in 1950, *Alice in Wonderland* in 1951, *Peter Pan* in 1953, and *Lady and the Tramp* in 1955. But these led to few toys. Toymakers apparently found more potential in older characters that parents could share with children. Toy licensees were more common for images of Disney films made before the war. The reissue of *Snow White* in 1952 prompted Whitman Publishing to feature Snow White painting kits and sewing cards. These old Disney characters had an added advantage over the new: those children who had been given Mickey Mouse dolls and Snow White sand pails in the 1930s had become parents and were shopping for toys in the 1950s. Similarly, Campbell Kids dolls reappeared in 1947 and again in 1956, revived with the help of TV soup commercials. And Ideal reissued its famous Shirley Temple dolls in 1957, coinciding with the appearance of Shirley's childhood movies on television. Parents bought nostalgia for their own childhoods with these reissues while giving what for their offspring was a fresh fantasy.[27]

Not all character licensing involved this cross-generational appeal. Cowboy images in the form of Roy Rogers and Hopalong Cassidy attracted the new generation on television and then on play suits, guns and holsters, playsets, and games. Hopalong Cassidy banks and even plastic flashlight guns appeared in 1951. But there was nothing about these products that threatened parental authority or sensibilities. In 1953 Roy Rogers Enterprises reduced the number of its licenses to weed out shoddy merchandise and offered a "Pledge to Parents" as a guarantee of quality. At the end of his TV shows, William Boyd's Hopalong character offered little sermons on right thinking and acting for little cowpokes. How could anyone doubt that "his" cap guns were just as wholesome?[28]

Inevitably, early children's television inspired character licensing. But the TV personalities that found their way onto toys evoked the images of nurturing, if fun-loving, adults, not a separate or menacing world of youthful fantasy. Buffalo Bob was the fatherly figure who hosted the Howdy Doody TV show, a well-known children's program featuring marionettes. Howdy Doody dolls and games appeared soon after the show was launched in 1947 and were a staple in Sears catalogs from 1951 to 1956. Pinky Lee, that frantic children's TV host dressed in a pinstriped suit, was featured in games and other toys. Lee looked and acted like a vaudeville head-liner, hardly a threat to grown-ups.[29]

Other toys that captivated the postwar generation of kids were intended to amuse the whole family. The slinky of 1945, the frisbee of 1957, and the hula hoop of 1958 were in a long line of novelties dating back to the Diabolo of 1908 and the pogo stick of 1921. They were for backyard play, allowing children to demonstrate their skill at hula hooping but also to teach their parents how to do it.[30]

Parents remained all important to toymakers. This was no better illustrated than in the continued attraction of educational toys. Playskool's catalog of 1950 appealed to the trained parent by prom-ising the "right toy for every age." And for parents not familiar with child-development ideas, the catalog included lessons in enlight-ened parenting. Play was declared to be the "foundation of a well adjusted, balanced personality in later years." Playthings were ar-ranged in age-appropriate groupings: bright objects of infancy, pull toys for toddlers, nesting blocks, pegboards, and picture puzzles for ten- to fifteen-month-olds. For the dramatic play of three- to six-year-olds, the catalog proposed simple toy workbenches, peg tables, and a Super Freight Train of plain wood (signals, decor, and color "could only limit or confuse the play of the youngsters"). Best of all were blocks to teach spatial relations. "Many progressive parents make up their children's sets by selecting individual units" of various sizes. But if the parent was unsure, prepared packages included the "correct balanced assortment." The ideal was not too many toys at a time, but a good selection updated with each devel-opmental stage.[31]

Playskool's approach had remained a constant in educational toys since the beginning of the century. But the tradition of devel-opmentally specific and plain toys took on a decidedly sophisti-cated cast in postwar companies like Creative Playthings. A 1963 catalog bragged, "We have traveled the world to bring you the best in toys." It offered "timeless" plain blocks with modernistic models of Buckminster Fuller's geodesic domes and construction toys "de-signed by an architect with mathematical and geometric learning implications." Parents bought these toys to give children a head start in the competitive world of modern learning. But Creative

Playthings also offered replicas of turn-of-the-century toys—dissected maps, toy printing presses, steam engines, Noah's arks, carom boards, magnetic toys, and even reproductions of mechanical banks and horse-pulled cast-iron fire trucks—appealing to older Americans for holiday gifts to grandchildren. For girls' dramatic play, they offered washboards and wringers as "time-tested favorites." Creative Playthings combined progressive education, aesthetic snob appeal, and nostalgia.[32]

Fisher-Price, hardly a proponent of the plain-blocks philosophy, still prided itself on resisting mere novelty and said so in its motto, "Good toys never die!" In 1955 it continued to feature Snooper Sniffers (a pull-along dog first made in 1937) and Busy Bees (with revolving wings, dating from 1944). Herman Fisher insisted that a toy that lasted from "one child to another" guaranteed a loyal market of parents. Tinkertoy ads appealed to "mothers and dads [who] know from their own experience [that] Tinkertoys mean endless fun." Walco Products offered "Indian beads" that gave children a "sense of achievement and creativity." These crafts represented "democracy at work—in play." Children who worked together to make headbands and belts were learning the "first and most important lesson in relationships": how to cooperate. The Progressivist philosophy of John Dewey still lived in the appeals of this maker of children's crafts.[33]

Benjamin Spock offered readers of *Ladies' Home Journal* in the holiday season of 1961 a familiar refrain: "The less specific [the toy] is, the more it stimulates a child's imagination." He even argued that the best toy was the wooden block (preferably 5½ by 2¾ by 1⅜ inches in size)—even though he conceded that boys needed trucks to affirm their masculine identity and girls required toys allowing them to imitate mother's "caretaking activities." But the novelty doll with its gadgetry was "unnecessary" and would not give girls "long-range satisfaction."[34]

Spock's critique of the flashy and flimsy toy was, however, rare in the popular magazines of the 1950s. *Parents' Magazine* insisted that boys "needed" western outfits and guns to help them let off aggression and to get "vicariously around their feelings." Preschool toys were unquestionably "scientifically correct." Girls ages six to eight naturally wanted baby dolls, especially the new soft-skin and wettable type, while the Teddy bear was the "favorite stuffed animal of all times." Articles advising on Christmas purchases stressed that givers should know the needs of the child, but they also gushed about the latest toy soda fountains and plastic doll houses. Their understanding of toys was conventional, and most of all accommodating to toy advertisers, hardly a guide to parents to take heed of novelty playthings.[35]

Still, playthings were supposed to be tools of good parenting. Toymakers recognized this in their advertisements and in their product lines. Despite all the differences from earlier toys, the playthings of the decade after World War II were mostly sold to adults, people who had grown up in the Depression or earlier. This may explain a lot of the "tradition" in the products offered. It hardly made adult choices wise or even well considered, but it did mean that toys were largely gifts of one generation to the next.

Origins of the TV Toy

Television took the toy beyond the worlds of parents, trained salespeople, educational experts, and, most of all, tradition. The new medium made possible a constantly changing culture of play that appealed directly to the imaginations of children. Over time this led to the predominance of fantasy-fad toys stimulated and sustained by the media celebrities whose appeal was primarily to the young. In the 1930s children's magazines, comics, and especially radio had fostered a distinct child's culture but a limited one. Old-fashioned periodicals like *American Boy* reached only a middle-class elite with their philosophy of self-improvement. From the late 1930s comic books attracted a broader audience with their lurid colors and superpower stories. In the 1930s and 1940s radio offered children's programs in the after-school hours. Licensed products emerged from the radio heroes. Nevertheless, the radio, without a visual image, was a poor medium for selling toys directly to children. By contrast, in the 1950s television became the ideal pipeline to the child. Advertising could give a dramatic image of the plaything, making it accessible to children too young to read. Also, unlike comic books, it was set in a legitimizing environment—in the family living room on Daddy's favorite new toy.

Yet toymakers were rather slow to discover the potential of TV advertising even though the networks featured prime-time children's programming in the early 1950s. Probably because of the expense of early television, the earliest ads were for educational toys that appealed to affluent parents. In 1951 Halsam Products sold its block sets on ABC's *Fun Fair*. And Playskool promoted Lincoln Logs in 1953 on *Pioneer Playhouse*. From 1952 the kindly figures of Miss Frances (of *Ding Dong School*) and Captain Kangaroo were used to sell toys. Frances Holwich, a professor at Columbia University's Teacher's College, allowed American Character Dolls to perch a Tiny Tears doll on a book while she read a story to the doll on her live TV show. This touching scene was used in an advertising campaign, during which Miss Frances made appearances at department stores. Bob Keeshan's Captain Kangaroo character was not above riding on an AMF Deluxe Tractor during his show in 1957. This type of "host" advertising would be banned in the 1970s, but it surely attracted young children who watched these beloved adults on TV in the 1950s. More important, parents were a major share of the audiences of these programs. Toy companies used TV first to sell to adults.[36]

In fact, adult entertainers promoted toys to parents beyond the confines of children's television. Talk show hosts Art Linkletter and Arthur Godfrey endorsed miniatures. Linkletter lent "his face, his name . . . his popularity . . . to Hubley's new Tiny toys." The sales pitch was simple: "The kids love Art. Their parents love him." A small maker of musical toys offered a child's version of Arthur Godfrey's "Uke" in 1952. Emenee Industries promoted Pinky Lee Xylophones and Gene Autry Cowboy Guitars. They even featured the image of the veteran Vaudevillian Jimmy Durante on the "Hotcha cha Uke."[37]

Toymakers early recognized the profit in licensing television characters. Tom Corbett, Space Cadet, was transformed into dolls and cardboard playsets in the early 1950s. Superman capes appeared shortly after the television show in 1952. The sheer imitative power of early television prompted the Desilu company to promote a Ricky Jr. doll in 1953. Desi Arnaz and Lucille Ball were convinced that the appearance of their baby on the *I Love Lucy* show made this doll a sure hit. Advertisements to dealers claimed that more would see Ricky Jr. than ever saw Shirley Temple. In October 1954 the appearance of a segment of Disney's new movie *Davy Crockett* on TV created a craze for coonskin caps, toy guns, playsets, and games depicting this frontier hero. Disney's hit peaked by the summer of 1955, but it prompted a wave of toy merchandising on western themes that lasted into the early 1960s. Disney went after the same appeal when the old Davy Crockett, Fess Parker, appeared in 1964 as Daniel Boone. But the western theme had faded by then and character licensing had turned to science fiction and superhero figures.[38]

Early TV was a fad accelerator, more efficient than seaside boardwalk crowds or even movies and radio in spreading a craze. But these fads were still part of an intergenerational world. The power of licensing was not lost on ABC, which by 1957 had a Character Licensing Department eager to sell *Maverick* and its other westerns to toy and clothing makers. The period from 1951 to 1962 saw such merchandising agencies increase from three to eighteen. But these were still hit-or-miss efforts and licensing was incidental to the TV program, not its reason for being.[39]

Direct advertising of toys to children became systematic with the first airing of the *Mickey Mouse Club* in October 1955. It was at first an hour-long program beginning at 5 P.M. when children usually controlled the TV dial. It gained an unprecedented audience of children—16.5 million by early 1956. The program created a craze for Mouseketeer memorabilia that allowed the young to participate in the TV fantasy. Within scarcely three months, Benay-Albee Novelty Company had shipped 550,000 Mouseketeer hats. While adults (and many children) felt the black-eared beanies made the wearer look ridiculous (and this may have been part of the attraction to parents), many children loved them. Mattel, Knickerbocker, Gong Bell, and many others produced a wide range of Mickey Mouse Club items—"Theater" playsets, the Mousegetar crank music box, water pistols, and a variety of toddler push toys. Most Mickey Mouse toys were directed toward young children and sold to parents as child quieters or as impulse purchases sparked by a pleading child near the checkout line of the grocery or drug store. All this was in the mold of the earlier Teddy Bear craze—as much adult celebrations of childhood as expressions of a distinctive youth culture.[40]

But the Mickey Mouse Club did more. It created a new context for selling toys directly to children. The program used old movie cartoons, as did other children's shows, but its central feature was the child performers with whom young viewers could identify. Annette and Cubby were stars, not merely an appreciative audience like the peanut gallery of Buffalo Bob's marionettes on the *Howdy Doody Show*. The two adult performers (Jimmy, a fun uncle type, and Roy, a kindly and vigorous grandfatherly personality) were more co-participants than parental figures. The real authoritative voice was in the advertising. Newspaper reviews of the program's debut complained about the hard sell directed to children. As important, the selling was often done with the voices of children.[41]

Mattel set the pace. Ruth and Eliot Handler risked their family business to purchase three commercials every weekday for a year on the *Mickey Mouse Club*. This flew in the face of conventional wisdom. Everyone knew that profit from toys did not warrant such expensive advertising and that commercials were effective only at Christmas and then only if directed at their purchasers—adults. Mattel's opening advertisement in the autumn of 1955 was for the burp gun, a cap machine gun reminiscent of a World War II weapon. The commercial featured a boy imagining he was hunting for elephants in his living room. This made the child and his imagination the message of the advertising. Within six weeks of commercials, a deluge of orders for the guns reached Mattel, causing a shortage at Christmas.

In 1957 Mattel launched another hit, the Fanner 50 smoking cap gun. As the advertising executive Cy Schneider notes, the Fanner was not sold by being associated with an admired adult cowboy. Rather Mattel's commercial featured a boy twirling his gun and demonstrating make-believe gun play. Beginning in 1959 advertisements for the Barbie doll suggested that the doll was a real person with whom children could identify. Some commercials featured unstaged girls' play and invited membership into a Barbie fan club. Thanks to TV, Mattel's sales rose from 6 million in 1955 to 49 million in 1961. Mattel's success on the *Mickey Mouse Club* prompted sponsorship of *Matty's Funday Funnies,* a half-hour show at 5 P.M. The boy figure in Mattel's logo served as the host of "Casper the Friendly Ghost" cartoons and Mattel commercials.[42]

Soon other companies followed Mattel's lead. By 1959 toymakers promoted their products to retailers by bragging about how much they advertised them on children's TV. The playthings themselves took a back seat to the promise of saturation television "reselling." Transogram Toys did not even bother mentioning its products when it announced its TV budget in a March 1961 promotion to retailers. Especially big advertisers in these years were Ideal and Kenner. But even the venerable Lionel advertised heavily, and Marx, the old holdout against advertising, finally gave in. Louis Marx produced his own TV program, *Marx Magic Midway,* a Saturday morning show featuring circus acts and Magic Marxie, a cartoon sales figure imitating Mattel's Matty. Appropriately, A. C. Gilbert sponsored *Discovery,* a weekday scientific adventure program, to showcase its products to 8 million viewers. These companies imitated Mattel's attempt to create a year-round toy market and to win children to brand loyalty.[43]

These sales tactics often worked. In 1958 a *Playthings* survey of toy stores found merchants eager to order TV toys. "Anything advertised on televisions sells," noted one buyer. Manufacturers grew increasingly sophisticated, scattering commercials on local stations rather than paying network rates. As the 1960s wore on toy companies no longer felt the need for a prestige program associated with their name. Instead manufacturers pushed play novelties in hard-sell, saturation advertisements on Saturday morning cartoon shows. Doll companies like Grant Plastic, Doll Bodies, and A and H Dolls, which failed to buy TV time, quietly disappeared as the ubiquitous Barbie ruled the screen and the toy shelves.[44]

Estimated personal consumption of toys and sport supplies rose from $5.78 billion in 1950 to $15.24 billion in 1970 (in 1982–1984 dollars). This translates into a rise from $142.96 to $252.26 in constant dollars spent per child under fifteen. Most of this rise occurred in the 1960s (67.5 percent compared to only 5.7 percent in the 1950s).[45] Television was clearly a powerful marketing tool. The traditional pitches to parents increasingly took second place to direct appeals to youthful longings and fantasy. It was no longer even necessary to have an adult like Miss Frances serve as salesperson. Toy companies sold directly to children, bypassing parents and their child-development experts.

By the mid-1960s, however, retailers' enthusiasm for TV advertising was turning to wariness. During the Christmas season of 1963 toy stores found that they had overstocked TV toys and had to sell half of the $55.4 million worth of them as "loss leaders." Trade surveys revealed that retailers preferred Fisher-Price's steady staples with an assured adult market to TV toys that sold large numbers but earned little profit. A buyer from the Newberry dime store chain complained in 1964 that the industry needed to produce a $5.95 toy with play value. He admitted that retailers let "ad agencies do too much thinking for us." Even the trade press was willing to admit that many toys advertised on television were too similar in their gimmickry and that companies relied too much on ads and not enough on product development and efficient distribution.[46]

Despite these setbacks, manufacturers were addicted to the tube. In 1967 Kenner was back to bragging that it was going to spend 35 percent more on TV than it had in 1966. And the strategy paid off with hits like the Easy-Bake Oven. Toy licensing of television characters continued unabated, with about fifty companies competing. In 1971 Mattel spent over $20 million on TV ads and Hasbro almost $6.5 million. Total spending on TV rose by 38.5 percent between 1967 and 1971, to nearly $79 million. In 1969 Bernard Loomis of Mattel produced *Hot Wheels*, a TV cartoon series, to advertise a new line of mini-cars. This crossing of the boundary between advertising and programming was pioneering but premature. Government pressure stopped Mattel from advertising the toy on the program, and the show soon disappeared. Still, TV toys were to here stay, no matter how great their threat to the retailers' bottom line.[47]

Increasingly sophisticated research on the impact of advertising on children taught the toy industry that playthings no longer had to appeal to parents' nostalgia or concern for their child's development. By the 1960s toymakers were designing their products to attract and stimulate the imaginations of children. Children, in turn, were skillful salespeople to their parents.[48] The connection of the toy business to adults and holiday gifts was beginning to fray.

Tradition and Transition

In the ten years after 1955 TV changed the way playthings were sold. But TV advertising to children did not by itself radically change the kinds of toys available. Old toys survived along with the new. Throughout the 1960s Sears catalogs offered Noah's arks, carom games, Uncle Sam banks, toy steam engines, microscopes, erector sets, miniature guitars, and puppet theaters, appealing to parents and grandparents who wanted to give toys they themselves had known as children. The mixture of a romanticized future and past that had dominated boys' toys in the 1950s continued. Excitement about the space program prompted the manufacture of the Cape Canaveral Rocket and Missile Launcher, "Mr. Atomic" Japanese tinplate robots, and various flying saucers. Sears also stocked Roy Rogers Double-R Bar Ranch sets, gun-and-holster sets, and plastic soldiers for reenacting "The Greatest Battles in History."[49]

Barbie had an important space in the girls' dolls section of Sears stores, but she shared it with updated versions of companion dolls like Chatty Cathy (Mattel), Kissy Dolls (Ideal), and Tiny Tears (American Character). Sears continued to sell old favorites like Raggedy Anns and even Kewpie dolls. And the 1950s emphasis on kitchen and dollhouse play scarcely changed in the 1960s. Even after Barbie took the doll world by storm in 1959, grandmothers and mothers fought back with preferences for the dolls of their childhoods. In 1973, for example, Montgomery Ward resurrected the Bye-Lo Babies and Shirley Temple dolls of the 1920s and 1930s. In 1978 Vogue dolls reintroduced Ginny, a hit in the mid-1950s.[50]

In the 1960s and 1970s the idea of play as a glue bonding family members together had hardly died. In 1960 silly putty was touted as the "fascinating toy for the whole family." Tyco, maker of race cars, promoted father-son play in *Boy's Life, Life,* and *Look* with ads telling the boy to "get to know your old man." Makers of trolls and other mini-fantasy figures sold them as hobbies that encouraged mothers to share time and interests with their daughters. And by 1973 Schaper Plastics was able to turn a 1950s fad toy into a "classic" by reminding parents of their "cherished memories" of playing Cootie and suggesting that "now it is time to share these moments with your children."[51]

The onslaught of television scarcely touched educational staples in the 1960s. Fisher-Price regularly advertised in women's magazines and on family TV serials like *Bonanza* and *Green Acres*. The new toy on the block, Lego, first manufactured in 1954 in Denmark, appeared in the United States in 1962. Early advertisements appealed to the discerning parent, not to the child. One ad from a 1964 issue of *Parents' Magazine* is particularly striking: "Let somebody else's child get his kicks tracking a little kid through a gun sight. War isn't very adventurous any more. There's more adventure in a medical lab or at the U.N. That's why we make Lego. And why you should buy it." This toy placed "no limits on what you can build." Legos promised to "develop the child's critical judgment, manual dexterity, and ability to think for himself." At the same time, educational toymakers appealed to retailers with the promise of full mark-up and year-round sales. Educational alternatives to the novelty toys sold on TV not only survived but thrived.[52]

Even toy companies that advertised to children—Hasbro, Kenner, and Mattel, for example—used TV to sell quite traditional parent-pleasing toys. In 1960 Hasbro's big success was Fizzies Fountain, which made "real pop" from tablets deposited in a dispenser. All the big companies continued to sell odd assortments of playthings. In 1963 Kenner still offered girder and panel sets, play drills, paint sets, and toy movie projectors that had been introduced in the mid-1950s. Toys remained gadgets, sold to parents for children who were expected to imitate adults.[53]

Even the advertising message stayed within the bounds of tradition. TV commercials for the 1963 erector set still stressed features like working conveyor belts and "automatic programming" machines. Early G.I. Joe advertisements emphasized not combat fantasy but "the greatest realism" in the soldier's uniforms and the "greatest equipment" that allowed the boy to "set up battle action whenever you want." Fathers appeared in commercials sharing in their sons' fun with the Dick Tracy Wrist Radio. Even the famous musician Louis Armstrong was seen on the screen telling little girls, "Suzy Cute needs a Mommy. Suzy Cute needs you!"[54]

The oft-declared guru of the toy industry in the early 1960s was Marvin Glass. This independent inventor was anything but a Santa Claus. At the age of forty-five in 1960, Glass chained-smoked, had been married four times, claimed to read Plato and be an enthusiast of Beethoven, and worked odd hours inventing toys out of a suite in a seedy Chicago hotel. Glass had no faith in children's opinions: the young were "too insecure to be innovators." It was the parents who wanted novelty. And that is what he provided. He was convinced that the best toys related to real life, so he kept abreast of trends. But the child also wanted playthings that put "his energies and his body to work." Mr. Machine, a windup "robot" that could be taken apart, fit the bill. Other Glass inventions (the Mouse Trap Game, Kissy Doll, and Moody Mutt) equally combined whimsy with mechanical wonder. Glass mocked the corporate "statistical approach, the toy testing approach" and pursued his idiosyncratic grasp of children's delight.[55]

But the statisticians would eventually prevail. Statistics reduced the risks of high-volume production, expensive advertising, and low profit margins. And these changes had as much impact on the contents of the toybox as did TV advertising. One place where accountants appeared early was in the new discount toy supermarkets. In 1956 and 1957 Child's World and Toys "R" Us first opened their doors. Sid Shneider built a string of 40,000-square-foot Child's World stores on the edge of suburban shopping malls in New England. Others joined by the early 1970s, including Toy Country USA, launched by American Medical Services, a nursing-home chain in search of a business in a "free enterprise community." As early as 1974 the superstores were using computers to monitor sales and orders, keeping close control over inventory. They relied on low-wage staff with little training or knowledge of toys. Increasingly, TV commercials directed at children were depended on to do the selling. Family toy stores gradually fell by the wayside or converted themselves into children's furniture stores or upscale shops for educational toys. By 1980 47 percent of the dollar value of toys was sold in discount or toy superstores.[56]

Consolidation was even more evident among manufacturers. With the passing of the old generation of toymakers (especially Gilbert in 1961 and Marx in 1972), old companies were bought out by investors with little experience with toys. Failure soon followed. In 1965 CBS bought Creative Playthings and later Ideal toys (only to sell them in the 1980s). Playskool was sold to Milton Bradley in

1968. In 1969, five years after buying American Flyer, Lionel Trains was itself sold to breakfast-food maker, General Mills. More dramatic were General Mills's purchase of Kenner and Parker Brothers in 1967 and 1968 and Quaker Oats's acquisition of Fisher-Price in 1969.[57]

These buyouts and mergers created an intensely competitive climate that greatly affected the contents of the toy shelves. With the demise of the old companies often came an end to their commitment to a particular age sector or toy tradition. Even survivors were forced to diversify into a full line of toys. Remco, the model vehicle specialists, branched out into dolls. Hasbro and Mattel ventured into craft sets. Companies that did not adapt failed. Transogram, for example, disappeared in 1970. And the 1970s produced shooting-star companies that overextended themselves in TV toys or made poor business decisions. Mego, for example, invested heavily in character licenses for action dolls (Superman, Casper, Cher) but died in 1982, buried by Kenner's Star War figures. The toy industry had always attracted gamblers. But the stakes were much higher now, and the incentive increased to pick winners rather than to meet the developmental needs of children. These changes in the business culture of manufacturers contributed much to the alienation of parents and the decline of traditions of toymaking that dated back to the beginning of the twentieth century.[58]

Barbie, G.I. Joe, and Play in the 1960s

Television and the new business climate in the toy industry alone did not transform the meaning of play. Toys were changing because American society was changing. By looking at the two most important trend-setting toys we can find clues to these changes. Much has been written about Barbie and G.I. Joe as icons of popular culture. But Barbie and G.I. Joe were also toys, and like other toys they were mostly given to children by adults.

Barbie began her career as a stiff plastic dress-up figure. Ruth Handler often claimed that she invented Barbie to fill a void in girls' play . Girls wanted a less cumbersome and more fun version of the fashion paper doll. In using paper dolls as a model Mattel was in effect redirecting doll play away from the friendship and nurturing themes of the companion and baby dolls that had predominated since the 1900s. In the nineteenth century paper dolls were used to display the latest styles and to portray royalty and famous actresses, especially in magazines devoted to fashion. They were associated with an adult world of quasi-aristocratic consumption. They had little to do with domestic or friendship themes. Paper dolls and their focus on fashion were an important part of girls' play in the first half of the twentieth century, but they were only a minor part of the toy business.[59]

Mattel, however, put fashion doll play at the center of the industry. The idea of making the paper fashion doll three dimensional was hardly new. Even the association of doll play with consumption was not innovative. It had been built into the concepts of dolls from Patsy to Toni. But Barbie was not a child doll dressed in children's fashions. Rather Barbie was in the shape of a young woman with very long legs and an exaggerated hourglass figure. She looked neither like the little girl who owned her nor like the little girl's mother. She was neither a baby, a child, nor a mother but a liberated teenager, almost a young woman. Handler admitted that even in this her creation was not so original. She "borrowed" the look from a German dress-up doll she and her daughter Barbara had noticed on a vacation in Switzerland. But she marketed it on a grand scale at a perfect point in the history of American childhood: at the end of the 1950s.[60]

Barbie was an early rebel against the domesticity that dominated the lives of baby-boom mothers. It may not be surprising that some of the first generation of Barbie owners became feminists in the late 1960s and 1970s. The revolt against, at least, the momism of the feminine mystique was played out with Barbie, who never cared for babies or children. But Mattel's doll was also an autonomous teenager with no visible ties to parents in a time when the earliest of the baby-boom generation were just entering their teens. This crop of teenagers, coming of age in a more affluent United States, had more choices than their parents had had and were freer of adult control. To the eight-year-old of 1960, Barbie represented a hoped-for future of teenage freedom. It was this attraction of Barbie that long survived the maturation of the baby-boom generation. It is also not surprising that when Mattel market-tested Barbie it found that mothers were not nearly so positive about the doll as were their daughters. Mothers recognized that this doll was a break from the tradition of nurturing and companion play and that girls apparently welcomed it.

Despite all this, Barbie hardly "taught" girls to shed female stereotypes. Rather she prompted them to associate the freedom of being an adult with carefree consumption. With her breasts and slender waist, Barbie came literally to embody the little girl's image of what it meant to be grown up. At the same time, in her contemporary fashions, she represented the up-to-date. Barbie did not invite children to be Mommy, nor was she the child's friend in a secret garden of caring and sharing. She was what the little girl was not and, even more important, what her mother was not. She was a fashion model with a large wardrobe designed to attract attention. Instead of teaching girls how to diaper a baby or use floor cleaners, Barbie play was an education in consumption—going to the hairdresser and shopping for that perfect evening gown for the big dance.Even when she had a job (model, stewardess, or later even a doctor), her work and life had nothing to do with the jobs of most women. Barbie was never a cashier at Wal-Mart or a homemaker.

If Barbie taught that freedom meant consumption, the Barbie line was designed to maximize parents' real spending. Playing consumer required that Barbie have a constantly changing wardrobe of coordinated clothing and accessories. Clothing sets were often much more expensive than the "hook," the doll itself. The first Barbie advertising brochure featured, for example, a Barbie-Q Outfit, Suburban Shopper, Picnic Set (with fishing pole), Evening Splendor (complete with strapless sheath), and even a Wedding Day Set. By the early 1960s Barbie had play environments, for example the Barbie Fashion Shop and Barbie's Dream House.[61]

Barbie's glamour required constant purchases of dolls and accessories. Playing grown up meant that Barbie had to have a boy friend, Ken (introduced in 1961). Because Barbie seemed to be six to seven years older than her owners, Mattel introduced in 1964 a little sister, Skipper, with whom the children could identify. Naturally Skipper developed her own entourage of "friends." In 1975 Mattel carried the transition doll to its logical conclusion with "Growing Up Skipper." Six-year-olds could mechanically reenact their growing-up fantasy: when her arm was rotated, Skipper grew taller and developed breasts.

Barbie also needed "friends" to shop and have fun with. Mattel manufactured an endless array of Midge, Francie, and Stacey dolls, all "sold separately." Like Barbie's clothing, they changed with the times. While Midge (1963) was the "freckled-faced and impish" girl next door, Francie (1966) and Stacey (1968) reflected the impact of English styles and music in the age of the Beatles. In 1968 Christie, a black friend for Barbie, was introduced, reflecting changing American race relations. Ken vanished suddenly in 1969 (apparently too stodgy an image to fit the long-haired Vietnam era) only to reappear two years later looking much more husky and hip.[62]

Mattel tapped into a young girl's fantasy life to create a demand for possessions. Company researchers watched girls play and noted that they enjoyed hair and dress-up games as well as acting out shopping, travel, and dating. They designed accessories to provide props for these play activities. And if the child did not immediately know what the story lines were to be, Mattel provided them on the back of the packages.

Barbie's impact on the traditional doll industry was enormous. Only 60 doll companies remained in 1969 of the more than 200 that existed when Barbie appeared in 1959. Barbie helped reduce the share of baby dolls from 80 percent of dolls in 1959 to only 38 percent in 1975. Barbie's success inevitably prompted much imitation. Ideal produced Tammy (who conceded the existence of parents with Mom and Dad dolls). American Character offered Tressy, with "hair that really grows." Topper's Penny Brite and the "perfectly proportioned" Tina of Ross Products were others. None survived long in a field dominated by Barbie.[63]

Mattel succeeded keeping successive generations of little girls wanting Barbie and not some other fashion doll. Ruth Handler resisted the temptation to give Barbie a fixed personality or even a "look." Handler liked to say this allowed girls to imagine what Barbie was really like. But from a marketing standpoint this made Barbie a fixture, even a "clothes hanger," upon which accessories could be draped. Partly because she came first, Barbie became the trademark fashion doll. All others were imitations. And Barbie never grew old or out of date as did the dolls made in the image of ephemeral glamour queens like Farah Fawcett-Majors. Barbie was the eternal star—despite her changeable hair and skin color. Barbie was still Barbie.

Mattel even succeeded in persuading little girls to "trade in" their old Barbies for a discount on a new look in 1967. Adults found this strange—voluntarily parting with a "loved" doll. But the girls saw it differently: they were simply trading in an old model for a new, much as their parents traded in their flashy 1959 Chevys for the more sedate look of 1960s models. Barbie's environment—clothes, hair, playsets, and friends—changed with adult fashion. But Barbie's face and shape remained a constant symbol of growing up. Thus Mattel created that elusive and contradictory prize—an ephemeral classic—and in doing so reshaped the play of American girls. A doll that mothers at first disliked became the doll that mothers had to give to their daughters.[64]

Hasbro's G.I. Joe mirrored the success of Barbie by becoming a perennial fad. It achieved this feat, at first, not by challenging expectations of fathers as Barbie broke with the doll culture of mothers, but by affirming the values and experiences of many fathers. Like so many other contemporary toys, G.I. Joe was inspired by a TV series, an action-adventure show, *The Lieutenant* (1963), that was supposed to appeal to adult men. But the program failed even before the toy appeared. G.I. Joe was not tied to any specific media personality or story. He represented the average soldier, evoking memories of fathers' experience in World War II and the Korean War. The original G.I. Joe of 1964 shared with Barbie the critical feature of being a dress-up doll, although marketed as "America's Moveable Fighting Man." At twelve inches, half an inch taller than Barbie, G.I. Joe was suitable for costuming in the uniforms of the four American military services (sold separately). Again like Barbie, G.I. Joe was accessorized. Hasbro adopted what was often called the "razor and razor blade" principle of marketing. Once the boy had the doll he needed accessories—multiple sets of uniforms, jeeps, tents, and, weaponry.[65]

Still, Joe was not simply a boy's version of Barbie. The obvious historical precedent was the cast-metal soldier, very different from the paper doll. Miniature soldiers had been part of boy's play for centuries. The object was to reenact the drama of present and past battles. G.I. Joe added to this traditional game by giving boys articulated figures with a man's shape and musculature. The Joes were a major improvement over cheap and impersonal plastic soldiers that stood on bases. Joe took the play beyond the traditional deployment of infantry, cannon, and cavalry. Detailed "Manuals," accompanying the doll, marched "Joe through basic training up to combat readiness," showing the boy how to pose his toy to crouch in a trench or throw a grenade. Joe changed war games from the pleasure of acting the general—arranging soldiers and weapons on a field of battle—to playing the soldier, the G.I. whom the boy dressed and posed. This probably made war play far more appealing to young children because they could identify with the individual soldier. Joe may have contributed to the decline of other forms of boys' play, at least temporarily, insofar as erector sets almost disappeared and Tinkertoys and Lincoln Logs were relegated to preschoolers in the G.I. Joe era.[66]

Nevertheless, the early G.I. Joe did not challenge traditional war play as Barbie displaced baby doll and companion doll play. G.I. Joe's success was based on a boy's identity with the all-male world of heroic action aided by modern military equipment and gadgetry. The play was conventional, featuring males bonding in adventure. This was a womanless world. Boys rejected the idea of a female nurse when it was introduced to the G.I. Joe line in 1965. These boys could play war the way their fathers might have fought it in World War II or in Korea. And they could dress their Joes in battle gear similar to that worn by conscripted uncles or older brothers serving their two-year stints in the army of the mid-1960s. The object was not the clash of enemies (as would be the case with later action figures). Even though boys made their Joe dolls fight each other, Hasbro offered soldiers from only one side. The point was to imitate the real world of adults in the military. GI Joe still connected fathers with sons.

Again in contrast to Barbie, G.I. Joe went through major changes. By 1967 as the Vietnam war heated up and adults such as Benjamin Spock attacked war toys, sales decreased. Beginning in 1970 Hasbro responded by transforming the "fighting" Joes into an "Adventure Team." Joes searched for sunken treasure and captured wild animals. As the Vietnam war wound down to its bitter end in 1975, it was awkward to sell military toys glorifying contemporary jungle warfare. While veterans of World War II and even Korea might enjoy giving their sons toys that memorialized their own youth, the situation for fathers who had reached manhood during the Vietnam era was very different. Most of these men wanted to forget the Vietnam war (whether they fought in it or opposed it), not to give their sons toys recalling this military disaster or any real war.

In 1976, with the Vietnam War in the past, G.I. Joe became "Super Joe" and shrunk to eight inches (because of higher costs for plastic). He no longer could be dressed. He returned to the role of a fighter, but he did not rejoin the ranks of enlisted men. He no longer was part of a world that fathers, uncles, or older brothers had ever experienced. Instead he was a high-tech hero, no longer connected to a troublesome reality. His laser beams and rocket command vehicles helped him fight off aliens, the Intruders. Added to his team was Bullet Man, the first of a long line of superhumans. The object of play was to pit good guys against bad guys, not to imitate real military life. But even these changes could not save Joe. From 1978 to 1981 the "Great American Hero" disappeared from store shelves to be pushed aside by an even more fantasyful line of toys based on George Lucas's *Star Wars*.[67]

With Barbie little girls combined growing up with feminine consumerism. This gave Barbie a permanent aisle of hot-pink packages in every serious toy store. G.I. Joe began as a celebration of an all-male world of realistic combat. But Joe encountered deeper contradictions in the 1960s than did Barbie and was forced to flee into fantasy. Still, both toys became models for toy play and consumption that still prevail today. They did so by breaking away from the worlds of parents.

Monsters, Space Guys, and the Appeal to the Child

Hasbro's G.I. Joe and Mattel's Barbie embodied major changes in toys and childhood in the 1960s and 1970s. But revolutionary approaches to toy design came from other, some long departed, companies like Revell, Aurora, Mego, and even Louis Marx. Their playthings challenged the expectations of parents even more sharply than did Barbie and the later G.I. Joe. These toys appealed to a child's quest for autonomy and uninhibited imagination and even acted as wedges between parents and children.

Leading the trend were boys' toys based on monster and grotesque images. In 1961 Ed Roth, a drag-race personality, introduced a disgusting and nasty figure, Rat Fink, on T-shirts. This character, a kind of anti–Mickey Mouse, appealed to a counterculture of hotrod enthusiasts. In spite of its origins, Revell licensed Roth's concept for a special series of race-car models marketed to children in 1962. "Big Daddy" Roth's image on packaging promoted hotrod miniatures driven by Rat Fink, grotesque monsters, and a scruffy Roth himself. Revell gave these adult-defying models names like Drag Nut and Mother's Worry. Hawk Models soon followed with Weird-Ohs and Aurora Plastics came out with Godzilla's Go-Cart and other monsters in race cars.[68]

In the 1950s model-building companies offered a hobby for both fathers and sons. By the mid-1960s they were promoting toys designed to irritate parents. Marx introduced a new line of friction cars called Nutty Mads featuring Gutterball Annie and other sports jokes. This was mild compared with the Blame Its line of figures. The "I Didn't Do It" and "I Didn't Push Him" figures offered images of children with sheepish looks who obviously did do it. The Born Losers collection of model kits featured an image of Hitler with a gun at his head. And Remco's Horrible Hamilton series of giant bugs were designed to delight boys while horrifying parents. The success of small companies with the grotesque and defiant inspired Mattel to make the Thingmaker in 1964, a kit to mold plastic images of dragons, trolls, and insects. Mattel's Vucuforms gave children the opportunity to pour "plastigoop" into molds to make Creepy Crawlers. But Mattel's designers topped themselves with the Incredible Edibles of 1967. With this toy the child could annoy both parents and younger siblings not only by making insects from molds but by eating them. It is impossible to say how many of these toys were actually purchased by children. But they were advertised to children in Sunday newspaper comics, boys' magazines, and comic books.[69]

Surely a leader in the trend was Aurora Plastics. In the 1950s Aurora had specialized in military vehicle models and miniatures of historic figures (for example, a Gold Knight of Nice and a Roman

Gladiator). But by 1960 it shifted to fantasy with models of movie monsters. Soon Aurora and *Famous Monsters of Filmland* magazine offered children prizes for making dioramas of monster settings. In 1965 Aurora borrowed ideas from these submissions to introduce a new series of models. This was an old trick of Gilbert's in promoting elector sets, but Aurora took it in a very different direction. Children were asked to construct mechanical images not of the adult world but of gruesome fantasy. In 1964 Aurora made itself notorious to parents by marketing models of a guillotine (complete with beheadable bodies). This toy caused such an uproar that it was removed from the shelves after seven months. But in 1971 Aurora returned with a series of models labeled The Chamber of Horrors. Most notable were the Hanging Cage, Pain Parlor, and Gruesome Goodies. Scantily clad female victims were featured, making the series, bragged Aurora, "Rated X for excitement." In 1965 Aurora marketed a Wacky Back Whacker (a spanking machine).[70]

Aurora's objective was probably not to appeal to childish sadism (or masochism); it was to entice the child's imagination and to give young people what they, not their parents, wanted. In their quest for a youth market, Aurora and other toymakers may have helped heighten differences between the generations by tapping the macabre for entertainment. At the same time, parents and other relatives accommodated the wishes of children and bought these toys. At least some adults tolerated this trend and even found it amusing.

More subtle was the appearance of comic book figures. Marvel Comics licensed its characters as toy figures as early as 1946. But only in the mid-1960s did these personalities become a permanent part of the toybox. Then Marvel's Fantastic Four and Spiderman appeared as miniatures. *Batman,* the short-lived TV spoof of 1966, was quite successful when licensed in the form of puppets, magnetic playsets, and many other toys. Superman won repeated exposure on TV and movies (1978, 1981, and 1983). Perhaps the best-known example of comic book toys of the mid-1960s was Ideal's Captain Action. This doll was Batman, Superman, and other superheroes all in one. With interchangeable faces and costumes, the child could rapidly shift from one comic-book story line to another. Captain Action competed with G.I. Joe, but his powers flowed from comic-book fantasy. By 1972 Mego was selling a wide range of superheroes in eight inches of plastic. In 1977 it added a Wonder Woman figure to compete with Barbie. In that year Mego also offered a new toy concept, the Micronauts, figures and space vehicles that had to be assembled and could be wound up. In anticipation of the action figure of the 1980s, the Micronauts dueled with one another. Space Glider, the good guy, was to fight Acroyear, the bad guy. The toy developer Neil Saul explained the phenomenon this way: children did not want toys that represented a "real person." Rather they desired an "excitement that can only come from the unreal."[71]

By the late 1970s toymakers understood that fantasy conflict could produce an emotional intensity absent in toys that merely reflected present-day technologies or invited children to dream of realistic careers. Because they were unbounded by the ordinary limits of humanity, comic-strip action toys were more thrilling than playthings that celebrated historic or contemporary heroes. As the popularity of Buck Rogers had shown thirty years before, toys based on conflict and heroics attracted children. But why was "excitement" more appealing to the young than anticipating their future in a real world of adults? Perhaps adults no longer knew how to make that future appear attractive to children. The sales pitches of A. C. Gilbert in the 1920s that promised engineering careers to boys who constructed erector sets would have seemed naive by the 1960s. Anyway many adults saw childhood as a time for fun, at least when at play. But toymakers in the 1970s adopted a one-sided and exaggerated view of playthings, understanding them as vehicles of children's imagination and enjoyment while increasingly ignoring the rights and responsibilities of parents to shape that imagination and enjoyment.

Toymakers argued that they merely met the demands of the youth market. When they isolated children from adults, they found the young wanting superpower fantasy and excitement. Bernard Loomis, a key player in the toy industry in the 1970s and 1980s, noted that these new figures were merely modernized lead soldiers.[72] But in the modernization toy manufacturers made miniatures of historic armies into superhero fantasy figures separate from the world of adults. The secret of the link between the "unreal" and "excitement" was that fantasy became more intense and pleasurable the more it was alienated from adult reality.

Aurora may have gone to extremes in appealing to the child's market. But it fit a trend that affected the entire toy industry. From the 1960s Mattel and Hasbro used sophisticated market research to identify children's longings and fantasies for toy development. Instead of questionnaires that depended on reading and reasoning skills, researchers used "letters to Santa" to identify children's desires. They observed children playing with the manufacturers' products away from parents—not just to test durability but to discern "play patterns" that could be incorporated into future products. They concluded that little girls wanted dolls with exchangeable clothing and with long hair to comb. They found that children did not identify with a name brand (thus Hasbro did not emphasize a company logo). Nor did they desire the product as such, be it a doll or a toy vehicle. They identified with a fantasy character that the toy embodied. Barbie and G.I. Joe were not merely dolls but represented fashion models or soldiers. Like Marvin Glass and older toy inventors, Mattel understood that toys should be an extension of contemporary popular culture. But the stress was upon images and stories that were a part of a specifically children's world of fantasy.[73]

Even the makers of preschool toys, long associated with a market of "progressive" parents, began to shift perspective. In 1973 Seymour Gartenberg of Creative Playthings admitted the old company "philosophy was really that of adults intellectualizing what children wanted." In the future Creative Playthings would test toys on children. Soon after, this company featured a "flight simulator" in imitation of video games and Disney images on music toys. In 1974 Playskool offered McDonald's Restaurant playsets. This was a sharp departure from the old developmental toy philosophy.[74]

The fact that these educational toy companies had been taken over by growth-oriented companies in the late 1960s is surely important in understanding this change. CBS (owner of Creative Playthings) and Milton Bradley (which controlled Playskool) realized there was a limited market of affluent parents interested in "improving" their children. Moreover, adults' faith in the old educational toy had probably declined. One sign of this is the role of public television's *Sesame Street*. This daily program, which first appeared in 1970, had little in common with the plain-wooden-blocks philosophy of the past. Its makers, the Children's Television Workshop, used fast-paced cartoon and puppet characters to teach letters and numbers to three- and four-year-olds. They began selling licenses of the Sesame Street characters to manufacturers as early as 1971 in lieu of revenues that commercial programmers earned from TV advertising. They were careful licensors, insisting that toys displaying the images of Bert and Ernie be "educational" and not advertised directly to children. But the difference between Mickey Mouse and Oscar the Grouch licenses would have been lost on most children and adults. Even the Lego, obviously the successor to the Tinkertoy and erector set, changed. In the obvious interest of increasing sales, Lego appeared in kits in 1966, transforming the infinitely adaptable block into a single-purpose model, and Lego kits increasingly featured fantasy space and adventure themes.[75]

The tradition of austere and functional preschool toys and the educational philosophy from which it sprang largely disappeared. The child's freedom to imagine became sovereign and the vehicle for the flight of fancy was the character toy. The parent increasingly was left out of the picture except as the purchaser, the go-between in an exchange between toymaker and the child.

Challenges and Limits of the TV Toy

The magic of TV advertising, of licensing, and, in general, of appealing directly to children guaranteed growth in the toy industry for almost fifteen years after 1955. But beginning about 1968 toymakers were besieged along many fronts, and this turnabout culminated in the late 1970s in a serious challenge to the linchpin of their industry—TV advertising to children. In the midst of the Vietnam war, a new surge of public opposition to war toys appeared. Sears removed toy guns from their catalogs and stopped advertising them (even though they still were sold in stores). Bloomingdale's and other retailers took them off their shelves. Even a toy distributor from Maine campaigned for "Toy Disarmament," promising to send his stock to a bonfire and calling on children to add theirs to the blaze. Benjamin Spock's new edition of *Baby and Child Care* insisted that parents should show disapproval of "pistol play" in children. No longer did he argue that toy weapons displaced aggression and were an inevitable part of the boy's identity formation.[76]

In May 1971 Aurora's torture toys sparked a picket line organized by the National Organization for Women and Women Strike for Toys. Nabisco, which had just bought the company and was seeking a "cleaner" image, immediately ended production of these celebrations of gore. Instead, it had the new Aurora manufacture race cars powered by air balloons. A year before, Edward Swartz had published his first list of dangerous toys along with *Toys That Don't Care*. He claimed that 700,000 children were hurt annually by poorly made playthings. From 1970 the federal government began an aggressive program of monitoring toy safety (banning thirty-seven products the first year). One week before Christmas of 1971, the Federal Trade Commission (FTC) hit Mattel and Topper with warnings that some of their commercials were deceptive. Public protest and consumer activism were taking their toll.[77]

Toy industry executives took notice of these criticisms. Sid Shneider of Child World stores admitted at a 1970 meeting of the Toy Manufacturers' of America (TMA): "In the past we have created too many meaningless and expensive toys, too easily breakable, too briefly entertaining, and we have too often promoted some toys on television that did not deserve shelf space." Shneider and others expected a "consumer revolution" in the 1970s to make manufacturers more sensitive to parental values and toy quality. The TMA hired Robert Barbash of the Institute for Motivational Research to study parental expectations. He found that age guidance and convenient packaging would help ease their anger. But in 1972 the TMA took a more confrontational approach, urging members to take on the consumerist movement. In particular, it attacked Edward Swartz for what it called his exaggerated claims about dangerous toys and for his conflict of interest as a product liability attorney.[78]

The toy industry was under attack from other quarters as well. The oil embargo of 1973 dramatically raised plastic costs and priced many toys out of the market. Looming on the horizon was a declining birthrate. Births dropped from 4.27 million in 1961 to 3.14 million in 1975. Obviously the long-term solution for maintaining sales was more toys per child. But how was the industry to achieve this when materials were more costly? Toys had long been a highly unpredictable business. In the TV era they had become even more so. Toymakers were beginning to realize that the payoff of advertising a single toy on TV was diminishing. In the early 1970s retailers were again complaining of low profit margins on TV toys. After a bad sales year in 1970, Mattel and other major companies tried to diversify in order to avoid the roller-coaster ride of profits and losses. Ruth Handler claimed that Mattel bought Ringling Brothers' Circus in 1971 as a vehicle for toy advertising should activists succeed in banning toy commercials on TV. But few of these investments succeeded. In 1974, after record losses, government investigators accused chief financial officers at Mattel, including Ruth Handler, of illegal bookkeeping. Stockholders forced out the founders of America's most successful toy company.[79]

In the midst of these troubles appeared an even greater threat to the industry—the video game. In 1972 Nolan Bushnell founded Atari to manufacture arcade games. But soon Atari and its competitor Magnavox were making home video game consoles that plugged into television sets. With their swiveling "joysticks," players moved electronic good guys across the screen in search of electronic bad guys to zap. By 1976 Coleco joined the rush, and the next year hand-held and TV electronic games were pushing toys off the shelves.[80]

In those difficult times the toy industry faced its greatest crisis— new regulations on TV advertising. Action for Children's Television (ACT), founded in 1968 by Peggy Charren, called for the elimination of children's TV commercials altogether as an intrusion on parental rights. "Would any mother let in a man at the front door who says he wants to show some new toys to her three year old?" asked ACT president Evelyn Sarson in 1971. To avoid government control, the Association of National Advertisers developed voluntary guidelines in 1972 (with monitoring conducted by the Children's Advertising Review Unit of the Better Business Bureau from 1974). Advertisements were to avoid disdain for adults, were not to exploit children's anxiety about being accepted in their peer groups, were not to encourage unrealistic expectations about what the toy could do, and were to clearly state what items were "sold separately." At the same time, the National Association of Broadcasters recommended that stations reduce advertising from 16 to 12 minutes per hour of children's programming on weekdays and 9.5 minutes on weekends. It also condemned "host" advertising (Captain Kangaroo selling toys on his own program, for example), and program-length commercials (shows featuring toys in the story lines). The Federal Communications Commission (FCC), in turn, adopted these rules. Some companies, like Kenner, responded to parental criticism of gender stereotyping by showing girls in commercials that formerly had been directed only to boys.[81]

But these efforts were insufficient. Partly because of to pressure from ACT and other consumer groups, in February 1978 the Federal Trade Commission (FTC) agreed to open an inquiry into a prohibition of children's TV advertising. Although consumer groups had originally targeted ads for sugared cereal and candy, the FTC extended the scope of the potential ban to include all advertising to children. An FTC report argued that commercials directed to children under eight years old were inherently deceptive because children did not understand their purpose. The report noted that children saw 20,000 commercials a year and that infants were attracted to the ads long before they noticed programming. To ban them was not a violation of First Amendment rights because such commercials fit the legal definition of an "attractive nuisance." In any case "the state has a legitimate interest in curtailing speech that interferes with the paramount parental interest in the child rearing process." This was an extraordinary attack on a previously unquestioned given in American business—that children, like adults, were markets. It was a defense of parental rights in an arena where those rights had long been ignored.[82]

The possibility that the toy industry's pipeline to American youth would be closed drove industry leaders into action. The editor of *Toys, Hobbies and Crafts,* Ian Gittlitz, complained that if toy commercials were to be banned, why not outlaw Santa Claus? After all, children did not understand that stores hired Santas to sell toys. TMA officials mounted a lobbying effort in the summer of 1978. When a formal hearing took place in March 1979, executives from

Ideal, Mego, Kenner, and Mattel were there to defend TV advertising. They argued that TV toys created volume sales and that this meant lower prices. Without TV commercials toy retailers would not have the sales traffic necessary to stay in business. If such advertising support was banned, children's television could not be financed. Anyway, as Martin Abrams of Mego argued, children were smarter than consumerists like Charren believed. They knew the difference between a commercial and a program. Pressure from the TMA and other corporate interests led Congress in 1980 to eliminate FTC authority to ban commercials deemed unfair, and the issue of TV advertising to children was quietly dropped. The industry won total victory.[83]

The toy industry was vastly different in 1978 from what it had been in 1950. The toy companies that had shaped the meaning of play in the first half of the twentieth century had largely disappeared. And new toymakers had supplanted many specialized firms and accumulated the resources necessary to reach a mass market. In the process of consolidation, however, they had lost some of the old loyalty to developmental toys. Even more, toymakers had largely abandoned their commitment to serve the values and desires of parents.

The toy business remained anchored in television. And TV advertising meant that toymakers could speak directly to children while parents slept on Saturday morning or rushed to make dinner on week nights. Toy companies continued to listen to the young in their marketing research. TV helped create a link between an ever-changing and inexperienced audience of the young and an industry intent upon maximizing sales. This further eroded the connection between parents and their children's play. Thus toys of adult nostalgia—from Betsy Wetsys to Mickey Mouse tin windups—gradually declined. Also passing from the scene were the miniatures of adult life—the Amsco dish sets, the scale-model earth-moving trucks, and the historical battle playsets. Even educational toys, the plain wooden blocks and pegboards that affirmed parental control over the development of children, gave way.

But it was not simply TV advertising and profit-hungry novelty-makers that transformed the toy. If playthings like Barbie and the later G.I. Joe no longer imitated adult roles and experiences, this was not simply because toymakers were exploiting youthful rebellion. Parents purchased Barbies and Captain Actions because their children wanted them. For them, good parenting meant making children happy. Few complained about the decline of dollhouses and erector sets. Parents at least tolerated doll play that glorified an insatiable consumerism. They permitted boys to play at destruction rather than construction and accepted war games in a fantastic world divorced from the real world of bullets and battles.

New toys thrived in part because parents were no longer certain about appropriate sex roles in adult life or the proper uses of war and violence in play. No longer did they buy toys that claimed to prepare girls to be good mothers and wives or boys to become successful men of work and science. Even the toy soldiers that glorified the wars of fathers no longer worked by the late 1960s because of the controversies over Vietnam. Parents were less willing to give children toys that claimed to teach the young to follow in their parents' footsteps. They had lost confidence that they knew what their children's path to maturity should be. In their uncertainty, instead of creating new models of adulthood in play, parents of the 1960s and 1970s tolerated an increasingly escapist play.

Thus Captain Action replaced Hopalong Cassidy; Barbie bested Betsy Wetsy; and Sesame Street Pop Up Pals swept away simple wooden trains. Some of the new toys tweaked the sensibilities of grown-ups; others simply affirmed a separate world of children's fantasy. New playthings embodied dreams of growing up fast to a glamorous world of consumption or a heroic realm of power and control that escaped reality. Of course, all adults did not abandon the attempt to preserve the past, introduce a real world, or develop skills with gifts of toys. And a few parents resisted playthings that seemed to teach values they despised. Some even went after a key element in the change—the TV advertisement itself. But neither the commercials nor the new toys that they promoted were stopped. And these facts made possible the extraordinary toys of the 1980s.

7 SPINNING OUT OF CONTROL

By THE 1980s play was divorced from the constraints of parents and their real worlds. Toys that evoked memories of real wars, western adventure, or dreams of future space exploration gave way to action figures, combinations of clichés torn from any realistic context. The dolls and playsets that encouraged girls to act out their mothers' roles were replaced by Barbie's fantasies of personal consumption. Preschool play, once the realm of blocks, pull toys, and teddy bears, now featured junior versions of fashion and action play. Educational toys were increasingly marginalized. Even Lincoln Logs and Tinkertoys were edged off store shelves by fantasy playthings.

The new toys might be understood as modern versions of Kewpies, Shirley Temple dolls, and Davy Crockett caps, relics of an earlier media age. However, the fantasy playthings of the 1980s and 1990s represent something more. Toys have become part of a vast interconnected industry that creates novel fantasies for profit. This industry encompasses movies, TV shows, videos, and other media. It embraces licensed images that appear on everything from caps and lunch boxes to toys. Those fantasies designed for the youth market celebrate a world free from real adults.

Beginning in the late 1970s, fantasy toys were divided into three well-defined categories built around fashion, action, and "friendship," designed for girls, boys, and preschoolers. All of these had their story lines for which elaborate assortments of figures, accessories, and playsets served as props. These playthings invited dramas of grooming, combat, and caring that toymakers found children enjoyed. But these dramas no longer portrayed the child's future adult roles and the ideals of parent-child bonding. Little girls combed the manes of pastel-colored plastic ponies. Gone were the instruction booklets from Aunt Patsy telling the girl how to be a good mother. No more did toy advertising call on sons to invite their fathers to help build erector sets. The war play of action figures was unintelligible to fathers. One toy executive in 1983 claimed that 90 percent of toy consumption was driven by children's wants; toymakers convinced themselves that they served children's desires, not those of adults.[1]

The toy industry did not merely impose this new regime on children and parents. The changing character of playthings mirrored a wider transformation of consumer goods in American culture. With aggressive advertising and creative packaging, cars, cosmetics, and clothes came to symbolize power, sex appeal, health, and participation. Children learn similar lessons from the mass media: that toys can enhance their status with their peers, tell the world they are grown up, and give them a feeling of power. Most of all, toys express children's freedom from adult tutelage. The old view that children should learn from the past and prepare for the future is inevitably subverted in a consumer culture where memory and hope get lost in the blur of perpetual change. The toy industry exploits these trends, but it did not create them.

Parents participate fully in the consumer culture, but many are disturbed by its manifestation in children's playthings. Adults often have lamented the increased size of the modern child's toybox. And indeed toy spending has risen dramatically—from $6.7 billion in 1980 to an estimated $17 billion in 1994. Contemporary children receive more, but less expensive, action figures and fashion playsets as compared to the one-time purchase of high-quality and costly fire engines or dollhouses. But, when adults complain about an overabundance of toys, they may be reacting more to the nature of fantasy playthings than to their quantity.[2]

It is important to understand both the business and cultural roots of the dominance of fantasy/fad toys today. Each element of this fantasy industry has a history, but their full integration only occurred in the late 1970s. This industry has had a mixed record in selling its vision of play to American children, but it has greatly changed the meaning of play in our time.

A New Toy Industry

The origin of the era of action-figure fantasy cannot be linked to any one toy such as Barbie or G.I. Joe. Rather the new phase began with fundamental changes in the toy industry's relations with the media, licensing agencies, and the public. Two critical events occurred in the late 1970s: the defeat of reformers' attempts to prohibit toy ads on television (1978–1979), and the appearance of "Star Wars" toys (1977–1978). The silencing of media critics capped years of difficult relations between toymakers and parents. It signaled a shift toward a far more market-oriented children's media in the 1980s. It led to program-length commercial TV shows created by toy companies to promote toy lines—in which the difference between advertising and entertainment disappeared. Television shows became a vehicle for creating and managing toy fads, thus opening the door to a full integration of the toy industry and media fantasy.

The extraordinary success of the Star Wars action figures in the wake of the hugely successful movie of 1977 displayed the full commercial potential of this integration. The toy industry learned to create a line of goods that miniaturized the characters and props of a movie. This was the first of many systematic efforts that joined media fantasy creations and the toy industry around a line of simple injection-mold figures and accessories. Increasingly, at the core of this association were licensing agents who brought potential partners together. The characters and stories of the fantasy media dominated the play of children of all ages. This was a world without real adults or parent surrogates. Long gone were the Miss Franceses and even the Buffalo Bobs. Communication between fantasy toymakers and children was direct and unmediated by parents.

The defeat of the media critics created an environment conducive to fantasy novelties, and Star Wars provided the formula. The voices of concerned parents were largely lost in the rush to woo children through unimpeded TV advertising. Manufacturers did respond to the criticism that some toys were dangerous to small children by simplifying construction. Playthings changed from gadgets with many moveable parts to figures representing glamour, power, or friendship of which only the arms, legs, and heads could be moved. In response to opposition to toy guns in a time of mounting urban violence, weapons appeared less often for direct use by the child but rather in the hands of $3\frac{3}{4}$-inch figures, which the child directed into battle. Unlike the G.I. Joe of the 1960s, who seemed to glorify real war, science fiction figures from the late 1970s fought in fantastic miniworlds of rocketry and lasers where the child could not fully identify with the creature or the violent acts he performed. Action figures turned green and purple; many were only half-human, fantastic animals, or even robots. They were not communist or capitalist, foreign or American, black or white. They were otherworldly and unreal.

The toy industry also avoided the increasingly bitter debate about women's roles in society. Young girls' play with baby dolls suggested a narrow training for motherhood that offended some. These dolls did not disappear, but minidolls built on fantastic stories of "friendship" introduced a less controversial theme in girls' play. The stories of Care Bears who cared for one another and Rainbow Bright who brought beauty to the world threatened no one. The toys derived from these stories were as abstracted from the real world of family care and future roles as the boys' action figures were from worlds of real work and war. Children were no longer to play house or play war. They were to stage the friendships and fighting of tiny figures.

The new toy industry was a response to the opportunities and challenges of the 1970s. But it had deeper roots in problems that American toymakers had faced since the beginning of the century. The key difficulty had always been finding winners in a very unpredictable toy market. This was more complex than simply meeting changing consumer demand. Toymakers produced the demand for playthings as well as the playthings themselves and had done so systematically since the early years of the century. They appealed to parents' childrearing ideals to create markets for toys. Horsman adapted new romantic images of childhood to sell character dolls. Milton Bradley borrowed ideas from child-development experts for its kindergarten toys. Manufacturers created new rites of passage by which electric trains or baby dolls, for example, were associated with stages in growing up.

From the beginning, the modern American toy industry was also part of an expanding fashion culture based on seasonal changes in goods whose purchase enhanced the buyer's status. Teddy bears, for example, did more than express a romantic view of childhood. They meant that their owners belonged to a special community of teddy-bear owners. The seemingly infinite flow of playthings represented the new and the current. The fashion toy always needed to be updated and upgraded. These playthings had an advantage over the staples that promised child development or marked rites of passage. They could be sold to a wider age group, and they could bring a premium price because they were greatly in demand.

Still, the toy as fashion created its own dilemmas: How was the manufacturer to know what version of the new and current would form a community of buyers? Would consumers identify with a doll in the image Judy Garland after having given their hearts to Shirley Temple? How were toymakers to tap into or create a fad? In a 1990 book the inventor Eliot Rudell identified the central task: "We are looking for the same energy and appeal that is coming at our users from everything else around them." The successful plaything had to be connected to an ever-changing world. The object was "catching the wave." A toy failed, noted Playskool's Steven Schwartz, either because it was "too similar to something that has been done before [or because] *nothing* like it has ever been done before." Success meant being on time, hitting the moving target of mass appeal. And few toymakers were good shots.[3]

These were constant issues throughout the twentieth century, but the pressure to confront them increased in the 1970s. The market for traditional developmental toys shrank when the baby boom turned into a baby bust. Rites-of-passage toys such as electric trains, Flexible Flyer sleds, Daisy Air Rifles, and erector sets declined in popularity as they no longer satisfied the overstimulated imaginations of American middle-class boys. The same could be said for the dollhouse for American girls. The empty spaces these playthings left encouraged the manufacture of fad toys, and finding winners grew more important.

A perennial problem of the toy industry was seasonal sales. From the 1880s toys were an essential part of ritualized giving to children in the December holidays. But the industry chafed under the constraints of seasonal buying. Manufacturers and retailers cheered when fads occasionally sparked off-season sales. The teddy bear fad of 1906–1907 instilled the hope that novelties could create a continuous flow of sales and cash. The Snow White phenomenon of 1938 created an off-season craze, but it did not last. Toymakers were forever searching for possible ways to increase year-round sales.

One way of creating and sustaining fads was to spend more money on advertising and product development. This required that revenue be liberated from manufacturing costs. Toy companies began to subcontract production to cheap labor sites abroad. From 1981 to 1993 toy imports rose from $1.49 billion to $8.49 billion. In 1993 73 percent of toys sold in the United States were manufactured abroad ($3.77 billion worth in China). Offshore manufacturing also became profitable because the time and money consumed in communication and transport declined and quality controls in foreign factories improved. Major companies like Mattel devoted considerable managerial energy to accelerating the efficiency of offshore manufacturing in the late 1980s. As manufacturing reduced costs by moving abroad, the number of toy warehouses and discount chains grew, and this increased the pace of sales. By 1993 Toys "R" Us alone controlled 21.5 percent of U.S. toy sales, and discount giants (Wal-Mart, K-Mart, and Target) sold another 25.8 percent.[4] The toy industry was participating in a new era of "fast capitalism"—the increasingly rapid shift from one product line to another on a virtually global scale.

With production and distribution costs reduced to a minimum, toymakers could concentrate on creating winners and doing so throughout the year. Mattel had found in the mid-1950s that advertising directly to children was more effective in creating demand than in appealing to parents and that year-round advertising worked. Direct advertising to children had helped to control the market and had extended sales beyond the holiday season. Such advertising "helped" both retailers and final consumers select from the thousands of toys seeking markets. As the manufacturers loved to point out, advertised toys had a lower markup than unadvertised ones. The expense of advertising was offset by greater quantities with lower unit costs. As for retailers, they used advertised toys as loss leaders to attract buyers to their stores. By the 1980s, except in specialty stores, sales staff played almost no role in introducing the parent (or child) to an appropriate toy. Instead, advertising did the selling. Store staff merely shelved and cashiered. This strategy worked well in the era of TV.[5]

But selling to children posed special problems. Toy companies were less successful in building brand-name loyalty than were car or home appliance firms. Youngsters with no memory or interest in the reputation of toy companies had no reason to be loyal to a company logo. All they cared about was the current product. More important, advertising—even with its many appeals to peer conformity and the imagination—was not always enough to create a blockbuster toy. Toymakers liked to emphasize that commercials may create a demand but play value alone will sustain it.[6] The problem was how to get children to continue to play with a particular toy.

From the toymakers' point of view the ideal was not merely to publicize a product but to shape play patterns to maximize sales. In order to do so they abandoned the notion that the toy was merely a gadget in which interest quickly expired. Instead merchandisers saw the possibilities of making an expandable line of toys into a tangible expression of a collective fantasy. The ideal then was to induce children to play out a story with props requiring the purchase of the company's product line. Companies found they could economize on advertising and enhance sales at the same time by pushing a toy personality or category like Barbie and linking it to a vast variety of play products associated with her "world." Once the basic toy had been sold to children, each extension of it could follow with relatively little advertising cost. This pattern was as old as the Schoenhut Humpty Dumpty Circus of the first decade of the twentieth century. But it became far more sophisticated and nearly universal in toy marketing in the 1980s.

The key to the new approach was to associate the toy line with a mass-media character or story line. Manufacturers formed alliances with makers of children's movies, TV cartoons, comic books, and even greeting cards. They used an increasingly imaginative array of outlets (from fast-food toy premiums to Barbie boutiques) to convince children that their toy concept was in fashion. The ultimate goal was a managed fad, a carefully fabricated and sustained demand for a particular toy.

Ironically, the age of the managed-fad toy allowed speculative toymakers to flourish while also encouraging the consolidation of the toy business. The cost of entry into the toy trade had always been low. A winning idea and sufficient capital to make molds and to subcontract out production did not require the resources of General Motors. Thus it was relatively easy for new companies to compete or old companies to move into new product lines. New firms like Worlds of Wonder and Playmates appeared from nowhere with the smash hits of Teddy Ruxpin and Teenage Mutant Ninja Turtles. And Coleco shifted from video games to their opposite, Cabbage Patch Kids, with little difficulty.

However, if new companies could rocket to success with a fad, only a big firm could live for long on novelty. The ability of a company to mount massive advertising campaigns and diversify guaranteed survival. The British and French toy industries built around high-quality small-batch production, for example, suffered irreparable harm in the early 1980s because they lacked the means to diversify to cover losses on bad bets. And fads also faded quickly, as the makers of hula hoops and coonskin caps discovered in the mid-1950s. Dependence upon a blockbuster could quickly turn a company to bankruptcy when overhead costs necessary to support a hit become an impossible burden. The bigger the blockbuster, the harder the maker often fell.[7]

The best solution was to create a staple fad. This was a toy that tapped into the elusive social appeal and timeliness of a winner but also survived long enough to support the heavy costs required to sustain a fad and launch the next one. Worlds of Wonder (WOW) and Coleco had extraordinary success with fad toys in the 1980s. Coleco's Cabbage Patch Kids, those soft baby dolls with distinctive dimples, and WOW's electronic talking bear, Teddy Ruxpin, were the envy of the industry when they appeared in 1983 and 1985 respectively. Yet Coleco, despite acquisitions designed to diversify, was forced to file Chapter 11 for protection against creditors in 1988. The same fate had befallen WOW a year earlier. Of the upstart companies, only Lewis Galoob survived. And it did so only by forcing out the son of its founder, David Galoob, in 1991.[8]

The logic of the staple fad and of risk reduction encouraged consolidations. In 1970 Hasbro's young chief, Stephen Hassenfeld, bragged that in "five, ten, fifteen years from now, I'd like to be the General Motors" of the toy business. And Hassenfeld largely succeeded. In 1984 Hasbro bought the venerable game company Milton Bradley and with it gained Playskool. In the 1980s Hasbro also brought in remnants of Ideal and Knickerbocker toys. Sales nearly doubled from 1984 to 1988. In 1991 Hasbro won the bidding for Tonka, an established maker of toy trucks, which brought with it Kenner and Parker Brothers. Hasbro made some wise choices (such as avoiding the temptation to enter the electronic game competition in 1981 that produced huge losses for Mattel and Coleco). But it also made mistakes. Thanks to diversification, however, Hasbro could avoid the perennial problem of toymaking speculators—having all their eggs in one basket. Acquisition of Milton Bradley, for example, reduced Hasbro's reliance on revenues from G.I. Joe, which dropped from 36 percent to 14 percent of total sales between 1982 and 1986 even though G.I. Joe income more than tripled during that period.[9]

If Hasbro largely won the buyout game, Mattel was not about to be left behind. It radically expanded its foreign market in the late 1980s, beating back all comers with the perennial Barbie. In 1993 it finally won control of the prized preschool market with its purchase of Fisher-Price for $1.1 billion. Mattel expected 30 percent of its revenues from this acquisition, especially in sales abroad in non-Christian areas where sales were less dependent upon Christmas.[10]

These once upstart novelty-toy companies prevailed over the old family companies with the skillful manipulation of novelty, TV advertising, and financial power. They took over key companies with traditions of family games and infant play products.[11] Bigness helped reduce risk and create demand—even if it seemed also to diminish parents' control over the consumer choices of their children. But inevitably, with the concentration of the industry, the diversity and integrity of toys declined. Indeed, toys became more conventional, more apt to fit a formula, in the 1980s than they had ever been before.

The Managed Fad: Licensed Images and the Program-Length Commercial

From the 1890s, when Palmer Cox's Brownies first appeared on bowling-pin sets and puzzles, toys have been associated with characters licensed from literature or media. But the role of "personalities" in toys has never been greater than in the 1980s. So important were they that in 1981 a special character-licensing fair took place for the buying and selling of fantasy images. By 1983 toy-trade magazines published licensing supplements or even spun off separate magazines to inform the industry on new characters for sale. This was in response to a threefold increase in the sale of licensed merchandise between 1978 and 1983. About 60 percent of toys sold in the United States by 1987 were based on licensed characters, compared to roughly 10 percent in 1980.[12]

Until the 1980s a personality generally emerged from a successful comic strip, cartoon, movie, or TV program and then was offered as a license. Toy companies used the image of Mickey Mouse or Hopalong Cassidy to sell ordinary sand pails and cap pistols only after the characters had become children's "friends" in movies and on TV.[13] The character's personality may have been embodied in the toy (a Zorro mask and sword, for example), but only occasionally did toymakers offer miniatures of the licensed character's imaginary world as playsets (for example, the Roy Rogers Circle Bar Ranch). More commonly the licensed image was simply printed on a traditional toy or game. Licensed toys had limited value to manufacturers and retailers. Licensing usually added about 10 percent to manufacturers' costs, and if the licensed character lost its appeal, so did the toy. Retailers like Sears often avoided licensed toys, just as they avoided name-brand goods. They preferred low-cost house products, and some retail chains even "knocked off" licensed toys with look-alikes. Most of all, traditional licensing did not resolve the problems of risk to the licensee, because no one could predict with certainty whether a licensed toy would win the hearts of kids and become a fad.

But a subtle change occurred in character licensing in the late 1970s. Character images no longer acted merely as a friendly salespeople inspiring familiarity and trust. Instead, they increasingly merged with toys. These playthings in effect captured an image linked to a story created by the mass media. So a Star Wars figure invited the child to reenact a scene in the movie. The licensed toy became a prop that emerged simultaneously with a media fantasy. The story and the toy were one. Both were consumed together. This pattern had emerged as early as 1938 with Disney's *Snow White*. But the merger of toy and fantasy became the norm in the 1980s.

TV played a major role in advancing this form of character licensing. The defeat of regulation over TV advertising to children led to both the decline of traditional children's programming on the networks and the erosion of the distinction between children's shows and advertising. In September 1981 Mark Fowler, President Reagan's new head of the Federal Communications Commission (FCC), opposed the existing regulation of children's television. Fowler insisted that broadcasters should be treated as businesspeople and not be expected to serve as trustees of children's culture.[14]

From December 1983 the FCC no longer required commercial stations to air children's shows. This move coincided with a declining interest of the TV networks in traditional children's programming because of falling advertising revenue. *Captain Kangaroo*, a staple on CBS since the mid-1950s, was relegated to early morning in 1981 and then quietly canceled in 1984. The hours per week that the average network station devoted to children's programming dropped from 11.3 to 4.4 between 1979 and 1983. The reason was simple. Action-adventure series like *A-Team* attracted a more diverse and more prosperous audience than did children's shows, and thus advertisers were willing to pay higher rates for commercials. Meanwhile in August 1984 the Federal Trade Commission (FTC) ceased enforcing a children's TV advertising policy in effect since 1974. This move unshackled the "creativity" of toy commercials. More important, these policy changes opened the door to programs created to promote toys, a door that had been closed since the FCC opposed Mattel's *Hot Wheels* show in 1969.[15]

Peggy Charren's Action For Children's Television petitioned the government to eliminate deception in toy ads and to end cartoon programs that promoted toy lines. But in April 1985 the FCC affirmed the right of toy companies to produce "merchandise supported children's programming," citing these manufacturers' otherwise insufficient access to advertising time on TV. In any case local broadcasters had the right to decide the entertainment value of their programming.[16]

Toy companies had a strong incentive to develop toy-based shows. Reduced children's programming on network TV put the companies in an awkward position. They feared they were losing a vital pipeline to the imagination of youth. But syndication came to the rescue. With syndication independent producers sold their programs directly to individual stations, bypassing the networks. When toymakers joined with animation companies to produce and syndicate their own series, they gained some notable advantages over traditional advertising on network programs. Syndication gave them assured access to advertising time on children's shows. In a half-hour segment the toy producer/advertiser would often get two minutes of commercial time while the station would have four minutes to sell to local business. But syndication did more than guarantee toymakers an opportunity to sell on TV. According to the advertising expert Hal Katz, it gave them "unparalleled control over the editorial content of the programming on which [their] commercials appear[ed]."[17] They could produce cartoon series whose stars were their own toy figures.

The result was the program-length commercial (PLC). These toy-based programs were sometimes simply specials, introducing a toy line in the form of a cartoon feature or even a miniseries. But even more useful was the half-hour cartoon show that kept the toy line regularly in front of the child. The PLC reversed the traditional relationship between licensed characters and toys. They were not simply entertainment featuring characters that gained popularity and thus a market for licensing as toy concepts. These programs were "originally conceived as a vehicle for providing product exposure to the child audience." In the 1983–84 season there were already fourteen PLCs. The best known were *He-Man and Masters of the Universe* (Mattel), *G.I. Joe: A Real American Hero* (Hasbro), *Care*

Bears, and *Strawberry Shortcake* (Kenner). By the fall of 1985 all top-ten bestselling toys had cartoons that featured them. As late as the fall of 1987 twenty-four of thirty-five cartoon series had toy tie-ins.[18]

Critics of this practice abounded. Dr. William Dietz of the American Academy of Pediatrics complained that toymakers "sell a product while claiming to be entertainment and I think that is unconscionable." A hallmark of traditional broadcasting, noted Cynthia Alperowicz of Action for Children's Television, was the distinction between "commercial speech and editorial speech." And the PLCs violated it. PLCs stacked the deck against parents by manipulating young children into wanting a particular toy while ostensibly entertaining them. A children's programming official from CBS admitted that toy-based shows were "the tail wagging the dog." One PLC maker, Filmation, in response to criticism that its programs encouraged children to identify fun and play with conflict, hired a Stanford University professor to review shows for violent antisocial content. He persuaded Filmation to add thirty-second moral "tags," which often appeared at the end of a cartoon segment. The journalist Tom Engelhardt responded that exhortations to "be polite, be happy, respect your elders, don't fight" were mere "predictable permutations" pasted onto violent cartoons. But Tonka Toys defended the PLC: "An American child really needs that story line to help it play and one of the ways to do that is with a TV program." In any case, Kenner noted, the PLC had a "payoff" of increased sales that forced all competitors to join in order to survive.[19]

Animation companies like Filmation, Marvel, and DIC worked closely with toy companies to produce these shows. In the fall of 1987 DIC cranked out over 330 hours of animation on contract from toymakers. Originally a French company, DIC was purchased by the American Andy Heyward in 1986. Heyward solicited toy companies with offers to create animations of their planned lines. In this way the entertainment and toy businesses were merged. DIC put up little or no money in its productions for Mattel and Hasbro. The price of this risk-free business was that DIC allowed the toymakers to participate in all phases of production. The veteran animator Joseph Barbera complained that story line and character development were sacrificed to the display of the toy. But TV stations accepted toy-based programs because they were cheap. Also, because toy companies heavily promoted these shows, stations seemed assured of high ratings. In some cases toy companies even offered TV stations a royalty on toy sales in their viewing area in exchange for a time slot.[20]

Toy companies got a full half-hour of advertising time with these programs. They were also sometimes spared licensing fees. These toys were not spinoffs of successful shows whose characters were developed, and thus owned, by Disney or other fantasymakers. Instead they often originated with the toy company. Indeed, "reverse licensing" became possible when toymakers like Mattel and Hasbro sold rights to use their toy characters to other manufacturers. Like Disney in the 1930s, Mattel carefully monitored the quality and marketing of their Masters of the Universe licensees.[21]

The main advantage of the PLC was that it helped to manage a toy fad. The TV show gave children a set of fantasy situations and personalities upon which to model play. Even more, that play could be orchestrated through the careful exposure of the story line on TV. By the mid-1980s this marketing formula had been perfected. The main player was often a toymaker. But sometimes it was a media company collaborating with a toymaker and other licensees. There was an art to the "timing" and coordination of a licensed property. After all, the appeal of licensed character, no matter how cute or heroic, was only temporary. Because the lead time for most product lines was twenty-one months (according to *Playthings* in 1984), the appearance of a new character-based toy and its PLC had to be coordinated.[22]

One example is the effort of King Features to launch a character-licensing program for a team of superheroes called Defenders of the Earth in 1986. King began with a TV special in April presenting the adventure story of the Defenders and their struggle against alien forces. At the same time, King worked with Galoob toys to create an action-figure line around these superheroes. Galoob had already launched an advertising campaign the previous December. Marvel Comics joined the team with a comic book. Galoob and King Features took a group of costumed Defenders on a tour of malls in thirty "Nielsen market cities" in March. Following this came major

TV commercials. The long-awaited TV series appeared in September. In anticipation of the holiday rush for Defenders of the Earth toys, Western Publishing created "Point of Purchase" displays expected in stores by October.[23]

The toy executive Bernard Loomis revealed the industry's confidence that fads could be managed when he argued that toys succeed primarily because manufacturers "fall in love with something and make a commitment to it." Company promotion, not public taste, was critical. Loomis knew of what he spoke. He had been key to the success of toys as varied as Hot Wheels, Star Wars, Strawberry Shortcake, and Care Bears.[24]

To the fantasy story were attached "licensed accessory products." The toy was a prop of the imagination. Even when manufacturers did not invent the story (as in the case of Mattel's licensing of the Smurfs), the toy was to give "children creative ways to enjoy their whimsical friends all week long." The "back story" of the media fantasy was the leverage that the toy industry used on retailers and licensees. As one Care Bear movie advertisement to potential licensees noted, "Don't miss it. Millions of kid's won't." Michael Georgeopolis of United Media Enterprises summed up the matter in 1983: "The very idea of translating a character concept to playthings is the essence of the toy business." This would have been news to A. C. Gilbert and even Louis Marx. The new characters were imbedded in stories that invited reenactment and required an ever-increasing number and variety of props to sustain the play. The managed fad created a world unto itself shared by children and a profit-hungry toy business.[25]

Miniworlds of Fantasy Play

No American child in the years between 1977 and 1983 could have avoided George Lucas's *Star Wars* trilogy. American boys, especially, were inundated with toy figures, vehicles, and playsets built around the rivalry of Darth Vader and Luke Skywalker. By 1987 some ninety-four figures and sixty accessories had been manufactured by Kenner, Lucasfilm's exclusive toy licensee. The first two Star Wars movies earned $870 million by 1983 when the final one was released. But the licensed products raked in $2 billion. While delays in production prevented most eager buyers from getting their Star Wars figures in time for the holidays in 1977, a full range of licensed products were already in stores by the time *The Return of the Jedi* appeared in May 1983. Jedi drinking glasses, toothbrushes, and cookies as well as Darth Vader telephones made Star Wars characters ubiquitous. And although these licensed products were in effect free commercials for Star Wars toys, Kenner still spent $12 million in an advertising campaign in 1983. In an effort to revive the sales magic of the movie, Lucas reran *Star Wars* and *The Empire Strikes Back* on TV in early 1984. Each film featured new "toyetic" personalities, vehicles, and other gadgets—easily converted into molded plastic. The first film produced toy robots (R2-D2 and C-3PO), bad guy "Storm Troopers," and, of course, heroic Luke Skywalker and Princess Leia. Later films added TIE Fighters, Scout Walkers, and Ewoks. These toys gave a generation of American youth the opportunity to reenact their favorite scenes from the movie. Star Wars surely set the pace as fantasymakers rushed to invent knockoffs of this science fiction classic, each with accompanying lines of toys.[26]

The impact of *Star Wars* is best seen in the transformation of Hasbro's G.I. Joe line.[27] After years of seeking an answer to antimilitarism, Hasbro discontinued Joe in 1978. But the success of Kenner's Star Wars toys and a political climate after Ronald Reagan's victory in 1980 more sympathetic to military spending gave Hasbro the opportunity to reintroduce G.I. Joe in 1982. Luckily, they relaunched Joe in the lull between the second and third Star Wars movies. But this time he was neither a soldier doll nor an adventurer but part of a team of fantastic fighters in a Mobile Strike Force. These characters with charming names like Flash and Grunt faced COBRA, an equally determined cadre of bad guys, in futuristic battle gear and settings. No longer was Joe an individual. G.I. Joe was only a trademark, covering a number of constantly evolving matched teams of foes, each with their own accessories of firepower and vehicles. And the Joes had shrunk to the $3\frac{3}{4}$-inch height made standard by Kenner's Star Wars figures. They were cheap to make, easy to collect, and appropriate for "miniworld" play.

The new G.I. Joe became the bestselling toy of the 1982 holiday season. No wonder. Hasbro had launched a $4 million advertising campaign for the 1982 holidays designed to reach 95 percent of the country's five- to eight-year-old boys fifty times. By 1983 Joe had a TV show. In 1984 G.I. Joe logos appeared on fifty licensed products. By 1988 Hasbro claimed that two-thirds of American boys between the ages of five and eleven owned Joes.

Critics complained that G.I. Joe and other action-figure lines celebrated the United States as high-tech world policeman—especially when COBRA figures looked like Arabs. Jay Roth of Playco Toys admitted that the new military toy lines were designed to represent "agents of police activity that incorporate Star Wars–type weapons in the tradition of good guy–bad guy clash." Of course, Hasbro's Stephen Hassenfeld insisted that G.I. Joe had no connection with any effort to glorify the American invasion of Grenada, for example. But G.I. Joe and his many imitators combined what toymakers saw as the future of American military hardware with the play appeal of the clash of good against evil. Yet Hasbro took poetic license in its renditions of futuristic weapons. The political meaning of good vs. evil was also vague, if not completely absent. It was hard to tell the good guys from the evildoers.[28]

This was not morality play or political play. It was conflict play. There was memory neither of that "good war" against fascism fought by children's grandfathers nor of the confused and for many "bad" war of Vietnam that their fathers had fought, avoided, or protested against. Nor was the war play really based on the Reagan arms buildup or spats with petty dictators. It was about pure fantasy conflict. These toys did not indoctrinate children with political ideology. These toys offered boys no more than a simple vision of "good" vs. "evil" in a fantasy world where violence was a constant. The lesson learned may have been that the world is a violent place where superheroes equipped with superweapons must be free to combat the forces of chaos. But these toys certainly did not orient children to the real world of international politics.

The theme of violence was pronounced but, because it was so unrealistic, it was easy not to take seriously. Action figures used wildly imaginary weapons, and conflict was reduced to the scale of the playsets. Hasbro did not produce or license G.I. Joe toy guns even though the Joes used them in their tiny hands. Children were not invited to "play war" in person with Joe's toy machine guns and grenades. They were to direct a stage play of utterly unreal war with minidolls as the actors. War play was completely divorced from the "national narrative" of good Americans vs. Indians and foreign enemies. Parents no longer dressed their children like soldiers or even gunslinging cowboys. Instead of turning their backyards into play battlefields or dueling with cap guns and holsters in family dens, boys were allowed to collect tiny warriors that reminded no adults of any war they had known about. The conflicting feelings of adults toward the military were avoided, and most parents ignored their children's war play[29]

Star Wars and G.I. Joe were just the beginning. Mattel's He-Man and Masters of the Universe, appearing in 1982, closely paralleled the Star Wars formula: the youthful, blond, and muscular He-Man and his team of good guys (Man-At-Arms, Man-E-Faces, Ram Man, the fighting falcon, Zoar, and Teela, a warrior goddess) fought the aged, bony, and evil Skeletor and his horde (Beastman, Trapjaw, Tri-Klops, the "feathered fiend," Screech, and Evil-Lyn, another goddess warrior). A major feature of Mattel's line was Castle Grayskull, shaped like a mountain with a dungeon tower, a landing platform for a "Fright Fighter" vehicle, and a "Viper Tower" (with a "vicious serpent head" that children could spin). Grayskull was the center of the fray in a "fantastic universe beyond all time." "Who will control its hidden secrets and mystical power?" Mattel asked children. "You decide!" He-Man reached the pinnacle of *Toys and Hobby World*'s "Top TV Toys" list in June 1983 (even beating Star Wars). That year Mattel sold 23 million Masters of the Universe action figures. But Mattel went much further when, in the fall of 1983, it delivered a daily syndicated cartoon starring He-Man.[30]

There were many imitations. The best known were based on a Japanese toy novelty—a die-cast vehicle that turned into a semi-human robot warrior with a few deft tugs on wheels and other parts. The first of these was Hasbro's Transformer line, appearing in 1984. The back story, the adventure that gave the toy characters their roles and situations for children to reenact in play, has a familiar ring to it. The citizens of Cybertron were divided into the "good" Autobots and the "evil" Decepticons who, having landed on earth, made war on each other. The Autobots naturally took the shape of cars and the Decepticons, airplanes. Each transformer came with a "Tec Spec Chart" detailing its amazing capacities and a "Bio Card" featuring its "personality." To the Transformer line inevitably new toys were added. Annual model changes took on the character of an arms race: Dinobots (robot dinosaurs) allied with the Autobots in 1985; in 1986 the Decepticons responded with their own animal transformers, the Predacons and Sharkicons. When, also in 1986, Constructicons helped the Decepticons build fortresses and Runamuck provided spy services to the evildoers, and Arialbots (air vehicles) came to the aid of the Autobots.[31]

Inevitably others tried to cut into Hasbro's Transformer market. The venerable makers of matchbox cars offered the new generation Voltrons, and Kenner made a line of transformers called the Centurions. Tonka produced a *GoBot* magazine in 1986 to promote their transforming robot line. This magazine mixed fantasy with factual stories about the planets and reports about the high-tech future of robotics. One story invited children to "imagine your toy GoBots coming to life." Retailers found that children came to their stores knowing precisely which transformer they wanted to buy and cajoled parents at birthdays and holidays to purchase the larger sets. By the beginning of 1985 these toys were cutting sharply into sales of electric trains, die-cast cars, and trucks. So rapidly did the media blitz hit, with each line of transformers having its own TV show, that by the fall of 1985 one retailer mused that "everyone now seems to have the older ones."[32]

Fantasy figure play did not always require a TV cartoon to enliven it. Some toy lines violated the trend toward distinctly children's fantasy by drawing their characters from comic papers familiar to parents. In 1984 Kenner followed its amazing success with Star Wars with a Superpower Collection which included Superman, Batman, Robin, Superwoman, Aquaman, and Hawkman. But sometimes figures drawn from adult fantasy were radically transformed when made into children's toys. Coleco turned an R-rated movie about a counterterrorist loner, Rambo, into a standard action figure line. "Our beloved country (and, indeed, the entire world) has been thrown into peril by international terrorists," trumpeted the publicity launching Rambo action figures. But in imitation of the new G.I. Joe, the Rambo line pitted teams of fighters against each other: the enemy force called S.A.V.A.G.E. (Secret Army of Vengeance and

Global Evil) and headed by the "evil GENERAL WARHAWK" fought Rambo and his Forces of Freedom. And Coleco told its story on a TV cartoon that shaped the play to now well developed expectations.[33]

Drawing upon the action-figure formula, toymakers also shaped little girls' play around licensed characters and fairytale story lines. In 1980 a studio at American Greeting Cards (known as Those Characters from Cleveland) developed the image of a cute redheaded girl in old-fashioned clothes called Strawberry Shortcake.[34] This was something of a specialty at American Greetings. In 1967 this company featured the homespun image of Holly Hobbie on greeting cards. It was so successful that in 1973 Holly became a licensed character for dolls and plush toys. Strawberry Shortcake similarly exploited a sentimental theme of innocent girlhood. But the new image was a far more sophisticated product. Those Characters from Cleveland used the strawberry theme after survey research showed that little girls identified with strawberries. The character was designed to convey emotions of "security and affection."

More important, from the beginning Strawberry Shortcake was created not merely as a greeting card theme but as a licensing property to be used in toys, dolls, and juvenile furniture. Those Characters from Cleveland charted a three- to five-year product-development cycle. They recognized the synergy created in multiple licenses. In a 1984 publicity brochure they bragged: "The cumulative effect of advertising by *all* licensees and the licensor creates an overall impression that $1 + 1 = 3$." Strawberry Shortcake also differed from Holly Hobbie in other ways. She quickly found "friends": Lime Chiffon and Raspberry Tart joined her in the magical realm of Strawberryland. Kenner won the license to re-create all of these characters in injection mold plastic. And in 1980 Strawberry Shortcake and her pals appeared on TV. In 1983 the line was freshened up with six new friends, including Crepe Suzette with her French poodle and Almond Tea with her pet Marza Panda. As minidolls and playsets, Strawberry Shortcake became a girls' version of Star Wars—a miniworld of playacting fantasy stories.

Following on this success came American Greeting's Care Bears, again in association with Kenner toys. In 1982 Those Characters from Cleveland tested a number of prototypes before finding the perfect look for Kenner's array of hard plastic minidolls. Licensees and American Greetings spent $122.5 million to launch a wide-ranging product line (everything from school supplies to plush animals) for 1983. Although in the teddy bear tradition, Care Bears had more in common with the new G.I. Joe. The Care Bears were a collection of twelve figures with moveable limbs. Each was distinguished by a symbol on the belly signifying a different positive emotion. A child could hardly play with just one or two. Like the action figures, the bears were to work as a team to overcome the killjoy Vovocaine Numb and other grinch-like figures. In the spring of 1986 a Care Bear movie was released, supplementing the six TV specials that had appeared by the previous fall. Each reinforced the story of the bears that cared enough to bring love to the world. A major competitor to the bears was Hasbro's My Little Pony line of pastel minifigures. These diminutive horses with their long and colorful manes combined "friendship" and grooming play. Forty million units were sold between 1983 and 1986. In hopes of extending the line, Hasbro produced a movie in June 1986 and a new secondary line, Flutter Ponies (Pegasus-like winged figures).[35]

Those Characters from Cleveland went on to develop *Herself the Elf*, a TV special aired in June of 1983. The Elf and her friends, Snowdrop and Woodpink, used their magical powers to make winds blow, birds chirp, and flowers grow. Besides teaching children the "miracles of nature," this special also introduced a line of minidolls and accessories from Mattel. The latter included a Floating Flower Shower, Flower Vanity, and a Doll 'n' Tote pink posie purse with a pocket for a tiny Herself the Elf. Hallmark got into the act with its Rainbow Brite line of figures (again with Mattel). Rainbow Brite brought color to the world from a land at the end of the rainbow. She and her friends prevailed with goodness over the bad (but stupid) Murky Dismal and his sidekick, Lurky. Similar was Hallmark's Rose Petal Place (codeveloped with Kenner). In this story line flowers magically became creatures that offered friendship to a lonely little girl in a special garden. Harmony reigned despite the evil spider Nastina. The Rose Petal characters were minidolls, each featuring a flower suggested by their names (Sunny

Sunflower and Lily Fair Iris, for example). They were dressed in flower colors and featured hair pieces reminiscent of flower petals.[36]

At one level these toys were little more than a commercial exploitation of familiar fairy tale themes. While the boys' action-figure industry mined the literature of science fiction, the greeting card companies dug up vague recollections of enchanted gardens, kindly animals, and talking flowers from fairy tales and especially Victorian romantic children's fiction. Lewis Carroll would have recognized his vision in the work of Hallmark and American Greetings even if he might have been appalled by the maudlin cast to the plagiarism. There is also a similarity between Care Bears and Brownies. The individual characters in both sets worked together for the common good and did so in a world largely free of adult authority.

But much had changed. The new figures were designed for girls only. The pastel colors, female figures, purse accessories, and hair play central to most of the new lines told parents and children for whom they were designed. And the psychological complexity of the early cartoon and storybook characters had disappeared. The impish but nice Brownies had turned into the saccharin Care Bears. The caring characters of the 1980s lived in a world where evil had been reduced to the killjoy, often a pitiful figure whose opposition to the happiness of a colorful world came only from ignorance or fear of caring. Gone were the terrors of wicked stepmothers and dangerous forests. These were not myths for children to work through their anxieties about family relations or fears of the unknown. They were radically simplified stories of make-believe worlds where friendship and joy reigned. Even the loving relationships of the Care Bears were removed from the girl just as the violence of the new war play was second hand to the boy. These characters were not huggable (although some later did appear in plush). Young girls were to direct a drama featuring loving characters without actually playing the roles themselves. No parent could object to Care Bears, but neither did these toys reach the emotional depths of traditional nurturing and companion dolls.

These new toys encouraged forms of play that were abstracted from the real worlds of family and household care. They did not invite girls to be "little mommies." But they also gave no hint of a modern woman's need to balance work and family. Strawberry Shortcake neither perpetuated old sex roles nor offered alternatives for a new age. These toys evaded the modern ambiguities of growing up female. But few parents seemed to mind. Perhaps they were unwilling to address those ambiguities, content to allow their little ones to remain in the secret garden of innocence. Even so, little girls learned more than sweetness; these toys taught them about fashionable colors, accessorizing, grooming, and the pleasures of collecting. It was a short step from the manes of My Little Pony to the hairdos of Barbie.

Not all toys for little girls fit into this mold. The Cabbage Patch Kids craze of 1983–1984 did not feature hard plastic minifigures. Nor did it require a cartoon or, at first, a line of accessories or "friends." The Cabbage Patch dolls were in some ways a throwback to the soft character dolls of the 1910s made by Horsman and Martha Chase. They were "ugly" baby dolls and were to be cuddled. But this extraordinarily successful doll still was part of the growing fantasy industry. It appeared first in 1977 in craft shows, the creation of a twenty-seven-year-old soft-sculpture designer from Georgia named Xavier Roberts. The doll's success led Roberts to develop an extraordinary marketing ploy. He converted an old medical clinic in his small Georgia town into "Babyland General Hospital" where staff made the dolls and Roberts offered them for "adoption" for fees of $125. Customers were charmed by the idea that the Kids were orphans found in an "enchanted cabbage patch." Their "wistful expressive faces" brought out a protective sentiment in many buyers. This gimmick was not unprecedented. The ugly Billiken doll of 1908 had also been "adopted." But free publicity on national TV daytime programs created a frenzy for the doll. Amy Carter, Diana Ross, and even Burt Reynolds became adoptive "parents." By August 1982 Roberts had sold manufacturing rights to Coleco. Still, the appearance of Cabbage Patch Kids on store shelves created veritable stampedes in November and December of 1983. By the end of 1984 20 million had been sold.[37]

The appeal of Cabbage Patch Kids was obvious. Children found this "huggable" doll a welcome change from the stiff plastic that dominated doll play in the 1980s. But, like the teddy bear craze of

1906–1907, this doll also attracted adults. At the height of the craze, Cabbage Patch dolls were bought by women with no children. A few enjoyed the playful illusion that these dolls were babies. Some placed them in infant car seats and took them to the mall. But most adult women liked them because they reminded them of their own baby doll play and their desire that their children share in this experience.[38]

Inevitably Coleco, a company deep in debt because of failed video games, tried to extend the Cabbage Patch magic. In 1984 it offered "Preemies," Kids that looked like premature babies, to appeal to the nurturing play of children and adults alike. Coleco also introduced a line of "Posable Art Wear" for the Kids already adopted. In 1986 it tried other "huggables" like the Koozas, Wrinkles, and Furskins. But none had the success of the earlier Cabbage Patch Kids, and nothing could save the company from bankruptcy.[39]

Another variation on the theme of fantasy toys was the fashion doll. It did not require the licensed character and media-based back story. Barbie, at least, provided her own. The boxes containing Barbie merchandise gave a brief story to guide play. And Mattel's perennial fad did just fine without the orchestrated media exposure needed by He-Man. Nevertheless, while Barbie had bested all competitors in the 1960s and 1970s, in 1986 she met a new rival in Jem.[40] In contrast to other Barbie imitators, Jem's maker, Hasbro, fully exploited the new sales strategy developed for the action figures. Hasbro touted her as the "most dynamic introduction to the fashion doll category in almost 30 years" when presenting her at the Toy Fair of 1986.

Jem was first of all transformable with the aid of a magic earring which changed her from Jerrica Benton, successful businesswoman and owner of her own music agency, into Jem, lead singer in a "truly outrageous" rock band. Naturally, Jem's band, the Holograms, had a rival in a punkish group called the Misfits. With their blue-and-yellow hair and wildly shaped guitars, the Misfits were chaos incarnate as compared to the more sedate stage costumes of the Holograms. The Misfits were managed by Eric Raymond, fierce rival of Jerrica and her Star Light Music Company. Adding to the charm of dual roles, Hasbro invented Rio, the only other male in the line. Rio served as both Jem's road manager and Jerrica's boy-friend. Hasbro's publicity asked: "Will Rio ever find out that the two special ladies in his life are one in the same?"

Naturally Jerrica/Jem came with contrasting fashions for her two identities. Special accessories included the Star Stage that doubled as a playset and as a cassette recorder for listening to rock songs specially written by Hasbro staff. This toy giant convinced itself that it had found a gold mine with this attempt to appeal to the "music and fashion conscious girl of the 1980s." A TV show followed (airing most places on Sunday mornings at 10:30 A.M.). It featured some 195 "original" songs in its first 65 episodes. At first Jem/Jerrica sold rather well, rising from nineteenth on *Toy and Hobby World*'s list of top selling toys in March 1986 to tenth by October. But by June 1987 she had dived to twentieth, thereafter quickly falling into the discount bin. The concept may have been simply too complex for the five- to nine-year-old girls for whom the doll was designed. And the accessories required for the full effect may have been too costly for most parents.

The next year Hasbro tried the far more modest Maxie, a teenage doll. She was prettier and more wholesome looking than Jem. Maxie was the "California high school" girl, easier for middle-class girls to identify with (and for parents to accept) than the "truly outrageous" Jem. Still, with only $7 million in advertising (compared with the more than $20 million committed by Mattel to Barbie in 1988), it is not surprising that Maxie too soon disappeared.[41]

Jem may have failed, but Hasbro scared Mattel into at least a temporary revamping of the Barbie image. In 1987 Barbie went on TV with a show featuring her own band, the Rockers. Barbie was no longer simply a symbol of growing up in consumerist freedom. She was another fantasy personality with a back story upon which to model play. Fashion, friendship, and action each offered distinct "play patterns," for children of different ages and sexes; but all featured the character line with its fantasy story.[42]

Going to Extremes

By the mid-1980s the formulas that had brought success to Star Wars and Strawberry Shortcake had affected the entire toy market.

Major companies like Hasbro, Mattel, Kenner, and even Galoob and Tonka divided their offerings into sharply defined categories: male action figures appeared in garish green, purple, and black, while little girl's "friendship" toys could be identified by their sweet-smelling pastels. Mattel largely dominated a third category, the slightly older girl's Barbie aisle of hot-pink boxes. Sales of action figures outstripped those of science toys by twenty-eight times between 1984 and 1986. The wholesale value of dollhouses, the classic girls' "training toy" of the 1950s, declined from $114 million to $14 million between 1983 and 1988 while sales of fashion doll accessories rose from $65 million to $143 million.[43]

Older concepts in boys' toys were reduced to the clash of fighters. Tonka took the construction toy and made it into a set of action figures. Its Legion of Power offered five-year-olds and up the opportunity to piece together interlocking blocks into battle vehicles for the war between the planets of Prolon and Konn. Galoob turned "off the road vehicles" into predatory jungle animals ready for battle. And in 1986 Mattel produced the first interactive cartoon show, *Captain Power and the Soldiers of the Future*. A child owning Mattel's PowerJet equipped with electronic sensors could exchange shots with space warriors on the show. While these interactive toys were too expensive to displace action figures, they took fantasy violence to a new level by giving children a crack at the science-fiction killing they formerly only watched.[44]

Play figures no longer needed even to conform to the simplest laws of nature. The animal, mechanical, and human elements could be pasted together in whatever combination seemed to pack the most emotional or imaginative punch. By definition these toys were detached from the past of adults and the expected future of children. By the mid-1980s they were freed from any sense of time as toymakers combined the futuristic and prehistoric.

Coleco tapped the previous generation's fascination with the bizarre and exotic with its giant insects, the Sectaurs. These were action figures ridden by fighting men from the Shining Realm and the Dark Domain, battling on the distant planet of Sybion. The insects were changelings, which "telebonded" with Sectaur fighters (themselves semi-insects with their own antenna). Yet in advertisements the "human" Sectaur warriors were posed in heroic postures with raised sword and shield, reminiscent of Greco-Roman statuary. This was an image packaged to evoke multiple emotions—fright, fascination with the paranormal and futuristic, and identity with the classic image of male power and heroism. The message was not simply or even primarily that boys can be heroes. It was that boys can possess a package of excitement, the "kool stuff" embodied in the diverse meanings of the toy.[45]

In 1988 Tyco took this fantastic mixture even further with the Dino-Rider line. This series featured "scientifically accurate dinosaurs." Tyco hired Dr. Robert Bakker, an authority on dinosaurs, to participate in a media tour. Tyco noted that "kids know dinosaurs" and wanted realism. But these dinosaurs were ridden by space soldiers. Tyco publicity bragged that they had successfully combined the "two dominant fantasies of kids' play: the future and the past." The narrative provided was the typical stuff of fantasy: survivors of a devastated planet in the distant future were sent back in time to 65 million BCE. The good guys befriended plant-eating dinosaurs while the evil Krulos and his monster legions of Rulons enslaved meat-eating dinosaurs with "brain boxes." Typical was the Dino-Rider Brontosaurus, a realistic prehistoric figure but equipped with laser beams and missiles. The past and future, primitive and complex were blended in the Dino-Rider's rendition of battle play.[46]

Action-figure fantasy extended still further when it crossed into another commercial play category—the fashion fantasy of girls. Mattel researchers found that one-third of the viewers of the *He-Man* TV program were girls and that females bought 10 percent of the action figures in 1984 (out of $622 million in wholesale sales). Ever attentive to the possibilities of market expansion, Mattel and Galoob rushed to introduce a derivative action-figure line for girls. Industry researchers found that while girls embraced the idea of cosmic conflict, "they identify with a heroine who controls her environment, protecting it through cooperation, cleverness, and special powers instead of aggression." They found also that girls adopted a "more materialistic approach" to figure play, that is, they wanted their warriors to be well-dressed and to look nice.[47]

The result was Mattel's She-Ra, Princess of Power, and Galoob's The Golden Girl and Guardians of the Gems. These toy lines combined magic, adventure, and glamour, an assault of sorts on the gender divide. Female warriors clad in showgirl costumes were hardly new. Years earlier Kenner's Bionic Woman, a knockoff of the Six Million Dollar Man, was a superperson with "Bath 'n' Shower" and "Beauty Salon" accessories. The odd goddess or female team member that appeared in the boy's action lines usually looked like a beauty queen. She-Ra was the sister of He-Man after all. But now She-Ra got her own TV show and her own "enemy," Catra (who looked the part in her black fur pelt). Magic, more than muscle, gave She-Ra the edge. Her pink horse, Spirit, turned into Swift Wind when mask and wings were added; and her owl and swan helped too with their special powers.[48]

Golden Girl had her troop of Guardians and was aided by her unicorn, Olympia, to fight the bad girls headed by the Dragon Queen. The Golden Girl and her pals had weapons. But they also came with die-cast, gem-studded shields (which their owners could also wear as brooches). The success of Barbie was not forgotten. The Golden Girl and Dragon Queen had their own consorts (Prince Kroma and Ogra). The line featured three fashion clothing sets (Forest Fantasy, Glorious Glitter, and Festival Spirit) each with matching purses. The Golden Girl and Dragon Queen naturally had long-maned horses (fun to comb). And battle was in the defense of the "magical" Palace of the Gems. Galoob pulled out all the stops with the Golden Girl. The line combined action, magic, and fashion play. It packed into one toy line the "play values" of He-Man, My Little Pony, and Barbie.[49]

However, all this "fun" was just too much for girls in the mid-1980s. Neither line was very successful. Perhaps this was because they came close to self-parody by their exaggerations, almost caricatures, of what made the earlier action-figure lines successful. By mixing so many disparate elements together in order to attract children, they had lost track of what attracted children to toys in the first place.

The Teenage Mutant Ninja Turtles, however, transformed themselves from a spoof on action-figure themes into the most successful action-figure line of the late 1980s. According to the scenario developed by Peter Laird and Kevin Eastman for a comic-book series, pet-store turtles, doused by a mutagen, grew to human size, and learned the martial art of ninja from a rat. Like their teacher, they lived in the sewers of a big city and subsisted on pizza. In 1988 the Turtles themselves became a line of action figures when an obscure Hong Kong toy company, Playmates, picked up the rights. By the Christmas selling season the Turtles had become a hit. Within three years 80 million had been shipped to retailers. And Playmates claimed that 90 percent of American boys aged three to eight had one. By 1990 profits reached $156 million. Playmates president Chan Tai Ho hardly fit the mold. He had been a refugee from China in 1966. Before his success with the Turtles he had acted as subcontractor for American toymakers. By 1990 it was he who contracted out production of Turtles to mainland China.[50]

Why were the Turtles a hit? Their whimsical appearance and comical antics may have been a welcome relief from the grim faces and story lines of G.I. Joe and He-Man. They also delighted kids by their weird appearance, insatiable desire for pizza, and use of teenage slang. Playmates offered an accessory called the Flushomatic, a miniature toilet which when filled with "Retromutagen Ooze" could be "flushed" onto captive Turtles in a Torture Tray. This bathroom humor appealed no doubt to little and not so little boys just as it made mothers wince. By the fact of their own absurdity, the Turtles made fun of fantastic superheroes of the 1980s. Their popularity was witness to the decadence of the genre.[51]

But Playmates also knew how to play the new marketing games. The company decided early to produce five cartoon episodes of the Turtles to promote the story line. And in 1990 and 1991 it sponsored two feature-length movies about the Turtles to sustain sales. Chan followed the tried and true strategy of "model changes," constantly adding new Turtles (or "enemies") to spur fresh interest. But even the mighty Turtles fell, or rather gradually disappeared from the shelves over the winter of 1993–94. Playmates had long understood that day would come. Among its early projects to fill the gap were the Barnyard Commandos. Like the Turtles, this action-figure line satirized the action figure: "These guys are animals and that's no bull," went the advertisement promoting these teams of militarized farm animals. Pigs armed with "Pork-a-Pults" did combat with rams. Later Playmates tried Toxic Crusaders headed up by mop-toting Toxie, a 98-pound weakling hideously deformed by toxic wastes who fought the good fight for the environment against Dr. Killemoff and his evil friends. Even Hasbro stooped to self-satire with Bucky O'Hare, a goofy rabbit who commanded an "intergalactic crew to save the universe" from the planet-gobbling "Toad Menace." The era of action-figure fantasy culminated in toymakers' making fun of their own creations while trying to sell still more of them.[52]

The action figure dipped into the playthings of toddlers and even left its imprint on the educational toy market. As early as November 1982 Fisher-Price introduced the Adventure People line, complete with Alpha Star vehicles designed to tie in "with the space theme so popular in the action figure market." In 1983 a safe and simple line of Wild Dragsters was offered to little brother, preparing him for the day when he would be ready for the "grown-up" version. Fisher-Price designed a construction line, Construx, for five-year-olds. These models of sea-land adventure (amphibious vehicles) seemed to harken back to an earlier era. But by 1986 a new subline appeared, the Military Construx. Fisher-Price bragged that it was tapping into that "winning military theme" with models of mobile missiles. In 1988 Construx drew upon the fantasy-animal theme of older boys' toys with Terrordrone, an alien winged creature. Fisher-Price also continued to manufacture plastic looms and Jetport playsets, but when this respected company used war themes in the toys of toddlers, it had abandoned the idea of age-graded playthings.[53]

In 1985, shortly after Hasbro's takeover, a Playskool promotion promised "innovative Hasbro products" in the Playskool line. Playskool classics like inlaid blocks and wooden puzzles remained; and in 1986 Playskool won praise for its tough but cuddly preschool boys' doll, My Buddy. But by 1987 Playskool featured First Transformers (with no weapons) for one-and-a-half- to three-year-olds. By 1990 the Playskool version of those low-seated plastic tricycles ("big wheels") were emblazoned with Ghostbuster, Batman, and G.I. Joe logos. At the same time, Playskool relegated its Tinkertoys and Lincoln Logs (which had once been prized acquisitions) to one lonely page in a fifty-page catalog. For both Fisher-Price and

Playskool, the marketing advantage of selling fantasy directly to children undermined old commitments to providing parents with toys that taught.[54]

Other toymakers offered still more "imaginative" alternatives to traditional preschool play such as WOW's Teddy Ruxpin, the interactive plush bear, and Galoob's Smarty Bear with its "deep and soothing voice" that "responds to the sound of a human voice." These furry creatures with computer chips inside combined technological gadgetry with the traditional huggable plush at $60 to $75 each.[55]

Although beauty toys for preschool girls were hardly new, in the 1980s Mattel extended the fashion fun of Barbie into the little-girl market. Its Poochie of 1983 was to be a "new status symbol for young girls." This pink-and-white puppy appealed to preschoolers, but its "designer paws" added a grown-up theme. This logo appeared on comb-and-mirror sets, stamp sets, and other "personal musts" of fashion-conscious five-year-olds. Poochie and its accessories represented all the "sophistication and innocence of girlhood." Kenner's Shimmer minidolls of 1986 went even further. Part girl and part woodland animal, these figures had long hair, "pearlized and iridescent" skin, and removable clothing. Kenner bragged that Shimmer "combines beauty, hair play, mothering, and fashion play into an exciting fantasy that transforms little girls' dreams into reality." The always daring Galoob combined transformers and girls' fantasy playsets in its Sweet Secrets of 1985. Included in this line was the Locket-Bye-Baby, a wearable locket that when opened converted into a playset, featuring a baby in a playpen. Fashion, fantasy, and gadgetry were wrapped into these little-girl toys. In 1990 even Fisher-Price entered this field when it introduced the Just My Style line, complete with vanity, curling irons, and jewelry boxes. Playskool drew upon its parent Hasbro's My Little Pony concept when it produced the My Pretty Mermaid with "Fun to Style Hair."[56]

The idea that toddlers and small children should be protected from the experiences of older children and adults, a hallmark of childrearing since the days of Rousseau, was abandoned in these toys. In the 1980s the very idea of age-graded play was directly attacked when Mattel offered preschool toys that merged sophistication and innocence. When Mattel assured buyers that Barbies were suitable for children over the age of two, what they meant was that young children could hold the doll and that it was safe for them to play with—physically. Obviously, by offering play themes developed for the older child to the preschooler, manufacturers put profits earned by widening the market above loyalty to traditional childrearing principles. But the fact that Shimmers or Sweet Secret sets were offered at all indicates that very young children were exposed to ideas appropriate for older children through their big sisters or brothers and TV. Innocence was no more. The breakdown of developmental age categories reflected more than the merchandisers' greed or even parents' ignorance. It was the consequence of the pervasive presence of popular toys in media, stores, and catalogs which were accessible to all kids. The little ones could no longer be shielded from the wider world of fantasy.

Many parents continued to seek out playthings designed to enhance development. Thus traditional infant toys remained in Playskool and Fisher-Price catalogs. And new specialty companies, most notably Little Tikes, attracted discerning parents with well-constructed and safe plastic cars and houses for the two-year-old toddler. By 1990 Little Tikes was fifth in toy sales. The Childcraft company resurrected Hill building blocks and even manufactured progressive puzzles (developed by the Women's Action Alliance) showing men in nurturing roles to teach that "giving care to children is indeed the business of both sexes."[57]

Foreign companies stepped in to fill the gaps left by American toymakers in search of blockbusters. The German import Playmobil won loyal customers and doubled U.S. sales between 1987 and 1989 with attractive plastic playsets depicting historic castles and Eskimo villages. It even offered a western stockade as an updated version of the old Fort Apache playset. Gund, Inc., continued its tradition of classic plush animal toys, defiantly challenging "hard edge plastic, zapping electronics and military toys." Sweden's Brio offered sturdy wooden blocks and trains. Brio insisted that parents should not "purchase instant gratification" and offered advice on how to avoid the manipulation of advertisers. Brio even suggested that parents "set limits on the number of toys their children are given." The company went so far as to say in 1990: "Parents who buy good, open ended toys will find that their children need fewer toys and they will find that they are truly making a sound investment in their child's growth and development." But then Brio sold expensive toys. They appealed to improving and relatively affluent parents eager for educational playthings and toys that recalled their own childhoods.[58]

In the 1970s and early 1980s the Danish company Lego built a toy empire in the United States. It bucked the trend of action-figure fantasy. Instead it perpetuated the construction-toy tradition with its interlocking blocks. Lego used its European origins, museum and mall displays, and Legoland theme park to spread its reputation for quality and creativity. Its eye-catching red, yellow, white, and blue pieces could be combined into infinite forms and shapes which delighted children and gave them unrestricted opportunities to employ their skills and imagination. Lego's chief Godtfred Christiansen claimed his blocks provided "unlimited" and timeless play, stimulated activity without violence, and were gender neutral.[59]

However, while Brio and Playmobil were content to remain niche companies with their expensive lines of toys, Lego compromised with the American fantasy industry in the late 1980s. Despite Lego's continuing upscale image, the company used TV advertising to fight off "imitations" from Fisher-Price and Tyco. A 1987 promotional for Zack the Lego Maniac tried to make Lego "kool" to the action-figure crowd. Lego slipped into the tie-in game with teaser samples of Legos in kid's dessert packs. The claim that Legos offered unbounded creativity was increasingly hard to square with a sales program based on kits or "systems" designed to construct a single model. And the "timelessness" of Legos jarred against the sale of Lego Space Systems in 1984. While Lego did not provide a violent back story, many of these systems came with exotic weaponry. Some parents found Legos frustrating. When children treated Lego space warships like action-figure toys rather than models, they easily broke, obliging fathers and mothers to help put them back together (if the directions could still be found). In the face of competition Lego had adapted to the all-pervasive marketing techniques of the noveltymakers, sacrificing its initial educational value.[60]

Retrenchment and Returning Toys to Parents

Inevitably the feast of fantasy came to an end. Clearly there were limits to which different "play values" could be crammed into a single toy line. Imagine the confusion that the plush toys for 1986 must have caused children sorting through the Gummi Bears, Kissyfur, Popples, Keypers, Teddy Ruxpins, American Rabbits, Wrinkles, Star Fairies, Care Bears, Rainbow Brites, Robotmen, and Pound Puppies, as well as the standard Sesame Street, Charles Schultz, and Disney characters. Companies found it difficult to get store space for new lines with such crowded shelves. To be sure, retailers accepted $840 million worth of action figures in 1985. But when faced with the bewildering array of Centurions, Inhumanoids, Thundercats, and MASK figures, stores were hard-pressed to pick likely movers. Virtually all of these action figures and saccharin minidolls were backed by the same media formula, thus becoming indistinguishable. When fantasy was unhitched from any reference point and when any and all play patterns could be combined at will, confusion and boredom followed.[61]

In 1987 wholesale revenues from licensed toys dropped from $8.3 to $7.8 billion, the only decline since 1977, when this statistic was first collected. Ratings for syndicated action-figure cartoon shows declined by 37 percent from 1985 to 1987 (although there was a 50 percent increase in the number of programs). *Toy and Hobby World* noted that "glut" and "repetition" had taken their toll. A survey of retailers found that 85 percent believed the market for licensed toys was saturated in 1986 and 60 percent planned to decrease buying in 1987. Manufacturers' sales of action figures declined from $861 million in 1986 to $523 million in 1988.[62]

Toymakers faced an even bigger problem—the return of the video game after 1988 with an improved Nintendo Entertainment System. Indeed it is arguable that the action figure flourished in the mid-1980s in a lull between the video craze led by Atari between 1977 and 1982 and the revival dominated by Nintendo and Sega after 1988. In 1990 Nintendo outsold Hasbro and Mattel combined ($3.4 billion to $2.9 billion).[63] *Playthings* estimated that Nintendo took $1 billion from toy sales in 1987 and by 1990 had won 21 percent of the toy market. Nintendo products held the top spot in the toy hit parade through the early 1990s. Video games did what action figures did, but better. Many video games featured themes of conquest and clash with enemies as did the action figures, but the pace was set by the game's electronics, creating an experience of great emotional intensity.[64]

While the PLC toy was losing its luster, children's TV critics were again getting a hearing in the courts and Congress. Reformers rallied behind a bill sponsored by the liberal Senators Tim Wirth and Frank Lautenberg. Their Children's Television Act demanded that stations provide at least seven hours of children's programming per week. While Reagan had earlier vetoed this bill, his successor, George Bush, allowed reform legislation to become law in 1990. This law also limited commercials on children's programming to twelve minutes per hour on weekdays and ten and a half minutes on weekends. It also obliged the FCC to review children's educational programming before renewing licenses of broadcasters. Still, as late as 1991 the FCC claimed it could not distinguish programming that was "toy-driven" from shows with toy spinoffs. The FCC only banned toy programs from showing commercials of the toys they depicted.[65]

Although still tolerated, the Program-Length Commercial was in sharp decline as early as 1986. A focus group of children asked to view samples of toy shows from the 1987–88 season generally found them disappointing. One boy claimed he was "powered out" with transformer-type programs. In that year the popular shows were *Ducktales* and *Chip 'n Dale Rescue Rangers.* These were traditional cartoons produced by high-quality animators associated with Warner Brothers and Disney. Because of high ratings, toy companies eagerly bought commercial time on these shows in the traditional way.[66]

In the late 1980s toymakers attempted to bolster slumping sales by reviving time-tested toys.[67] They returned, at least in part, to addressing the desires and sentiments of long-neglected parents. Companies that had prospered with novelty throughout the 1980s reintroduced boys' toys from the earliest days of the baby boom. Matchbox's 1988 catalog stressed the die-cast vehicles that had launched the company in 1947. Galoob introduced Micro Machines, tiny vehicle playsets in the tradition of Louis Marx and Buddy "L."

Kenner revived Spirograph sets and dressed up the Play-Doh line. Fisher-Price returned to traditional infant and toddler toys with a enlarged line of those peglike Little People and their playsets. Etch-A-Sketch reappeared in TV advertising in 1990 after an eight-year hiatus. "Evergreens"—proven favorites from the 1950s and 1960s—like the board game Chutes and Ladders and even the ancient Uncle Wiggly were dusted off and returned to the shelves.

Some companies went back even further, refurbishing the toys of the 1910s. In 1987 Playskool made news when it reintroduced the cylindrical Tinkertoy container to attract the attention of parents nostalgic for their own childhood fun. Three years later the European toymaker Meccano announced that it was reviving the erector set in the United States. The revival of these playthings showed that adults still could insist that toys teach or relate to the real world (as they knew it).

In response to the excesses of the 1980s other toymakers turned to early fantasy toys, hoping to appeal to both adults and children. They dug up fantasy characters that adults remembered from their childhoods. *The Flintstones*, a stone-age cartoon situation comedy from the mid-1960s, returned in 1987 in a toy line called the Flintstone Kids. Children as well as parents connected with Fred, Wilma, and Bam Bam, because from 1985 the these characters had reappeared in TV reruns. Warner Brothers dusted off cartoon personalities from the 1930s and 1940s (Bugs Bunny, Porky Pig, and Daffy Duck) and transformed them into Tiny Tunes. And media empires like Turner Home Entertainment and Viacom sold toy companies licenses for characters from cartoon and movie classics like *Tom and Jerry*, *The Wizard of Oz*, and *Mighty Mouse* that children saw on cable TV. This strategy made economic sense. These products had been proven hits and they were cheap to deliver to the market—just like TV reruns. And, because they were *new* to the young, they could be sold to them as innovations. More important, they appealed, as had Mickey Mouse toys in the 1950s, to a cross-generational market.[68]

Traditional dolls also made a comeback. Wholesale sales rose almost $100 million between 1987 and 1988. Leading this revival were baby dolls. Tyco's Oopsie Daisy fell and cried, and its Shivers "shivered when cold." Ideal even reintroduced Betsy Wetsy. Hasbro did them one better with its Baby Uh-Oh, who was "full of Surprises." When she "drank" cold water, her diaper changed color suggesting that she had filled her pants. These dolls drew on an old theme—the marriage of gadgetry with appeals to "mothering."[69]

But toymakers also pushed simple dolls that appealed to a child's desire for attachment (and was approved by parents). Mattel reintroduced Raggedy Ann–style dolls in the form of that 1970s hit, Holly Hobbie. Kenner revived companionship with its Always Sisters dolls—a line of four "families" of doll sisters (two older sisters with fashion and vanity sets to share and one baby sister to care for). These dolls were to be "the sisters you've always dreamed of." Kenner appealed to conservative adult consumers with the Special Blessing doll, intended to "reinforce traditional values encouraged by parents." This fifteen-inch huggable doll was shown kneeling and with clasped hands as if in prayer. The doll even came with an inspirational booklet. Kenner bragged that it was responding to a Gallup poll that showed that 90 percent of adults wanted more emphasis on family values. For its part, Mattel offered a wholesome suburban family theme in its Heart Family dolls.[70]

Along with nostalgia and family values came a curious crossover product—collectors' dolls distributed by novelty toymakers. As early as 1987 Mattel marketed the Barefoot Children Collection from the village of Paderborn. These "life-like dolls in limited edition" were the "creations of Annette Himstedt," a "famous" European artist. Mattel followed three years later with the Corolle Collection, a revival of French "Bébé" dolls to be "loved for a lifetime." The dolls had pretentious French names like Bébé Chou and Nouveau-Né, and many featured "dainty outfits." These were updates of nineteenth-century European china dolls, offered in the mass market to women in search of a memory that long preceded their own childhoods.[71]

As interesting was Mattel's decision to feature collector-quality Barbies dressed in international costumes. Mattel's Barbie as Scarlet Collection appeared repeatedly in half-hour infomercials in 1994–1995. This $224.55 set featured four Barbies dressed as Scarlett O'Hara in *Gone with the Wind*. Because of their price, probably few of these dolls ended up in the hands of girls at play. But the commercial invited mothers to share the feelings of "security" and "happiness" they remembered from their own childhood play with Barbies with their daughters by collecting Barbie classics. As the celebrity host Leeza Gibbons said in the commercial, "life is a collection of memories," and Mattel had lots of them to sell. These revivals of baby-boomer toys and dolls had as much to do with meeting the emotional needs of adults as with resurrecting good playthings for children.

A far more serious break from the excesses of the 1980s was Pleasant Rowland's American Girl Collection (1986), a line of high-quality dolls and accessories depicting girls at various stages in American history and linked with a book series. The idea was to give girls interested in both reading and playing with dolls an "understanding of their pasts and a sense of pride in the tradition they share with girls of yesterday." The doll line was too expensive for many parents. But the play scheme represented a clear and opposing alternative to the Barbie. The books and other literature stressed a positive "can do" image of young girls rather than encouraging the child to identify with a "teen-age model." Instead of watching TV, the doll owner was to get her play narrative from reading. And in place of fashion play the American Girl Collection invited the historical reenactment of the lives of girls with families in realistic situations. But this product was an exception.[72]

The back-to-basics movement was a response to parental desires for toys that related to their values and memory. It was a recognition that the fantasy industry had reached an imaginative dead end. But if this movement was a reaction to the fads of the 1980s, it was itself a fad, repeated every few years when the toy industry was in a slump. The retro-toy trend was more parental nostalgia than a serious effort to revive the tradition of educational or developmental play. To succeed in that would have required really new toys designed to meet the needs of contemporary children.

In any case the back-to-basics toys did not last long. TV toy tie-ins arose again in 1990. As a Kenner executive noted, "recognizability" was essential. Hasbro's Pirates of Dark Waters, Tyco's Little Mermaid, and Mattel's Killer Tomatoes all came from TV or movies in the 1990–91 season. In the fall of 1992 Hasbro began airing a full-length animation based on the revival of the Transformers. They aimed to fill the vacuum left by the fading Turtles. Hasbro hoped that a new generation of young boys, who had never heard of this fad of the mid-1980s, would love these gadget toys just as had their older brothers or uncles. And following in the steps of the Chinese-owned Playmates came the Japanese company Bandai, which marketed the Mighty Morphin Power Rangers in 1993. A TV program featuring the kung fu fighting of these brightly colored figures in jumpsuits and helmets supported the toy and spread its wonders. Another foreign company, Toy Biz, licensed Marvel Comics X-Men (similarly made into a cartoon program in 1993). It followed this success with Spiderman in the fall of 1994. Wholesale deliveries of action figures rose again, reaching $1.17 billion in 1994.[73]

The action figure's return should surprise no one. Action figures rose when video games fell in the 1980s. They were part of the same play complex. Action figures largely replaced traditional toy guns (reaching twenty-three times the wholesale value of toy weapons at the peak of the action-figure craze in 1985). But when sales of the armed miniatures dropped by over two-thirds between 1985 and 1991, toy gun sales increased by 126 percent. The clash-of-powers play of the 1980s was never really challenged. It simply shifted from one play form to another.[74]

The ephemeral character of hit toys had hardly changed either. Half of the top ten toy lines of 1994 were new to the list. Only Barbie and G.I. Joe were long-time veterans. The licensed product was not dead. Indeed, with the proliferation of Disney and Warner Brothers stores in malls in the early 1990s, the licensing phenomenon became even more pronounced. These fantasy companies went directly to the public, selling, in 1995, 50 percent more per square foot of floor space than did the average mall store.[75]

Despite the revival of baby and companion dolls, Barbie had not lost her hold. In 1990 Barbie was doing a $700 million business (up from $135 million in 1980). Ninety-five percent of American girls aged three to eleven had at least one Barbie. The average owned was eight by 1993. That year F. A. O. Schwarz turned a section of its venerable store into a Barbie Boutique, featuring a full array of Barbie-brand goods from beanbag chairs and school supplies to expensive collectors' Barbies. The dazzling pink Barbie billboard beckoned adults perhaps even more than children. Mattel sought the other end of the market too in 1993 when it offered mini-Barbies to the preschoolers in McDonald's Happy Meals. If there was any fear that American girls had had enough of Barbie, she was making headway into the newly liberated Eastern European markets. By 1993 Barbie became a billion-dollar winner.[76]

The economic advantages of the "recognizable" toy based on TV fantasy were too great for any alternative to prevail. The plaything as a tool to reenact the past or prepare for the future had largely disappeared. The improving tradition of the educational toy had been marginalized or blended into the ethos of fantasy consumerism. The toy had ceased to be the token of special personal time—a transition from one childhood stage to another—or a marker of a special holiday season. Instead, those special toys, the erector sets or dollhouses, had been smothered under the pile. And holiday gifts were diminished by the constant festivals of consumption created by managers of fads and fantasy.

This surely has changed the meaning of childhood. When toys lost their connection to the experience and expectations of parents, they entered a realm of ever-changing fantasy. Indeed, the parent's gift to the child increasingly became not the learning of the future or reason or even the sharing of a joy of childhood. Parents instead granted children the right to participate in a play world of constant change without much guidance or input from adults. The events of the 1980s did not bring this change by themselves. But they seemed to have closed the door on the past.

8 MAKING SENSE OF THE MODERN TOYBOX

EVERY DECEMBER magazines run stories about the latest toys for holiday gift-giving. They report with wonder just how much the toy industry expects Americans to spend that year and speculate about which toy or novelty item is hot and why. Many articles also ask questions like why, for example, anyone would pay $30 for a "robot hamster" or why tried and true stuffed-animal characters should be stuffed with computer chips to allow them to "talk to each other." Each year the same issues return, reflecting Americans' simultaneous fascination and frustration with contemporary playthings. Many may admire the marketing savvy of the inventor who developed the Garbage Pail Kids—grotesque figures such as Arline Latrine, Heaving Heather, and Destroyed Lloyd, which mocked the sweetness of the Cabbage Patch Kids by emphasizing body fluids and violence—and proceeded to sell them to four- to eight-year-old boys. But just as many are appalled by toys whose only apparent appeal is that they come in the shape of some TV superhero (last year Power Rangers, this year, X-men) whose story the parent does not know or care about.[1]

Those adults who were children before the 1970s remember receiving erector sets and dollhouses as rites of passage. These were toys that grandparents had enjoyed as children and that seemed to tell the young something about what they could expect as adults in their future worlds of business and the home. These playthings crossed the boundaries of generations, even if they were not really "timeless." By the 1980s, however, the endlessly changing displays of action, fashion, and cuddly figures bore little relation to parents' childhood toys and had even less to do with children's actual future. Despite occasional reissues of older toys, the toy store has become unfamiliar territory to adults. They see the rows of aggressive purple-and-green action figures and conclude that these inhuman creatures teach violence or make children fearful. Some parents shudder at the long aisles of pink Barbies glorifying "perfect" bodies and vast glamorous wardrobes that can never be complete.

Yet toy sales per child continued to grow in the 1980s and 1990s. Parents cannot resist the pull of their children's wishes. And children get their wishes from TV advertisements. Mattel discovered as early as 1955 that commercials on the *Mickey Mouse Club* could create a mad rush for Burp Guns and Fanner 50s. Since 1959 Barbie commercials have fueled the fashion and shopping fantasies of American girls, winning Mattel sales of $1.1 billion by 1994—despite adult disapproval. In 1993 $790.4 million was spent on toy advertising, compared to only $221.6 million in 1983. Toy companies produced TV cartoons based on their own toy lines, which children watched in their homes and which spurred them to buy mountains of He-Men, G.I. Joes, and Power Rangers. The now nearly universal practice of packing toys in children's fast-food meals has made the toy fix as regular as the burger-and-fries habit. Media corporations like Disney and its toymaking partners have created an almost continuous buying season as they space their toy-inspired animations like *The Lion King* and *Pocahontas* throughout the year.[2]

But merchandisers cannot alone be blamed for the consumers' excess. Parents are not forced to buy. Even children grow skeptical of the claims of advertisements by the time they reach elementary school. A mid-1980s study found that preschoolers asked for only an average of 3.4 toys at holiday time but received 11.6. Other studies have shown that older children want more toys than do younger children, suggesting that when the young are given more toys than they ask for they expect more the following year. Clearly parents give more than their children demand and help to create higher expectations.[3]

Toy advertisers have long appealed to parents' pride as providers. Today they increasingly appeal to guilt feelings as well. As women have entered the labor force in unprecedented numbers, toymakers have encouraged mothers to buy toys to assuage their guilt about spending less time with their children. The steep rise in the proportion of working mothers with preschoolers (increasing from 11.9 percent in 1950 to 44 percent in 1978 to 58.9 percent in 1991) is merely one sign of change. Divorced parents similarly try to compensate for fragmenting the family and to compete for love and loyalty with gifts of playthings. In response to their ambivalent feelings about their performance as moms and dads, parents become yearlong, not just seasonal, customers.

Grandparents also contribute to the overflowing toybox. Longer-living adults have more time and money to spoil their grandchildren. They may feel that they are making up for what they could not give their own children years before. Or they may be compensating for the fact that they have so little contact with grandchildren, because of geographical mobility and dispersement, compared with families in an earlier age. So grandparents use Santa Claus and his bottomless sack of goodies to give of themselves through gifts instead of through their actual presence. Santa's loving image helps adults disguise from themselves as well as from the young the commercialism of their annual spending frenzy. They want children to have fun, to be free from the constraints of adult life, and they find an easy way to express these desires in the purchase of toys. The toy industry exploits these sentiments but does not entirely create them.[4]

Adults spend because they want to. This points to a basic dilemma faced by many Americans. They agree that children should be sheltered from many aspects of the adult world and that parents have the right to protect and nurture their offspring, free from unreasonable outside interference. Yet they bow to the pressures of marketing professionals who know how to appeal to the psychological proclivities of children as well as to delight their minds and senses. Many adults admire the novelties of the market at the same time that they raise concerns about the cost and appropriateness of these diversions for children. That ambivalence is manifested in a debate that is almost as old as the modern commercial toy itself—the clash between advocates of unfettered toy markets and child development professionals who are often critical of commercial playthings.

The critics complain that an unconstrained market in playthings denies children a childhood by overwhelming their young minds with packaged images and fantasies. While toy companies may have an interest in selling Barbies to parents of three-year-olds, this practice of broadening the market as far as possible threatens to make children grow up "too fast." The incessant bombardment of toy advertisements undermines parents' authority to teach restraint and deferred gratification. How, Neil Postman and other critics ask, can children be taught the discipline necessary to read critically and to think deeply if they are immersed in a culture that celebrates instant pleasure? How can they find wonder in a world that does not protect them from anything?[5]

The manufacturer has an economic incentive to fabricate toys and dolls that require add-ons. But this turns play into collecting complete sets of action figures or doll "families" rather than enjoying what one has. And in an era of increasing gender equality, critics charge that toymakers exploit the six-year-old's quest for gender identity by exaggerating boys' power toys and girls' make-up and fashion playthings. Similarly, toy companies indulge boys' fascination with toy weapons by providing more destructive and exotic weapons than any child could imagine. The conflict between the logic of the market and the rationale of the nurturing family is long and persistent.[6]

Distrust of the toy industry extends from those on the secular left to those on the religious right. Opponents of war toys charge that they teach violence as a way of resolving conflict. Critics denounce girls' toys for the image of women they project and the crude consumerism they encourage. In 1992 educators and women's groups were outraged at a talking Barbie that said "Math class is tough," suggesting that this might discourage girls from achieving in science and mathematics. In December 1993 a phantom group called the Barbie Liberation Organization secretly switched the voice boxes of talking Barbies with G.I. Joes, making Barbie say "Eat Lead, COBRA" and G.I. Joe ask "Will we ever have enough clothes?" The object of this trick on unsuspecting buyers was to underline how Barbie designers sought to "subjugate women and provide them with less opportunity."[7]

Conservative religious groups also attack the fantasy toy industry. In fact, one Evangelical Christian, Joan Robie, cites secular child psychologists and consumer critics in her attack. These religious conservatives despair when their sons' rooms look like combat zones and their daughters' rooms like beauty parlors: "God entrusts kids to parents, not Hollywood," they protest. Along with a general critique of the toy industry for encouraging unrestrained materialism and hobbling the child's imagination, some Evangelicals add that fantasy toys from Care Bears to He-Man encourage belief in magic and pagan mythology and thus undermine Christian parents' efforts to raise children in their faith.[8]

Some critics have countered the appeal of commercial and pagan playthings by creating toys in their own image and interest. Evangelical toy entrepreneurs have offered the Born Again Bunny (with a New Testament verse on the rabbit's ear), Grace the Pro-Life Doll, and Judah the Christian Soldier (equipped with a Breastplate of Righteousness and a Helmet of Salvation). A feminist manufactured "Proud to be Me" dolls in the shape of "normal" women rather than the anorectic Barbie. Others have returned to "time-tested" toys. Robie's list is revealing. It includes blocks, marbles, jump ropes, tiddly winks, pick-up sticks, miniature looms, doctor and nurse kits, pop beads, beauty kits, rubber dinosaurs, kaleidoscopes, harmonicas, and even Old Maid cards. These "timeless toys" are nothing more or less than the common playthings of an earlier generation remembered today by the middle-aged.[9]

But most critics go further, demanding that toys prepare children for adult roles and concerns. The educator Diana Green insists that "excellence [in playthings] requires arduous effort." Good toys must "prompt youngsters to teach themselves" and not be "instant gratifications." Today's children, Green argues, need to play with the toys that shaped successful people like yesterday's Thomas Edison or today's Colin Powell or Connie Chung. These playthings are a predictable melange of the improving and the enlightening:

Legos, Tinkertoys, blocks, UNICEF multicultural rag dolls, a Save the Forest game. The austere ethic of the educational toy of the 1920s survives in modified form in Green's proscriptions. So does a nostalgia for the toys of rugged individualists once glorified in the wares of A. C. Gilbert and Lionel.[10]

But can or should any contemporary child share in the nostalgia of the previous generation? In the late twentieth century there is little reason to assume that most adults or children are willing to give up the pleasures and rhythms of constant change for the didactic developmentalism of the educational toy of the 1920s. Toys cannot be expected to link the present either to the past or to the future when popular culture itself is so ahistorical. If some parents expect these things, surely few children do. The desires of these adults for skill-building play prevail only so long as their offspring are too young to shop for themselves. Once children are old enough to enter the world of the peer culture and of consumerism, educational toys have relatively little influence.

Defenders of the toy industry have been quick to point out that commercial toys do not necessarily conflict with "family values." They accuse critics of reading too much into these objects. To an educated adult the Barbie doll may symbolize a "life of meaningless surface values." But to the three- to seven-year-olds who receive Barbie in the 1990s, she is nothing more than a "fairy princess." Adults project upon toys their own anxieties about the contemporary culture, argues the anthropologist Brian Sutton-Smith. Can they then be trusted to interpret the child's experience of the toy?

Countering critics, defenders argue that children have their own instincts and impulses and do not need Hasbro or Mattel to introduce them to fantasy and aggression. The recent shift from the toy gun to the action figure could hardly be called an escalation of aggressive play since the fantastic miniworld of the figures is so alien to the real world of conflict and violence. Industry supporters claim that the young inevitably mix the magical with the mechanical, the past with the future, and overstress gender roles in their play. They argue that toy companies are only doing what kids would do anyway. And in any case fantasy has no long-lasting impact on children, for most of them grow up to be normal adults. When toymakers constantly introduce new products, they are only responding to the rapidly changing interests and sensibilities of children today.[11]

Perhaps the most common response of toymakers to their critics is that they are not ultimately responsible for the play of children; parents are. As the Toy Manufacturers of America noted in 1987, "Toy makers make the toys available, but it is parents who decide who plays with them and how." But this does not acknowledge that sophisticated marketing and advertising enable toy manufacturers to manipulate their audience. Long gone are the moralistic toymakers like Milton Bradley, who combined Puritan values with a love of games in his nineteenth-century board game, the "Checkered Game of Life." A *Dun and Bradstreet Report* article noted with a cheerful cynicism that a revived version of that game in 1960 abandoned Bradley's goal of "happy old age" for "becoming a millionaire." The toy industry seeks maximum market share, rapid turnover on merchandise, and, most of all, speculative profit based on making children desire and parents buy molded plastic figures at five or ten dollars apiece.[12]

The object of the toy and fantasy industries has been to maximize sales and profits, not to rear children. If this means exploiting emotions, generating insecurities, and promising instant gratification, so be it. This, of course, is true of most advertising. But marketing to children is different from selling to adults. The consumer here is not an independent, mature person. It is not just that the young lack the experience to see through the flimflam. They need positive guidance in order to learn how to make choices and decisions. They are not equal partners in the buyer-seller relationship. Thus certain constraints are called for.

Toymakers have found, however, that more products can be sold by appealing to novelty and immediate pleasure. Their research has isolated specific "play values" that children enjoy—ranging from hair-and-dress play to the clash of man against monster. Satisfying consumers' desires is a legitimate goal of business, but should toys appeal only to the childish imagination? Critics sometimes forget how important the new and fun are in expressing young people's quest for autonomy from their elders. But manufacturers also ignore or disguise their self-interest in pushing novelty items.[13]

The truth is neither that sideshow hucksters have captured our youth nor that the market provides what people really want. Adults are torn between a childrearing model that requires sheltering children from market-determined change and a culture of consumption that celebrates novelty and profit. This conflict is rooted in the joint appearance around 1900 of modern ideas about parenting and the novelty toy industry, which together shaped American childhood. The tension was subdued for decades by manufacturers' willingness to accommodate parental wishes. But when toymakers began to appeal directly to children they widened the gap between the concerns of parents and the interests of merchandisers. They reduced parents, as the buyers of toys, to acquiescent go-betweens in a transaction between the fantasy industry and the child. Toy manufacturers have broken their "contract" with parents to produce playthings that express parents' values and preserve children's innocence.

At least as important to parental frustration with contemporary toys is the fact that parents have lost a sense of what they want playthings to be. In the past toys provided continuity between parents' childhoods to those of their offspring. But in today's fast-changing world few adults can fully embrace yesterday or anticipate tomorrow. Many are no longer comfortable with play as a rehearsal for adult gender roles. But this leaves children with few models of the past or future even as it frees them from old constraints on their imaginations. In place of the traditional models of dolls and trucks, toymakers grow rich by producing magical pseudo-technology of violent conflict for boys and maudlin "caring" play and fashion fantasy for girls. These toys have not eliminated training in sex roles. They have only made male heroism more fantastic and female caring less grounded in reality. A culture that has long encouraged boys to worship gadgets and girls to fetishize clothing and appearance now also promotes the habit of unrestrained spending.

Toys are still at the center of the family's gift festival. At Christmas and Hanukkah parents and relatives shower the young with playthings, substituting, increasingly it seems, cost and quantity for meaning. But even the significance of the holiday is reduced as we mark time throughout the year with an unceasing flow of novelty purchases—*Pocahontas* figures this month, *Toy Story* characters the next. With the decline of special times for gift giving, each gift becomes just another addition to the toybox with a diminished relationship to the occasion for which it was given and even to the giver.

Still, despite the critics, many adults are not too perturbed by the constant change of contemporary toys. Parents, like their children, enjoy fads. And, even if parents cannot easily understand the appeal of a particular new toy, they do realize that novelty delights children. A large number of today's parents played with Barbie or G.I. Joe when they themselves were children. In 1995 Mattel reissued the first Barbie, appealing to nostalgic thirtysomething women. And the 1990s saw serious collectors' clubs devoted to G.I. Joe's heritage. These adults have always been immersed in a culture of the ephemeral and the fantastic. It is no surprise that they are not disturbed if their children also embrace that culture.

The only serious alternative to the novelty toy industry has been the educational playthings movement. And it never appealed to more than a small educated elite. Since the 1960s the movement's association with a Victorian Anglo-Saxon culture of austerity and relentless self-improvement has made it irrelevant except to well-to-do parents intent upon improving their children's skills. Even then the most rationalistic among us still enjoy fantasy. Can we impose a stoic ideal on children that we ourselves do not live up to? And if we try, do we not merely substitute, without clear justification, the domination of parents for that of the peer group and the media?

Opponents attack novelty toys, as did Patty Hill in the 1900s, for what these playthings teach children. But they still expect toys to teach some values, preferably their own. Some want to share their memories of growing up through the toys that they knew as children. Others want educational playthings that give their offspring an advantage in the world. The G.I. Joe and Barbie bashers want dolls that teach conflict-resolution skills and feminism. But ultimately we cannot satisfy all these goals through toys.

Critics probably take toys too seriously as determinants of personality and character. Playthings are only props on a wider stage of wills and motives. Opponents of novelty expect more from "good" toys than they can deliver and fear the worst from those adults consider "bad." But they properly argue that children are more than a mere consumer market and that parents are responsible for their upbringing. The progressive legacy of protecting the young from premature entry into the labor market needs now to be extended to include the consumer market. If there is no escaping the appeal of goods, equally childhood should be more than an education in shopping. Surely we need to go beyond the dichotomous language of austerity versus indulgence. The realistic approach is to be critical participants in our own consumer world, for it is a realm that children live in too. Adults must develop the skills to raise independent children in, rather than against, a culture of consumption.

We have seen that toys have become increasingly fantastic as they have become more numerous. The same could be said of adult goods. Commercial toys share with adult fashions a bias toward the new—even as both mine the past to evoke mood and sentiment. The use of goods to create feelings or to say something about ourselves runs throughout contemporary American society. These commodities have become more common and are enjoyed more frequently because we have more leisure time and affluence than our predecessors did. The same is true of children's consumer culture. In a sense the aristocratic youths' automata have become the plastic action figures of the sons of the working class. The occasional enjoyment of a bisque doll or a model Noah's Ark has become the unceasing diversion of TV, video games, and toys. Just as modern adults are drawn to stars and celebrities, so are children. Part of the "education" of the young is passing from the toddler "stars" of Barney and Big Bird to the gender-based celebrities of G.I. Joe and Barbie and eventually to the "real" stars of the movies, sports, and politics. In these ways, modern grown-ups and children share a common consumers' world. We need to understand and demand higher quality from both together. The toy problem is the consumer's problem.

For nearly a century parents have sent messages of love and

learning to children through mass-produced toys. And we are not about to change. Goods are ways of expressing care, individuality, and imagination. They help bind age groups in identity with a shared time and experience. Some consumer products may evoke memory of a past that otherwise would be a blur. This is one of the major attractions of toy collectors. These people recapture their youth and share a dream with others of their generation when they accumulate Louis Marx windups, Patsy dolls, or G.I. Joes and Barbies. The consumer culture may be ephemeral, but it produces objects that give fleeting time concrete meaning.

Still, we cannot forget that goods also divide us and stand in the way of our communicating with others and ourselves. We become especially sensitive to this when we, as adults, confront the toy store. There, if we are honest, we find children who remind us all too much of ourselves in their grasping for every sparkling package and promise of pleasure. We live in a fleeting culture divided into age and lifestyle groups. Toys throw this fact into sharp relief with their relentless celebration of novelty and appeal to gender divisions. Because modern toys link fantasy to the liberation of children from adult culture, they divide the generations.

We need to learn better how to read goods—including toys—and our attraction to them. We want toys to be gifts of ourselves even as we want them to give children freedom. There is nothing wrong with expecting them to do both. The trick is for adults to avoid the nostalgia trap and for children to recover an imagination more rooted in the real world. We should think much more about realistic work and sex roles appropriate for today and how play and toys can prepare children for meeting these modern needs. These are not easy tasks. But the alternatives of nostalgia for the toys of the past or passive acceptance of ever-changing fantasy toys solve nothing. We need to find playthings that give children a connection to the past and a constructive, but also imaginative, view of the future, and to encourage manufacturers to produce them.

Most important, we cannot use toys or any other goods as a substitute for genuine contact with the next generation. The piling up of gifts of playthings cannot replace actual time spent with children. Toys can and should represent parents' values and express a sharing with children, but they cannot be surrogates for real interaction between parents and children. The toybox alone does not shape childhood. Playthings must embody messages from the older generation to the next. But, especially in an age of mass consumption, the adult messenger must be there to give meaning to the things of play.

NOTES

1. Their Toys and Ours

1. Nancy Carlsson-Paige and Diane Levin, *Who's Calling the Shots? How to Respond Effectively to Children's Fascination with War Play and War Toys* (Philadelphia: New Society, 1990); C. Miller, "Flat Feet and Big Hips," *Marketing News*, Sept. 30, 1991, 2.
2. Leah Yarrow, "Should Children Play with Guns?"; Jean Mamollo, "Pistol Packing Kids," *Parents' Magazine*, Jan. 1983, 50–55.
3. Donald Heimburger, ed., *A. C. Gilbert's Heritage* (River Forest, Ill.: Heimburger House, 1983); A. C. Gilbert with Marshall McClintock, *The Man Who Lives in Paradise* (New York: Rinehart, 1954).
4. "Hasbro: Merging with Milton Bradley," *Business Week,* May 21, 1984, 90; "Hasbro Inc.," in *Notable Corporate Chronologies,* ed. Susan Martin (New York: Gale Research, 1995), 802–803; "Mattel Gets All Dolled Up," *U.S. News and World Report,* Dec. 13, 1993, 74–77.
5. Sydney L. Stern and Ted Schoenhaus, *Toyland: The High-Stakes Game of the Toy Industry* (New York: Contemporary Books, 1990); *Antique and Hobby Collectors* (July 1991), 39, 50.
6. Cy Schneider, *Children's Television: The Art, The Business, and How It Works* (Chicago: NTC Business Books, 1987), 19–21; D. Kunkel and D. Roberts, "Young Minds and Marketplace Values: Issues in Children's Television Advertising," *Journal of Social Issues,* 47, no. 1 (1991): 57–72.
7. Carol Markowski, *Tomart's Price Guide to Action Figure Collectibles* (Dayton,

Oh.: Tomart, 1992), 106–107; Toy Manufacturers of America, *Toy Industry Fact Book* (New York, 1993), 9, 21.

8. Anne Koopman, *Charles P. Lazarus: The Titan of Toys "R" Us* (Ada, Ok.: Garrett Educational, 1992).

9. James Forkan, "Toy Companies Use Tie-Ins to Pad Ad Efforts," *Advertising Age*, Aug. 12, 1985, 64; "Toys in Hamburgerland," *Newsweek*, Dec. 12, 1988, 50.

10. Toy Manufacturers of America, *Toy Industry Fact Book* (New York, 1987 and 1994), 3, 7; Richard Levy and Ronald Weingartner, *Inside Santa's Workshop* (New York: Henry Holt, 1990), 131.

2. Modern Childhood, Modern Toys

1. Marshall Field, *Marshall Field Toy Catalogue, 1892–1893* (rpt. Prairie Winds Press, 1969).

2. Max von Boehn, *Dolls and Puppets*, trans. Josephine Nicoll (London: Harrap, 1932), chs. 1, 2, 8; J. P. V. D. Balsdon, *Life and Leisure in Ancient Rome* (London, 1969), 115–126; Mark Golden, *Childhood in Classical Athens* (Baltimore: Johns Hopkins University Press, 1990).

3. Mihaly Csikszentmihalyi and Eugene Rochberg-Halton, *The Meaning of Things* (Cambridge: Cambridge University Press, 1981), 50–51; Brian Sutton-Smith, *Toys as Culture* (New York: Gardner, 1986), 138.

4. Roland Caillois, *Man, Play and Games*, trans. Meyer Barash (New York: Free Press, 1962), 58.

5. Ruth Freeman, *American Dolls* (Watkins Glen, N.Y.: Century House, 1952), 19; Caillois, *Play and Games*, 57–58, 111–140; Boehn, *Dolls and Puppets*, esp. chs. 6–8.

6. Antonia Fraser, *A History of Toys* (New York: Delacorte, 1966), 44, 61–62, 66; Boehn, *Dolls and Puppets*, 112; Karl Grober, *Children's Toys of Bygone Days*, trans. Josephine Nicoll (London: Badsford, 1928), 20–22; Philippe Ariès, *Centuries of Childhood*, trans. Robert Baldick (New York: Knopf, 1962).

7. Dan Foley, *Toys through the Ages* (Philadelphia, 1962), pp.13–18; H. Weis, *Jumping Jacks* (Trenton, N.J.: Edward Chilton Bros., 1945), 24–25.

8. Alfred Chapuis, *Automata: A Historical and Technical Study* (Paris: Droz, 1958); Mary Hillier, *Automata and Mechanical Toys* (London: Jupiter, 1976).

9. Constance King, *Antique Toys and Dolls* (New York: Rizzoli, 1978), 9–11; Lesley Gordon, *Peepshow into Paradise* (New York: Harrap, 1953), 105–121.

10. Ester Singleton, *Dolls* (New York: Payson and Clarke, 1927); Leonie von Wilckens, *The Dolls' House* (London: Bell and Hyman, 1980), 8, 61–62.

11. Grober, *Children's Toys*, 34–39.

12. Ibid., 18.

13. Wendy Levitt, *Folk Dolls* (New York: Knopf, 1982), 19, 30–69, 60–82.

14. Ruth Freeman and Larry Freeman, *Cavalcade of Toys* (Watkins Glen, N.Y.:

Century House, 1942), 64, 92–96; Grober, *Children's Toys*, 15–32; Boehn, *Dolls and Puppets*, 42–47, 162–170.

15. Foley, *Toys*, ch. 8.

16. Constance King, *Collector's History of Dolls* (New York: St. Martin's, 1977), esp. 81–82; D. Richter, *China, Parian and Bisque German Dolls* (Grantsville, Md.: Hobby House, 1976), 10–11; Singleton, *Dolls*, 51–55; Fraser, *History of Toys*, 47–53, 93, 103; Freeman, *American Dolls*, 20–38, 90; Grober, *Children's Toys*, 15–18, 31–36, 47–52; Boehn, *Dolls and Puppets*, 155–156, 162–170.

17. John Locke, *Some Thoughts on Education* (Cambridge: Cambridge University Press, 1968), 211–212.

18. Rousseau, *Emile*, cited in Sol Cohen, ed., *Education in the United States* (New York: Random House, 1974), 1207.

19. John Brewer, "Genesis of the Modern Toy," in Karen Hewett and Louise Roomet, *Educational Toys in America, 1800 to the Present* (Burlington, Vt.: Robert Hull Fleming Museum, 1979), 7–9; J. H. Plumb, "The New World of the Child in Eighteenth-Century England," *Past and Present* 67 (May 1975): 64–93.

20. Fraser, *History of Toys*, 63; Katherine McClinton, *Antiques of American Childhood* (New York: Bramhall House, 1970), ch. 12; Inez and Marshall McClintock, *Toys in America* (Washington: Public Affairs Press, 1961), 22, 67, 78–84; Freeman and Freeman, *Cavalcade*, 213.

21. Anne Scott MacLeod, "The *Caddie Woodlawn* Syndrome: American Girlhood in the Nineteenth Century," in Mary Heininger, ed., *A Century of Childhood* (Rochester, N.Y.: Margaret Woodbury Strong Museum, 1984), 97–108; Karin Calvert, *Children in the House: The Material Culture of Early Childhood, 1600–1900* (Boston: Northeastern University Press, 1992), 1–18, 47–51, 80–81, 110–119; Bernard Mergen, "Made, Bought, and Stolen: Toys and the Culture of Childhood," in Eliott West and Paula Petrik, eds., *Small Worlds: Children and Adolescents in America, 1850–1950* (Lawrence: University of Kansas Press, 1992), 86–94.

22. Blair Whitton, *Toys* (New York: Chanticleer, 1984), 436–437, 447; idem, *American Clockwork Toys, 1862–1900* (Exton, Pa.: Schiffer, 1981), 18–49.

23. Whitton, *Toys*, 436; Freeman and Freeman, *Cavalcade*, 211–227; McClinton, *Antiques*, 272–273; Bernard Barenholtz, *American Antique Toys, 1830–1900* (New York: Abrams, 1980); Don Cranmer, *Cast Iron and Tin Toys of Yesterday* (Gas City, Ind., 1974); Hillier, *Automata*, 83–93.

24. Freeman and Freeman, *Cavalcade*, 115–152, 321–335; McClintock and McClintock, *Toys in America*, 255–256; Hillier, *Automata*, ch. 2.

25. Daniel Rodgers, *The Work Ethic in Industrial America* (Chicago: University of Chicago Press, 1974), ch. 4.

26. Althof, Bergmann, *Illustrated Catalogue of Mechanical Toys* (1874; rpt. Antique Toy Collectors of America, 1975); Louis Hertz, *Handbook of Old American Toys* (Wethersfield, Conn.: Mark Haber, 1947), ch. 6.

27. Hillier, *Automata*, 88.

28. Erlich Bros., *Fashion Quarterly* (1880; rpt. in *Antique and Toy World*, Sept. 1990), 110–114; Automatic Toy Works, *Automatic Toy Works Illustrated Catalogue to the Trade* (New York, 1882), 3–10, 13; Hillier, *Automata*, 85–89; Whitton, *Clockwork Toys*, 90–92, 153–160, 184.

29. Joseph Schroeder, *The Wonderful World of Toys, Games, and Dolls, 1860–1930* (Chicago: Follett, 1971), 17; Francis Hughes, *Toy Catalogue* (Rochester, N.Y., 1890), 29.

30. Stevens and Brown, *Illustrated Price List of Tin, Mechanical and Iron Toys* (1872), 90–91, 98, 100–101, 28–31; Ives, Blakeslee and Williams, *Iron Toys, Wood Toys, Tin Toys: Games and Novelties* (1893; rpt. Coalport, Pa.: L. C. Hegarty, 1965), 56–58, 60–63; Erlich Bros., *Toy Price List* (1882), 3–4;

31. Gordon Craig, *Gordon Craig's Book of Penny Toys* (London, 1899); David Pressman, *The Book of Penny Toys* (London: New Cavendish Books, 1991).

32. Roger Silverstone and Eric Hirsch, *Consuming Technologies: Media and Information in Domestic Spaces* (London and New York: Routledge, 1992).

33. David Hounshell, *From American System to Mass Production, 1800–1932* (Baltimore: Johns Hopkins University Press, 1984); Alfred D. Chandler Jr., *The Visible Hand: The Managerial Revolution in American Business* (Cambridge, Mass.: Harvard University Press, 1978).

34. Sources for the paragraphs on the new shopping outlets include Chandler, *Visible Hand*, ch. 7; Susan Strasser, *Satisfaction Guaranteed: The Making of the American Mass Market* (New York: Basic Books, 1989), ch. 7; John W. Ferry, *A History of the Department Store* (New York: Macmillan, 1960), ch. 3; Godfrey Lebhar, *Chain Stores in America, 1859–1962* (New York: Chain Store Publications, 1963), 27–47; Daniel Boorstin, *The Americans: The Democratic Experience* (New York: Random House, 1973), 91–129.

35. William Leach, *Land of Desire: Merchants, Power, and the Rise of a New American Culture* (New York: Pantheon, 1993), 22, 44–45.

36. Boris Emmet and John Jeuck, *Catalogues and Counters: A History of Sears, Roebuck and Company* (Chicago: University of Chicago Press, 1950).

37. Susan Strasser, *Never Done: A History of American Housework* (New York: Basic Books, 1982), ch. 1; Frank Presbrey, *The History and Development of Advertising* (Garden City, N.Y.: Doubleday, 1929), 374–413, 419–420.

38. Presbrey, *Advertising*, 446–489; Strasser, *Satisfaction Guaranteed*, ch. 4.

39. Freeman and Freeman, *Cavalcade*, 258, 383; Hertz, *Handbook*, 6–7 and ch. 6; Constance King, *Metal Toys and Automata* (Secaucus, N.J.: Chartwell, 1989), 46–47; "Morton Converse," *Playthings* (hereafter *PT*), April 1908, 32; McClintock and McClintock, *Toys in America*, ch. 14.

40. Department of Commerce, *Census of the United States: Manufacturers: 1929*, vol. II: *Reports by Industry* (Washington, 1933), 1195 (figures include wagons and sleds); Laurence Greenfield, "Toys, Children, and the Toy Industry in a Culture of Consumption, 1890–1991" (Ph.D. diss., Ohio State University, 1991), 42–48, 102; Fraser, *History of Toys*, 206; Freeman and Freeman, *Cavalcade*, 356–366, 382–383.

41. McClintock and McClintock, *Toys in America*, 350; Sears, Roebuck and Co., *Catalogue* (Chicago, 1911 and 1931); Schroeder, *Wonderful World*, 11–20; Freeman and Freeman, *Cavalcade*, 378–380; Leach, *Land of Desire*, 85–87.
42. Greenfield, "Toys, Children," 114–115; Leach, *Land of Desire*, ch. 3; "The Lure of the Window," *PT*, Nov. 1909, 35–36.
43. Whitton, *Toys*, 116.
44. "Selling Toys to the Middle Classes," *PT*, Dec. 1912, 70; "The Advertisement," *PT*, Dec. 1909, 65; Daisy Air Rifle ad, *PT*, Jan. 1913, 34.
45. "Editorial," *Toys and Novelties*, June 1913, 70; "Mother Buys the Toys," *PT*, Oct. 1913, 88.
46. Horsman ad, *McCall's*, Dec. 1928, 72; Knapp Toy ad, *Child's Life*, Dec. 1931, 694; Lionel Trains ad, *American Boy*, Oct. 1918, 45; "Lionel Electric Train Catalogue" (1932), Warshaw Collection, Smithsonian Institution, Toys, Box 3, File 12.
47. Arcade ad, *PT*, Aug. 1919, 197; Effanbee Dolls ad, Oct. 1919, 7; Greenfield, "Toys, Children," 102.
48. "Shall It Be 'Uncle Sam's Day,'" *PT*, March 1916, 104–105; "Children's Day Is New," *PT*, April 1929, 65; "The Toy Department—12 Months in the Year," *PT*, Sept. 1910, 54–55.
49. Homer Sinclair, *Toy Manufacture and Marketing: A Text Book for Toy Producers* (Springfield, Ill., Phillips Bros., 1931), 16, 34–37, 52–56; "Fallacy of Price Cutting," *PT*, Oct. 1910, 64; "How the J. C. Penney Co. Views Toys," *PT*, July 1928, 75.
50. Ruth S. Cowan, *More Work for Mother* (New York: Basic Books, 1983); Phyllis Palmer, *Domesticity and Dirt: Housewives and Domestic Servants in the United States* (Philadelphia: Temple University Press, 1990); Strasser, *Never Done*.
51. E.g., Daniel Scott Smith, "Family Limitation, Sexual Control and Domestic Feminism in Victorian America," *Feminist Studies*, 1 (Spring 1973): 40–57.
52. Ann Douglas, *The Feminization of American Culture* (New York: Knopf, 1977), ch. 4; Mary Ryan, *Cradle of the Middle Class: The Family in Oneida County, New York, 1790–1865* (New York: Cambridge University Press, 1983), 163.
53. Sutton-Smith, *Toys as Culture*, chs. 2–3, 245.
54. Ryan, *Cradle of the Middle Class*, 98–100; Joseph Kett, *Rites of Passage: Adolescence in America, 1790 to the Present* (New York, Basic Books, 1977), ch. 5; F. J. Darton, *Children's Books in England: Five Centuries of Social Life* (Cambridge: Cambridge University Press, 1958), 298–314; William Dewees, *Treatise on the Physical and Medical Treatment of Children* (Philadelphia, 1826), cited in Heininger, *Century of Childhood*, 6–8; Sutton-Smith, *Toys as Culture*, 27, 225, 245.
55. Heininger, *Century of Childhood*, 3–6.
56. Horace Bushnell, *Christian Nurture* (1847; New Haven: Yale University Press, 1967), 292.

57. Anne Scott MacLeod, *A Moral Tale: Children's Fiction and American Culture, 1820–1860* (Hamden, Conn.: Archon, 1975), 20–24.

58. Brian Sutton-Smith and B. G. Rosenberg, "Sixty Years of a Historical Changing in the Game Preferences of American Children," in R. E. Herron and Brian Sutton-Smith, eds., *Child's Play* (New York: John Wiley, 1971), 33.

59. See Antique Toy Collectors of America, ed., *Crandall's Wholesale Price List for 1879–80*, with historical introduction by Blair Whitton.

60. "Crandall's Wide Awake Alphabet: No More Long Faces over ABC"; "Charles L Crandall Centennial Presents for the Little Ones"; and "Crandall's Latest! The District School" ads in the *American Agriculturalist* (July 1876 and 1877), Strong Museum.

61. "Crandall's Latest! The District School" ad; McClintock and McClintock, *Toys in America*, ch. 8.

62. Susan Manos, *Schoenhut Dolls and Toys: A Loving Legacy* (Paducah, Ky.: Collector Books, 1976); Elaine and Dan Buser, *Buser's Guide to Schoenhut's Dolls, Toys and Circuses, 1872–1976* (Paducah, Ky.: Collector Books, 1976); Carol Corson, *Schoenhut Dolls* (Cumberland, Md.: Hobby House, 1993).

63. Schoenhut ad, *PT*, May 1908, 10–11; Manos, *Schoenhut*, 10–11; Mary Hillier, *A Pageant of Toys* (New York: Taplinger, 1966), 97–100; Corson, *Schoenhut Dolls*, 8–16.

64. Corson, *Schoenhut Dolls*, 6–9; Schoenhut ad, *PT*, May 1908, 12–13.

65. Schoenhut, *Price List* (Philadelphia, 1915), 1–17, quotations 16–17; Schoenhut, *Price List* (Philadelphia, 1911), 3–17.

66. Schoenhut, *Dolls: Illustrated Catalogue* (Philadelphia, 1911), 3–17; Schoenhut ad, *The Delineator*, Dec. 1914, 43; Schoenhut, *Price List* (1915), 26–29; Schoenhut ads, "Ayer Collection," Smithsonian Institution, Box 138.

67. Schoenhut, *Price List* (1915), 26–29, 34–35.

68. Schoenhut, *Price List* (Philadelphia, 1928, 1930); Schoenhut ad, *PT*, March 1927, 9; Schoenhut ad, *Ladies' Home Journal*, Nov. 1925, 186.

69. William Waits, *The Modern Christmas in America: A Cultural History of Gift Giving* (New York: New York University Press, 1993), ch. 2; Penne Restad, *Christmas in America: A History* (New York: Oxford University Press, 1995), 17–41, 91–104; Stephen Nissenbaum, *Battle for Christmas* (New York: Knopf, 1996).

70. Paul Davis, *The Lives and Times of Ebenezer Scrooge* (New Haven: Yale University Press, 1990), ch. 1 and pp. 35, 85–87.

71. Marcel Mauss, *The Gift* (New York: Norton, 1967), 37, 69, 76; R. Belk, "A Child's Christmas in America: Santa Claus as Deity, Consumption as Religion," *Journal of American Culture*, 11, no. 1 (1987): 89.

72. Restad, *Christmas in America*, 57–74; Dan Miller, ed., *Unwrapping Christmas* (Oxford: Clarendon Press, 1993), 18–19.

73. Waits, *Modern Christmas*, 1–12; Miller, *Unwrapping Christmas*, 18–19; James Carrier, "Rituals of Christmas Giving," in Miller, *Unwrapping Christmas*, 66–70.

74. Thorstein Veblen, *The Theory of the Leisure Class* (1899; Boston: Houghton Mifflin, 1973), esp. chs. 3–4; Carrier, "Rituals," 64–65.
75. This is a major theme in Waits, *Modern Christmas*.
76. James Carrier, "Gifts in a World of Commodities: The Ideology of the Perfect Gift in American Society," *Social Analysis*, 29 (1990): 19–37; David Cheal, "'Showing Them You Love Them': Gift Giving and the Dialectic of Intimacy," *Sociological Review*, 35 (1987): 150–169; Belk, "A Child's Christmas."
77. Waits, *Modern Christmas*, bibliographical notes, 238–240.
78. "Should Santa Claus Be Banished?" *Parents' Magazine*, 1, no. 3 (Dec. 1926): 3.
79. R. Belk, "Materialism and the Making of Modern American Christmas," in Miller, *Unwrapping Christmas*, 75–104.
80. Leach, *Land of Desire*, 89–90, 337; Waits, *Modern Christmas*, 130–133; "Everybody Helps in Los Angeles," *PT*, Dec. 1930, 74.

3. Shaping the Child's Future

1. Roland Marchand, "Precocious Consumers and Junior Salesmen: Advertising to Children in the United States to 1940" manuscript.
2. "Premium List," *American Boy*, Nov. 1916, 45–49; "Awards," *Youth Companion*, Oct. 26, 1922, 618; "Lettie Lane," *Ladies' Home Journal*, Dec. 1912, 40.
3. "Scientific Toys," *Playthings* (hereafter *PT*), July 1934, 33–34; Lionel Trains ad, *American Boy*, Oct. 1918, 45.
4. "Seven Acres of Toys," *Literary Digest*, April 17, 1937, 38.
5. Patricia Tice, "Gardens of Change," in Jessica Foy and Thomas Schlereth, eds., *American Home Life, 1880–1930* (Knoxville: University of Tennessee Press, 1992), 190–208.
6. G. Basalla, *The Evolution of Technology* (Cambridge: Cambridge University Press, 1988).
7. *Popular Mechanics* (1912), 93, 122, 281; (1923), 139, 229, 278, 651, 789; Thomas St. John, *Real Electric Toy Making for Boys* (New York, 1905); Margaret Marsh, *Suburban Lives* (New Brunswick: Rutgers University Press, 1990), chs. 2–3; Steven Gelber, "Homo Faber: Tools, Gender and Do-It-Yourself," manuscript.
8. Robert Griswold, "'Ties That Bind and Bonds That Break': Children's Attitudes toward Fathers, 1900–1930," in Eliott West and Paula Petrik, eds., *Small Worlds: Children and Adolescents in America, 1850–1950* (Lawrence: University of Kansas Press, 1992), 256–257.
9. Blair Whitton, *Toys* (New York: Chanticleer, 1984), 442; idem, *American Clockwork Toys, 1862–1900* (Exton, Pa.: Schiffer, 1981), 171–174.
10. Ives Manufacturing ad, *American Boy*, Nov. 1916, 23; Ives Toys advertising flyer (n.d.); *Lionel Electric Trains* (Chicago, 1931); American Flyer, *American*

Flyer Trains (Chicago, 1932), 7 (all in Warshaw Collection, Toys Box 2, File 10).

11. *American Flyer Trains*, 7; Ives Manufacturing Corp., *Ives Toys Make Happy Boys* (1923; rpt. Pittsburgh: House of Heeg, 1975), 24.

12. Hubley Manufacturing, *Catalogue of Iron and Steel Toys* (Lancaster, Pa., 1906, 1928), 3; Arcade Manufacturing Co., *Arcade Cast Iron Toys*, no. 40 (Freeport, Ill., 1932); Dowst Manufacturing, *Tootsietoys, 1933* (Chicago, 1933).

13. Lillian Gottschalk, *American Toy Cars and Trucks: 1894–1942* (New York: Abbeville, 1985), 1–34, 120, 172–173; Whitton, *Toys*, 297, 439, 315, 302; Butler Bros., *Toys for Boys* (1930; rpt. Chattanooga: Antique Research Publ., 1968), 17–30; Eduardo Massucci, *Cars for Kids* (New York: Rizzoli, 1991), 8–18; Anderson Electric ad, *PT*, June 1911, 163; Hubley Manufacturing, *Iron and Steel Toys* (1928).

14. On women and cars see Virginia Scharff, *Taking the Wheel: Women and the Coming of the Motor Age* (New York: Free Press, 1991).

15. Aero Flying Machine ad, *PT*, Feb. 1911, 103; American Aeroplane Manufacturing ad, ibid., 32; "Gimbel's Model Airplane League," *PT*, June 1932, 38; Keystone Toys ad, *PT*, Jan. 1930, 67; Metal Craft Corporation ad, *Junior Home* (Dec. 1928), 27–28; Ideal Aeroplane and Supply Co. ad, *St. Nicholas*, May 15, 1934.

16. Moline Pressed Steel Corp., *The Story of Buddy "L"* (East Moline, Ill., 1925, rpt. 1975).

17. David Pressland, *The Art of Tin Toys* (London: New Cavendish, 1992), 230; Karen Hewitt and Louis Roomet, *Educational Toys in America: 1800 to the Present* (Burlington, Vt.: Robert Hull Fleming Museum, 1979), 76–78.

18. Educational Committee of the Antique Toy Collectors of America, *American Live Steam Toys and Their Originators* (1978) 1–15; Ives, Blakeslee, and Williams, *Iron Toys* (1893; rpt. Coalport, Pa.: L. C. Hegarty, 1965), 56–58; Stevens and Brown, *Illustrated Price List* (New York, 1872), 90; Marshall Field, *Marshall Field Toy Catalogue, 1892–1893* (Chicago, 1892–93, rpt. Prairie Winds Press, 1969), 12–14; L. H. Mace and Co., *Illustrated Catalogue* (New York, 1907), 83.

19. Sears, Roebuck, *Toys, Games, and Playthings* (Chicago, 1919), 29; Weeden Steam Engine ad, *PT*, March 1948, 105.

20. Erlich Bros., *Toy Price List* (New York, 1882, rpt. 1970); Ives, *Iron Toys* (1893), 64–65; Marshall Field, *Toy Catalogue 1892–1893*, 21–35; E. I. Horsman, *Catalogue of Horsman Specialties* (New York, 1914), 32.

21. Joseph Schroeder, *The Wonderful World of Toys, Games, and Dolls, 1860–1930* (Chicago: Follett, 1971), 128–129; Alco Gas Appliances Dept. ad (Reflectoscope), *PT*, Aug. 1908, 12; J. J. Duck ad, *American Boy*, Nov. 1914, 33.

22. Whitton, *Toys*, 16; Erin Cho, "Lincoln Logs: Toying with the Frontier Myth," *History Today*, 43 (April 1993): 31–34.

23. Bureau of the Census, *Statistical History of the United States from Colonial Times to the Present* (Washington, 1965), 10, 71.

24. American Toy Shop, *"Tyro" Wooden Construction Blocks; Instructive, Scientific, Amusing* (Milwaukee, 1910); Structo Toys, *Illustrated Price List* (1931; rpt. Columbia, Md.: Greenberg, 1975); Structo ad, *American Boy*, Nov. 1916, 21; Sears, Roebuck, *Toys* (1919), 8–9.
25. See Ives Manufacturing catalog, *The Railroad That Six Boys Built: They Built Lots of Other Things Too* (Bridgeport, Conn., 1920); Ives, *Ives Toys;* Structo Toys, *Price List;* American Mechanical Toy Co., *The Toy for the Boy* (Dayton, Oh., 1915); American Flyer, *A Famous Railroad President: A Story for Boys* (Chicago, 1923).
26. Mysto Manufacturing ad, *PT,* Jan. 1911, 99; A. C. Gilbert with Marshall McClintock, *The Man Who Lives in Paradise* (New York: Rinehart, 1953), esp. chs. 1–3; William Bean, *Greenberg's Guide to Gilbert Erector Sets,* I (Sykesville, Md.: Greenberg, 1993), esp. 14–15, 39–41.
27. Gilbert, *Paradise,* 111, 138–139, 159–162, 258, 329–333.
28. E.g., A. C. Gilbert ad, *St. Nicholas,* July 1915, 45; "A Success Story," *PT,* Oct. 1916, 182; Gilbert, *Paradise,* 126, 131, 136, 156; A. C. Gilbert, *Manual of Instruction* (New Haven, 1915); idem, *Manual of Instructions: The New Erector Builds the Most Models* (New Haven, 1933); Meccano Co., *How to Make Models and Toys with Meccano* (Liverpool, 1915).
29. Gilbert ad, *PT,* Jan. 1921, 201–206; Gilbert ad, *American Boy,* Dec. 1920, 157.
30. Gilbert, *Paradise,* 135.
31. M. P. Gould, *Frank Hornby: The Boy Who Made $1,000,000 with a Toy* (New York, 1915), 4, 8–25; Meccano ad, *St. Nicholas,* Sept. 1915, 31.
32. Porter Chemicals ad, *Youth's Companion,* Dec. 7, 1922, 711; Porter Chemicals ad, *PT,* April 1929, 33.
33. Ives Manufacturing, *Ives Miniature Railway News* (Bridgeport, Conn., 1926).
34. Meccano, *Models and Toys* (1915, 1918); Meccano ad, *PT,* Jan. 1926, 189–190; A. C. Gilbert, *Manual of Instruction* (New Haven, 1915).
35. Schroeder, *Wonderful World,* 81, 127, 134, 141, 164–165, 207; Sears, Roebuck, *Catalogue* (Chicago, 1911), 865, and (1919), 28; James Spero, ed. , *Collectible Toys and Games of the Twenties and Thirties from Sears, Roebuck and Co. Catalogs* (New York: Dover, 1988), 19, 33, 70, 84.
36. Catharine E. Beecher and Harriet Beecher Stowe, *American Woman's Home* (Boston, 1869), 299, cited in Miriam Formanek-Brunell, *Made to Play House: Dolls and the Commercialization of American Girlhood, 1830–1930* (New Haven: Yale University Press, 1993), 11; Susan Strasser, *Never Done: A History of American Housework* (New York: Basic Books, 1982), ch. 7; David Hounshell, *From American System to Mass Production, 1800–1932* (Baltimore: Johns Hopkins University Press, 1984); Butterick Rag Doll ad, *Delineator,* Dec. 1907, 1085.
37. Formanek-Brunell, *Made to Play House,* 10–20; Max von Boehn, *Dolls and Puppets* (London: Harrap, 1932), esp. 157–161.
38. Erlich Bros., *Illustrated Catalogue* (1882).
39. Dorothy Coleman, *The Collector's Encyclopedia of Dolls* (New York, 1968),

143, 152; Madeline Merrill, *The Art of Dolls, 1700–1940* (Cumberland, Md.: Hobby House, 1985), 188–273.

40. Bureau of the Census, *Statistical History*, 22–23.
41. Dorothy Washburn, "Doll Oral History Project, Final Report," typescript, 1987, Strong Museum, 12, 20, 21, 36, and interviews #64, 6, and #49, 3–4. G. Stanley Hall found that 76% of boys played with dolls until age twelve. "A Study of Dolls," *Pedagogical Seminary*, 1 (Dec. 1896): 133–134.
42. Washburn, "Doll Oral History," 34, and interviews #63, 4–5, and #41, 6, 11.
43. Marshall Field, *Toy Catalogue* (Chicago, 1890), 1–8, and (1892), 11.
44. E.g., Strasser, *Never Done;* Ruth S. Cowan, *More Work for Mother* (New York: Basic Books, 1983).
45. Ives, *Iron Toys* (1893), 46; L. H. Mace, *Illustrated Catalogue* (1907), 54, 76–78; Hubley ad, *PT*, Jan. 1929, 10–11; Metal Ware ad, ibid., 87; Schroeder, *Wonderful World*, 240; Morton Converse, *Toys* (Winchendon, Mass., 1913), 10–11; *1914 Marshall Field Doll Catalogue* (rpt. Cumberland, Md.: Hobby House, 1980), 83, 91.
46. Flora Jacobs, *A History of Doll Houses* (New York: Scribner's, 1953), 170–177. R. Bliss was also a major innovator in folding cardboard dollhouses from 1895. Blair Whitton, ed., *Bliss Toys and Doll Houses* (New York: Dover, 1979), 10–20.
47. Schroeder, *Wonderful World*, 125; Sears, Roebuck, *Toys* (1919), 3; Structo ad, *Youth's Companion*, Nov. 30, 1922, 687; Chemcraft ad, *Youth's Companion*, Dec. 2, 1920, 752; Bureau of the Census, *Statistical History*, 133.
48. Christine Frederick, *Household Engineering* (New York: American Association of Home Economics, 1920), 8; Sears, Roebuck, *Catalogue*, no. 163 (Chicago, 1931), 656. See also Margaret Adams, *Collectible Dolls and Accessories of the Twenties and Thirties from Sears, Roebuck and Co. Catalogs* (New York: Dover, 1986).
49. S&G Importing ad for Pet's Toy Grocery, *PT*, July 1909, 33.
50. Formanek-Brunell, *Made to Play House*, 90–92, 104–105, 109–116; Merrill, *Art of Dolls*, 287–290, 358–362.
51. Horsman Dolls, *Horsman Rag Dolls* (New York, 1912), 2–4; "The Story of the American Doll," *PT*, Sept. 1938, 116–117.
52. Formanek-Brunell, *Made to Play House*, ch. 4; Inez and Marshall McClintock, *Toys in America* (Washington: Public Affairs Press, 1961), 364–365.
53. Horsman Dolls, *Catalog of Horsman Specialties* (New York, 1914), 6–8, 18–20; Horsman Dolls, *Rag Dolls; Sears, Roebuck, Catalogue*, no. 149 (Chicago, 1924), 515; no. 157 (1927), 624; no. 128 (1928), 476–488.
54. Berwick Dolls, *Famlee Doll Sets* (New York, 1925); Washburn, "Doll Oral History," 19, 21, 34, 43.
55. M. Kelly Ellenburg, *Effanbee—The Dolls with the Golden Hearts* (North Kansas City, Mo.: Trojan Press, 1973), 13–16; Patricia Schoonmaker, *The Effanbee Patsy Family and Related Types* (North Hollywood: Doll Research Project, 1971), 1–15 and 20–35.

56. Effanbee Dolls, "My Doll's Magazine" (New York, 1931); Schoonmaker, *Effanbee*, 50, 66; Polly Judd, *Composition Dolls* (Cumberland, Md.: Hobby House, 1991), 77–78.
57. Effanbee ads, *PT*, July 1928, 7, and Jan. 1929, 29.
58. Ellenburg, *Effanbee*, 87, 90; Schroeder, *Wonderful World*, 241.
59. Paul Bourcier, *Dolls and Duty: Martha Chase and the Progressive Agenda, 1889–1925* (Providence: Rhode Island Historical Society, 1989); Formanek-Brunell, *Made to Play House*, ch. 3.
60. Bye-Lo Baby ads, *Ladies' Home Journal*, Oct. 1925, 234, and *McCall's*, Oct. 1925, 98, and Nov. 1925, 90; Bubbles ad, ibid., Nov. 1927, in Ellenburg, *Effanbee*, 48.
61. Ellenburg, *Effanbee*, 17; Effanbee Dolls, *What Every Young Doll Mother Should Know* (New York, 1937).
62. Sears, Roebuck, *Catalogue*, no. 163 (Chicago, 1931), 1042; Effanbee ad, *PT*, Dec. 1927, 251; Nancy Gordon, *Woman's Body, Woman's Right: A Social History of Birth Control* (New York: Grossman, 1976), chs. 7–8; Carol McCann, *Birth Control Politics in the United States, 1916–1945* (Ithaca: Cornell University Press, 1994).
63. E.g., Effanbee ads, *PT*, Jan. 1924, 2–4; Feb. 1928, 11; Jan. 1929, 29.
64. Washburn, "Doll Oral History," interviews #60, 2–4; #47, 3; #40, 18, 53, 2.
65. E.g., ibid., 35, and interview #46, 1–4; Formanek-Brunell, *Made to Play House*, 27–29, 31–34, 166.

4. Freeing the Child's Imagination

1. David Nasaw, *Going Out: The Rise and Fall of Public Amusements* (New York: Basic Books, 1993).
2. Ives, Blakeslee and Williams, *Iron Toys, Wood Toys, Tin Toys: Games and Novelties* (1893; rpt. Coalport, Pa., L. C. Hegarty, 1965), 90–91; Blair Whitton, ed., *Bliss Toys and Doll Houses* (New York: Dover, 1979), 39, 71; Laurence Greenfield, "Toys, Children, and the Toy Industry in a Culture of Consumption, 1890–1991" (Ph.D. diss., Ohio State University, 1991), ch. 5.
3. Joleen Robinson, *Advertising Dolls* (Paducah, Ky.: Collector Books, 1980); Ruth Freeman, *American Dolls* (Watkins Glen, N.Y.: Century House, 1952), 11, 31–35, 64–68, 85–91; Miriam Formanek-Brunell, *Made to Play House: Dolls and the Commercialization of American Girlhood, 1830–1930* (New Haven: Yale University Press, 1993), 90–92.
4. Formanek-Brunell, *Made to Play House*, chs. 4–5.
5. Viviana Zelizer, *Pricing the Priceless Child: The Changing Social Value of Children* (New York: Basic Books, 1985), 3–21, 103–112.
6. William Leach, *Land of Desire: Merchants, Power, and the Rise of a New American Culture* (New York: Pantheon, 1993); "Editorial," *Playthings* (hereafter *PT*), June 1917, 60.

7. Humphrey Carpenter, *Secret Gardens: A Study of the Golden Age of Children's Literature* (Boston: Houghton Mifflin, 1985), 14–16, 23–44, 106–114.

8. Max Luethi, *Once upon a Time: On the Nature of Fairy Tales,* trans. Lee Chadeayen and Paul Gootwald (New York: Fungar, 1970), 44, 46, 51.

9. Formanek-Brunell, *Made to Play House,* ch. 7.

10. Bruce Whitehill, *Games: American Boxed Games and Their Makers, 1882–1992* (Radnor, Pa.: Wallace-Homestead, 1992); Parker Bros., *75 Years of Fun: The Story of Parker Brothers, Inc.* (Salem, Mass.: 1958), 20–24; Joseph Schroeder, *The Wonderful World of Toys, Games, and Dolls, 1860–1930* (Chicago: Follett, 1971), 78; Parker Bros., *Games* (Salem, 1891), 5.

11. Horsman ad, *PT,* Oct. 1909, 3; "Philadelphia," *PT,* Feb. 1908, 88; Schoenhut ad, *PT,* May 1908, 8.

12. Various Diabolo sets were offered by Parker Brothers, Milton Bradley, Horsman, G. Borgfeldt, and Art Novelty in *PT,* Jan. 1908, 29, 21, 3, 35, 47; "Imported Toys: Diabolo Doll!" *PT,* Feb. 1908, 84; ""Chronological History of *Playthings,*" *PT,* Sept. 1938, 98–114.

13. Roger W. Cummins, *Humorous but Wholesome: A History of Palmer Cox and the Brownies* (Watkins Glen, N.Y.: Century House, 1973); L. McCullock, "The Brownie Man, Palmer Cox," *American Collector,* 34 (Aug. 1976): 19–26.

14. Schroeder, *Wonderful World,* 94; Walbridge and Co., *Illustrated Catalogue* (New York, 1894), 26.

15. Kenny Harman, *Comic Strip Toys* (Des Moines: Wallace-Homestead, 1975), 5–7, 13–35, 51–56, 70–72; David Longest, *Character Toys and Collectibles* (Paducah, Ky.: Collector Books, 1992), I, 14–28.

16. "Domestic Toys," *PT,* Dec. 1909, 40, 86; Samstag and Hilder Bros. ad for Snookums, *PT,* Jan. 1910, 18; "Trade Notes," *PT,* June 1911, 198; Mysto Manufacturing ad, *PT,* April 1912, 192; Live Long Toy ad, *PT,* Jan. 1924, 152–153.

17. See, e.g., Arthur Berger, *The Comic-Stripped American* (Baltimore: Penguin, 1973); Reinhold Reitberger and Wolfgang Fuchs, *The Comics: An Anatomy of a Mass Medium* (Boston: Little, Brown, 1973).

18. Harman, *Comic Strip Toys,* 35–38; Freeman, *American Dolls,* 36; Longest, *Character Toys,* II, 129–130; Greenfield, "Toys, Children," 268–276; Madeline Merrill, *The Art of Dolls* (Cumberland, Md.: Hobby House, 1985), 386; M. Kelly Ellenburg, *Effanbee—The Dolls with the Golden Hearts* (North Kansas City, Mo.: Trojan Press, 1973), 59.

19. "Famous People and a Famous Line" ad, *PT,* Jan. 1926, 193, 131–134; W. C. Fields doll ad, *PT,* Jan. 1929, back cover.

20. Rosamund Humm, *Children in America: A Study of Images and Attitudes* (Atlanta: High Museum of Art, 1978), 10–33.

21. "Age of Billiken," *PT,* Nov. 1908, 70; Horsman ad for Billikens, *PT,* Sept. 1910, 35; Barker and Bennett ad for Killiblues, *PT,* Sept. 1909, 112; Horsman ad for Billikens, *PT,* July 1909, 2.

22. "The Kewpies' Christmas Frolic," *Ladies' Home Journal*, Dec. 1909, 28; G. Borgfeldt ad for Kewpies, *PT*, Jan. 1913, 20–21; Schroeder, *Wonderful World*, 195.

23. One example is Marshall Field, *1892–1893 Marshall Field Toy Catalogue* (Chicago, 1892), 20.

24. Pat Schoonmaker, *A Collector's History of the Teddy Bear* (Cumberland, Md.: Hobby House, 1981); Jurgen Cieslik, *Button in Ear: A History of the Teddy Bear and His Friends* (Julich, Germany: Marianne Cieslik Verlag, 1989), esp. 17–35; Linda Mullins, *A Tribute to Teddy Bear Artists* (Grantsville, Md.: Hobby House, 1994), 72–109; Mary Hillier, *Teddy Bears: A Celebration* (London: Ebury, 1985).

25. *Ladies World Magazine* (Dec. 1908), cited in Schoonmaker, *Teddy Bears*, 82.

26. "The Teddy Bear and the Doll at Christmas," *Ladies' Home Journal*, Dec. 1907, 80; Columbia Teddy Bear ad, *PT*, Dec. 1907, 109; F. R. Bird ad, *Delineator*, Dec. 1907, 1151.

27. Schoonmaker, *Teddy Bears*, 227–241, 250–252, 280–282; Mullins, *A Tribute*, 74–80.

28. Mace Co., *Illustrated Catalogue* (New York, 1907), 66–70; Butler Bros., *Toy Catalogue* (New York, 1910), n.p.

29. "Teddy Bears," *PT*, June 1908, 100; "Chronological History," *PT*, Sept. 1938, 100–102.

30. Strobel and Wilken ad for polar bears and Eskimo dolls, *PT*, Sept. 1909, 4; Steiff ad, *PT*, Nov. 1909, 18; F. W. Woolnough ad for Winnie the Pooh bears, *Child Life*, Dec. 1930, 700; Cieslik, *Button in Ear*, 139–169, 201–209.

31. All these uses of the teddy are portrayed in Butler Bros., *Catalogue* (1910).

32. Automatic Toys Works, *Price List* (New York, 1882), 3–7; Balch Institute for Ethnic Studies, *Ethnic Images in Toys and Games: An Exhibit at the Balch Institute for Ethnic Studies* (Philadelphia, 1990), 11–12; J. and E. Stevens, *Toy Catalogue* (1900), 18; Antonia Fraser, *A History of Toys* (New York: Delacorte, 1966), 189–191.

33. "The Christmas Doll," *Ladies' Home Journal*, Dec. 1914, 75.

34. Charles Best, *Cast Iron Toy Pistols, 1870–1940* (Englewood Colo.: Rocky Mountain Arms and Antiques, 1973), 191; Ives, Blakeslee and Williams, *Iron Toys* (1893), 82; Balch Institute, *Ethnic Images*, 32–35.

35. Horsman ad, *PT*, May 1911, 3; McLoughlin Bros. *Catalogue of New Books, Games, Etc.* (New York, 1887), 54; Schroeder, *Wonderful World*, 158, 209.

36. Mace, *Toy Catalogue* (1907), 115; On On Daga Indian Wigwam Co. ad, *PT*, March 1910, 91; Schroeder, *Wonderful World*, 151.

37. Ads for the Alabama Coon Jigger, *PT*, Jan. 1913, 167, April 1918, 43, and Jan. 1921, 16; Louis Marx ad for Amos 'n' Andy cab, *PT*, March 1930, 31; S and H Novelty ad, *PT*, April 1930, 131; Balch Institute, *Ethnic Images*, 11–12; Maxine Pinsky, *Greenberg's Guide to Marx Toys*, I (Sykesville, Md.: Greenberg, 1988), ch. 6.

38. There were exceptions. Note the S. and Bicker's Sales ad for a Sambo Target Game, *PT*, Sept. 1936, 26; Pinsky, *Marx Toys*, I, 11–12, 95–96, 77, 114; Schroeder, *Wonderful World*, 248; Butler Bros., *Toys for Boys* (1930), 30.

39. *New York Times*, May 11, 1930, cited in Greenfield, "Toys, Children," 260; Bureau of the Census, *Historical Statistics of the United States* (Washington, 1975), 73, 319 (figures exclude wagons and sleds); "Christmas Shopping," *Business Week*, Dec. 16, 1933, 14–15; "The Pick Pocket," *Toys and Bicycles*, April 1938, 117; "Guest Editorial," ibid., Oct. 1936, 24.

40. Roland Vaile, *Research Memorandum on Consumption in the Depression* (Washington: Social Science Research Council, 1937), 19, 28.

41. Pinsky, *Marx Toys*, I, 24; –Tootsietoy ads, *PT*, Feb. 1930, 88, and May 1931, 36–37; Dowst Manufacturing, *Tootsietoy Catalogue* (Chicago, 1933); Homer Sinclair, *Toy Manufacture and Marketing: A Text Book for Toy Producers* (Springfield, Ill., Phillips Bros., 1931), 64–69; Meccano ad, *Child Life*, Dec. 1935, 595.

42. Robert Griswold, "'Ties That Bind and Bonds That Break': Children's Attitudes toward Fathers, 1900–1930," in Eliott West and Paula Petrik, eds., *Small Worlds: Children and Adolescents in America, 1850–1950* (Lawrence: University of Kansas Press, 1992), 266–273; Glen Elder, *Children of the Great Depression* (Chicago: University of Chicago Press, 1974), 183–187, 192.

43. See, e.g., Edgar Dale, *The Content of Motion Pictures* (New York: Macmillan, 1935); Henry J. Forman, *Our Movie Made Children* (New York: Macmillan, 1934); Herbert Blumer, *Movies and Conduct* (New York: Macmillan, 1933).

44. Adam George, "Creative Merchandising," *PT*, Jan. 1934, 12; Famous Artist Syndicate ad, *PT*, April 1936, 183.

45. "Gearing Youth for To-morrow's Profits," *PT*, July 1930, 96–97; Orrin Dunlap, *Radio in Advertising* (New York: Harper and Row, 1931), 83; "On the Air," *PT*, Aug. 1930, 82; Marilyn Boemer, *The Children's Hour: Radio Programs for Children, 1929–1956* (Metuchen, N.J.: Scarecrow, 1989), 7–16.

46. "Mickey Mouse, Financier," *Literary Digest*, Nov. 1933; Norman Kline, *Seven Minutes: The Life and Death of the American Animated Cartoon* (London: Verso, 1993), 17, 53, 91–95.

47. G. Borgfeldt ads, *PT*, Jan. 1931, 65, March 1931, 64–65, and April 1931, 17; G. Borgfeldt ad, *Child's Life*, Dec. 1931, 702.

48. "Disney and Kamen Together 12 Years," *PT*, Aug. 1944, 81; "Kay Kamen Returns from Abroad," *PT*, March 1934, 96; "Europe Greets Walt Disney," *PT*, Sept. 1935, 65–65; "Kay Kamen's Plans," *Toys and Bicycles*, Aug. 1936, 24–25.

49. "Lord and Taylor's Toyland," *PT*, Dec. 1933, 15; "An Excellent Season," *PT*, Jan. 1934, 34; "Mickey Mouse Looks Forward to 1936," *PT*, Feb. 1936, 56–57; Cecil Munsey, *Disneyana* (New York: Abrams, 1974), 32, 39–48, 80–99, 109–100; Robert Heide and John Gilman, *Cartoon Collectibles: 50 Years of Dime Store Memorabilia* (Garden City, N.Y.: Doubleday, 1983), 101–102, 113–115.

50. Kline, *Seven Minutes*, 45. Alva Johnston, "Mickey Mouse," *Woman's Home*

Companion, 61 (July 1934): 12–13; "Mickey Mouse Is 8 Years Old," Literary Digest, 122 (Oct. 2, 1936): 18–19; L. Brugden, "Mickey Mouse," Scribner's 96 (July 1934): 40–43.

51. E.g., Ohio Art ad, PT, March 1934, 8; Fisher-Price ad, PT, March 1935, 106; Harman, Comic Strip Toys, 80–91.

52. "Creative Merchandising: Some Practical Ideas and Suggestions on Using Alice in Wonderland as a Promotional Feature," PT, Jan. 1934, 52; Columbia Pictures ad for Scrappy, PT, March 1935, 74–75; Terry Tunes ad for Kiko the Kangaroo, PT, July 1936, front cover; Paramount ads for "Gulliver's Travels" licensing, PT, April 1939, 9, July 1939, 105, and April 1940, back cover.

53. "Merchants, Markets, and Men," PT, Nov. 1937, 63; Madame Alexander ad, PT, Jan. 1938, back cover; "Walt Disney Contributes to the Toy Industry," Toys and Bicycles, April 1938, 122–123; "A Smash Hit in New York," ibid., Feb. 1938, 38–39; quotation: "Snow White Triumphant," PT, March 1938, 48–52.

54. "Walt Disney's $10,000,000 Surprise," Readers' Digest, June 1938, 25–26; Heide and Gilman, Cartoon Collectibles, 209–213.

55. E. E. Grumbine, "Juvenile Clubs and Contests," Printers' Ink Monthly, May 1936, 22, 23, 56, 57; idem, Reaching Juvenile Markets (New York, 1938), ch. 5.

56. Longest, Character Toys, II, 66.

57. "Dummy Dolls Deliver Dividends," PT, March 1938, 46–47; Longest, Character Toys, II, 45, 60–65.

58. "Kay Kamen's Plans," Toys and Bicycles, Aug. 1936, 24–25.

59. Ives, Blakeslee and Williams, Iron Toys (1893), 49–56; Kilgore ad, PT, Feb. 1911, 95; Richard O'Brien, Collecting Toys (Florence, Ala.: Americana Books, 1990), 301–302; Best, Cast Iron Pistols, 110.

60. Kilgore ad, PT, Sept. 1913, 87; Milton Bradley ad, PT, March 1916, 49; Liberty Toys ad, PT, July 1917, 101; C. R. Williams ad, PT, July 1917, 131; Milton Bradley ad, PT, Jan. 1920, 4.

61. Daisy Manufacturing ads: PT, June 1919, 73; St. Nicholas, Dec. 1907, 1; St. Nicholas, Nov. 1915, 23; American Boy, Oct. 1918, 38; American Boy, Dec. 1935, back cover.

62. Daisy ad, American Boy, Dec. 1934, back cover; Daisy ad, PT, Jan. 1935, 17; Hubley ad, PT, Jan. 1938, 15.

63. "They're After the Toy Gun," Toys and Novelties, Jan. 1936, 30–40; Nelson Crawford, "War Toys and War," Literary Digest, Sept. 4, 1937, 33.

64. "Readers' Protest," Toys and Novelties, Feb. 1936, 26–27; Rachel Palmer, 40,000,000 Guinea Pig Children (New York: Vanguard, 1937), 225–231.

65. Rapaport Bros. ad, PT, March 1935, 144–145; O'Brien, Collecting Toys, 175–176, 188, 197–210, 229–231; Peter Johnson, Toy Armies (Garden City, N.Y.: Doubleday, 1981), 105.

66. Grey Iron Casting, The Famous Greycraft Iron Men (Mount Joy, Pa., 1940).

67. The original story by Philip F. Nowland, "Armageddon-2419," appears in Buck Rogers: The First 60 Years in the 25th Century, ed. Lorraine Dille Wil-

liams (New York: TSR, 1988), 19–46; Crystal and Layland Payton, *Space Toys* (Sedalia, Mo.: Collectors Compass, 1982), 35–41; Boemer, *Children's Hour*, 66–70.

68. Daisy ad, *American Boy*, Dec. 1934, back cover; Payton and Layland, *Space Toys*, 41–42; Sackman Bros. ad, *Child Life*, Dec. 1934, 537; Rapaport Bros. ad, *American Boy*, Dec. 1935, 50; Tootsietoy ad, *PT*, June 1937, 1.
69. Mike Benton, *The Illustrated Superhero Comics of the Golden Age* (Dallas: Taylor Publishing, 1992), 15–30; Boemer, *Children's Hour*, 49–57.
70. Harman, *Comic Strip Toys*, 93, 105, 112; Longest, *Character Toys*, II, 79–84, 145, 138.
71. Sears, Roebuck, *Catalogue*, no. 171 (Chicago, 1935), 732; no. 173 (1936), 793; and no. 179 (1939), 896.
72. E.g., Ideal Toys ads, Jan. 1935, 23, March 1935, 24, and March 1936, 3; "Public Takes Shirley to Its Heart in April," *Toys and Novelties*, April 1936, 83; "Cash in on April's Double Header," *PT*, March 1936, 64.
73. Dorothy Washburn, "Doll Oral History Project, Final Report," typescript, 1987, Strong Museum, 2; Shirley Temple premium ad, *Child Life*, Dec. 1936, 537.
74. Johana Anderton, *Twentieth Century Dolls from Bisque to Vinyl* (Des Moines: Wallace-Homestead, 1974), 352–356, 336; Longest, *Character Toys*, II, 135–140.
75. E.g., Arcade Toy ad, *PT*, May 1934, 123; Mcloughlin Bros. ad, *PT*, March 1935, 157; Anderton, *Twentieth Century Dolls*, 153–154; Longest, *Character Toys*, II, 43–58, 65–68; Pinsky, *Marx Toys*, II, 70–71.
76. The Deanna Durbin doll of 1939 may have been that first teenage doll. "Dolls, What Will They Be?" *PT*, April 1939, 206–207.
77. *Historical Statistics* (1975), 319 (figures exclude sleds and wagons); "This Business of Christmas," *Current History*, Dec. 1937, 53–56; "Toy Volume up 10%," *Business Week*, Nov. 4, 1939, 28; "Guns and Dolls Sets," *Business Week*, March 15, 1941, 28.

5. Building Blocks of Character

1. Sidonie Gruenberg, *Your Child: Today and Tomorrow*, 2d ed. (Philadelphia: Lippincott, 1920), 140.
2. Patty Smith Hill, "Preface," in Charlotte Garrison, *Permanent Play Materials for Young Children* (New York: Scribner's, 1926), xi.
3. Ellen Key, *The Century of the Child* (New York, 1909), 183, 242–243. For the traditional view see, e.g., G. Stanley Hall's *Pedagogical Seminary* (1891) and *Child Study Monthly* (1895) as well as the advice manuals: E. L. Thorndike, *Notes on Child Study* (New York, 1903); William Shearer, *Management and Training of Children* (New York, 1904), 145–148.
4. Bernard Wishy, *The Child and the Republic: The Dawn of Modern American Child Nurture* (Philadelphia: University of Pennsylvania Press, 1968), chs.

2–5 and p. 84; Anne Rose, *Transcendentalism as a Social Movement, 1830–1850* (New Haven: Yale University Press, 1981), 52–56, 60–65, 80–84; Jacob Abbott, *Gentle Measures in the Management and Training of the Young* (New York, 1871), esp. 13–31, 92–93.

5. Key, *Century of the Child*, 100–101; "Editorial," *Parents' Magazine*, 1 (Oct. 1926): 1.

6. Susan Isaacs, *The Nursery Years* (New York: Vanguard, 1929), 2–3; John Watson, *Psychological Care of Infant and Child* (New York: Norton, 1928), 81–82.

7. Martha Wolfenstein, "Fun Morality: An Analysis of Recent American Child-training Literature," in Margaret Mead and Martha Wolfenstein, eds., *Childhood in Contemporary Cultures* (Chicago: University of Chicago Press, 1955), 169–170, 172–174; Arnold Gesell, *The Mental Growth of the Pre-School Child* (New York: Macmillan, 1925).

8. Laura Spelman Rockefeller Memorial Foundation, *Final Report* (New York, 1933), 7–9, 17–19; Orville Brim, *Education for Child Rearing* (New York: Russell Sage, 1959), 321–349.

9. Robert Lynd and Helen Lynd, *Middletown: A Study in Contemporary American Culture* (New York: Harcourt Brace, 1929), 151. White House Conference on Child Health and Protection, *The Young Child in the Home* (New York: D. Appleton-Century, 1936), 78, 237, 267.

10. Herbert Spencer, *The Principles of Psychology* (New York, 1873), 627–631; Abbott, *Gentle Measures*, 179–192; Karl Groos, *The Play of Man* (New York, 1908), 361–384, 395–397, 405.

11. G. Stanley Hall, *Youth: Its Education, Regimen, and Hygiene* (New York, 1918), 73–74; Luther Gulick, *A Philosophy of Play* (New York: Scribner's, 1920), 28, 89, 93

12. T. R. Croswell, "Amusements of Two Thousand Worcester School Children," *Pedagogical Seminary*, 6 (1898–99): 314–371; G. Stanley Hall and A. Caswell Ellis, *A Study of Dolls* (New York, 1897); J. H. Chase, "Street Games of New York Children," *Pedagogical Seminary*, 12 (1905): 503–505; Zachary McGhee, "Play Life of Some South Carolina Children," *Pedagogical Seminary*, 7 (Dec. 1900): 459–491.

13. William Forbush, *The Boy Problem in the Home* (Boston, 1915), 87–88; W. B. Forbush, *The Coming Generation* (New York, 1912), xviii, 16, 18, 117, 203.

14. Friedrich Froebel, *Education of Man* (1825; New York, 1895), 55; Heinrich Hoffman, *Kindergarten Toys and How to Use Them* (New York, 1874), 4–5.

15. Josephine Foster, *Busy Childhood: Guidance through Play and Activity* (New York: D. Appleton-Century, 1933), 16–22.

16. Hill, Preface, vii.

17. Jean Piaget, *Play, Dreams and Imitation in Childhood* (New York: Norton, 1961); Ethel Kawin, *The Wise Choice of Toys* (Chicago: University of Chicago Press, 1933), 23; Foster, *Busy Childhood*, 15–16.

18. Hall and Ellis, *Dolls*, 47, 49; Mary Read, *The Mothercraft Manual* (Boston,

1916), 286–291; Bureau of Educational Experiments, *Playthings* (New York, 1917), 4–5; Alice Sies, *Spontaneous and Supervised Play in Childhood* (New York, Macmillan, 1922), 51–75.

19. E.g., Piaget, *Play, Dreams,* 166; Susan Isaacs, *Intellectual Growth of Young Children* (New York: Schocken, 1930), ch. 1; Beatrix Tudor-Hart, *Play and Toys in Nursery Years* (New York: Viking, 1940).

20. Maude Nash, *Children's Occupations* (Boston: Houghton Mifflin, 1920), xii, 77; Hill, Preface, xi; Josephine Kenyon, "Parents as Companions," *Good Housekeeping,* March 1933, 108; G. T. W. Patrick, *Psychology of Relaxation* (Boston, 1916).

21. Read, *Mothercraft Manual,* ch. 13; Rose Alschuler and Christine Heinig, *Play: The Child's Response to Life* (Boston: Houghton Mifflin, 1936), ch. 4; White House Conference on Child Health and Protection, *The Home and the Child* (New York: Century Co., 1931), 5, 23–24, 39, 46–47.

22. E.g., Helen Curtis, "How a Woodshed Turned into a Jolly Little Playhouse," *Woman's Home Companion,* 57, no. 8 (Aug. 1930): 90; Children's Bureau, *Backyard Playgrounds* (Washington, 1923); White House Conference on Child Health and Protection, *Home and Child,* 61.

23. Nash, *Children's Occupations,* 200.

24. Cited in Antonia Fraser, *A History of Toys* (New York: Delacorte, 1966), 13.

25. Lesley Gordon, *From Peepshow to Paradise* (New York: J. De Graff, 1953), 35, 155; Blair Whitton, *Toys* (New York: Knopf, 1984), 14; Ruth and Larry Freeman, *Cavalcade of Toys* (Watkins Glen, N.Y.: Century House, 1942), 267.

26. Ebenezer Landells, *The Boy's Own Toy-Maker: A Practical Illustrated Guide to the Useful Employment of Leisure Hours* (London, 1860), vi–vii.

27. Ebenezer Landells with Alice Landells, *The Girl's Own Toy-Maker and Book of Recreation* (London, 1863), vi, 58; George Johnson, *Toys and Toy-Making* (New York, 1912); Mary Roberts, *When Children Play at Home* (Iowa City: University of Iowa, 1936).

28. Friedrich Froebel, *Pedagogics of the Kindergarten* (New York, 1912), 32.

29. William Kilpatrick, *Froebel's Kindergarten Principles Critically Examined* (New York, 1916), esp. 109–151; Evelyn Weber, "Play Materials in the Curriculum of Early Childhood," in Karen Hewett and Louis Roomet, eds., *Educational Toys in America, 1800 to the Present* (Burlington, Vt.: Robert Hull Fleming, 1979), 26–28; Maria Montessori, *The Montessori Method* (New York, 1912).

30. See Weber, "Play Materials," 26–34.

31. John Dewey, "Froebel's Educational Principles," in *The Middle Works,* vol. 1: *1899–1901* (Carbondale, Ill.: Southern Illinois University Press, 1976), 81–85.

32. M. Charlotte Jammer, "Patty Smith Hill and the Reform of the American Kindergarten" (Ph.D diss., Teachers College, Columbia University, 1960); Hill, Preface, xi, xiv–xvi; Patty Smith Hill, *A Conduct Curriculum for the Kindergarten and First Grade* (New York, Scribner's, 1923), 17–52.

33. Perris Leger, "Christmas Shopping for the Child," *Hygeia* 5, no. 12

(Dec. 1927): 608; Hill, Preface, xiv, xi; Patty Smith Hill, *Kindergarten Problems* (New York, 1912), 37–48.

34. Gulick, *Philosophy of Play*, 69, 73–75.

35. G. Stanley Hall, "A Story of a Sand Pile," *Scribner's*, 3 (June 1888): 690–696.

36. Kawin, *Wise Choice*, 14–15.

37. Psychologists used observations of block building and doll play to measure children's developmental processes. E.g., Frances Guanella, *Block Building Activities of Young Children* (New York, 1934); Harriet Johnson, *The Art of Block Building* (New York: 69 Bank Street Publications, 1945).

38. Tudor-Hart, *Nursery Toys*, 52, 58–59; Leger, "Christmas Shopping," 608.

39. Patty Smith Hill, "Avoid the Gifts That Overstimulate," *Delineator*, Dec. 1914, 22–23.

40. Read, *Mothercraft Manual*, 285; "Patty Smith Hill," *Playthings* (hereafer *PT*), Jan. 1921, 347.

41. Josephine Keyren, "Parents as Companions," *Good Housekeeping*, March 1933, 108, insisted that only if parents played with the child at home "could they expect to be real guides to him later on." But this view was surprisingly rare.

42. Hill, Preface, xvii; idem; *Conduct Curriculum*, xxi.

43. Hill, Preface, x, xi, xiv; Kawin, *Wise Choice*, 108; Nash, *Children's Occupations*, 199–200, 242.

44. Isaacs, *Intellectual Growth*, 104, 109.

45. Kawin, *Wise Choice*, 55–56.

46. See Margaret Marsh, *Suburban Lives* (New Brunswick: Rutgers University Press, 1990), chs. 2–3; Steven Gelber, "Homo Faber: Tools, Gender and Do-It-Yourself," manuscript.

47. Luella Palmer, *Play Life in the First Eight Years* (Boston, 1916), 214.

48. Palmer, *Play Life*, 214–217; Isaacs, *Nursery Years*, 124–125.

49. Gulick, *Philosophy of Play*, 69.

50. Helen Wooley, "Before Your Child Goes to School," *Parents' Magazine*, 1 (Oct. 1926): 8; Ellen Seiter, *Sold Separately: Children and Parents in Consumer Culture* (New Brunswick: Rutgers University Press, 1993), ch. 2.

51. Isaacs, *Intellectual Growth*, 20.

52. Weber, "Play Materials," 29; Freeman, *Cavalcade* 167–168, 340–350; "How to Use Plasticine as a Home Amusement" (Albany, 1908?), in Warshaw Collection, Smithsonian Institution, Toys 2, File 2; "Educational Toys," *PT*, April 1911, 60.

53. Holgate ads, *PT*, April 1932, 66, and Aug. 1932, 29; Playskool ads, *Parents' Magazine*, 3 (Dec. 1928): 5, 12; and 5 (Dec. 1930): 47; Playskool Institute ad, *PT*, April 1939, 105; Hewett, *Educational Toys*, 98–100.

54. Max von Boehn, *Dolls and Puppets* (London: Harrap, 1932), 183; Martha J. Chase, *The Chase Stockinet Doll: A Tradition in American Families* (Pawtucket, R.I., 1910).

55. "Announcing Fisher-Price" ad, *PT*, Jan. 1931, 108–109; John Murray and

Bruce Fox, *Fisher-Price, 1931–1963* (Florence, Ala.: Books Americana, 1987), xill; Halsam Products ads, *PT,* Feb. 1930, 89–91, and April 1937, 57.

56. E.g., the Dec. 1927, 1932, and 1938 issues of *Parents' Magazine.* See also "Playthings in Review," *Parents' Magazine,* 7 (Dec. 1932): 58.

57. "Educational Trends of Domestic Toys," *Toy World,* Oct. 1927, 32; "Fitting the Toy to the Child," ibid., 22–23; "The Right Toy for the Right Age," *PT,* Aug. 1932, 36–38.

58. Edith Boehm, "There's Money in Toys," *PT,* Jan. 1930, 266–267; "A Century of Progress in Toys," *PT,* Dec. 1933, 30–32; James Fri, "The Business of Christmas," *Current History,* Dec. 1937, 53–56.

59. Sies, *Play in Childhood,* 111–131.

60. Read, *Mothercraft Manual,* 287.

61. Foster, *Busy Childhood,* 77.

62. J. P. and Peggy McEvoy, "Talk with a Toy King," *Readers' Digest,* Jan. 1955, 125.

6. The Boomers' Box of Toys

1. Bureau of the Census, *Historical Statistics of the United States* (Washington: Government Printing Office, 1975), 15.

2. Stephanie Coontz, *The Way We Never Were: American Families and the Nostalgia Trap* (New York: Basic Books, 1992), esp. ch. 2.

3. Laurene Meringoff, ed., *Children and Advertising: An Annotated Bibliography* (New York: Children's Advertising Review Unit, 1980), 1–43; Gene Reilly Group, *The Child* (Darien, Conn., 1975).

4. "Happy Children Build Home Morale," *Playthings* (hereafter *PT*), May 1942, 38–39; "Appeal to the Stay at Homes," *PT,* June 1942, 26; "Toys," *Better Homes and Gardens,* Dec. 1946, 10–11.

5. Weeden Steam Engine ad, *PT,* March 1948, 105; Durable Toys ad, *PT,* March 1958, 158; Daisy Manufacturing ad, *Toys and Novelties* (hereafter *TN*), Jan. 1954, 95; Jack Tempest, *Post-War Tin Toys* (Radnor, Pa.: Wallace-Homestead, 1991), 80–97.

6. A. C. Gilbert, *Catalogue* (New Haven, 1949), 2; Revell ad, *TN,* May 1953, 145.

7. "Toy Empire Builder," *New York Times Magazine,* Jan. 10, 1954, 156; "Benjamin Michtom of Ideal Promotes Smokey the Bear," *TN,* Aug. 1953, 104; Judith Izen, *A Collectors' Guide to Ideal Dolls* (Paducah, Ky.: Collector Books, 1994), 20.

8. "Louis Marx Toy King," *Fortune,* Jan. 1946, 122–127; "Toys and the King" *Time,* Nov. 5, 1951, 110; "The Little King," *Time,* Dec. 12, 1955, 22–23, 92, 96, 127, 163.

9. See Gil Asakawa and Leland Rucher, *The Toy Book* (New York: Knopf, 1992), 22–23, 54–55; Bill Bruegman, *Toys of the Sixties* (Akron, Oh.: Cap'n Penny

Productions, 1992), ch. 1; idem, *The Aurora History* (Akron: Cap'n Penny, 1991), 8–9.

10. Bruegman, *Aurora*, 8–9; "Hasbro, Inc.," in *Notable Corporate Chronologies*, ed. Susan Martin (New York: Gale Research, 1995), 802.

11. Eliot Handler, *The Impossible Really Is Possible: The Story of Mattel* (New York: Newcomen Society, 1968), 1–16; Mattel ads, *PT*, March 1948, 215, March 1952, 57, and March 1955, 427–430; "Mattel Inc," in *International Directory of Company Histories*, Paula Kepos, ed., vol. 7 (New York: St. James, 1993), 304–307.

12. "National Toy Week," *TN*, Nov. 1954, 129; "Second Peak," *TN*, Feb. 1954, 172–173; "F. A. O. Schwarz," *PT*, March 1948, 436–437; "Surprise Inc.," *TN*, May 1956, 62–63.

13. "There's Fun in Millions in Toys," *Nation's Business*, Dec. 1953, 30–31; Department of Commerce, *Census of Manufacturers, 1963*, vol. 2: *Industrial Statistics*, pt. 2 (Washington: Government Printing Office, 1966), 39B-6 (figures include "durable toys" like wagons and sleds); "Self Service," *TN*, June 1954, 164.

14. E.g., "Toys Publicized Nationally by the Toy Guidance Council," *PT*, Dec. 1946, 156–157; "Toy Guidance Council Selects 104 Prestige Toys," *PT*, March 1956, 89, 138.

15. Bill Hanlon, *Plastic Toys: Domestic Dreams of the 40s and 50s* (Atglen, Pa.: Schiffer, 1993); M. A. Brown, "Plastics for the Toy Industry," *PT*, Aug. 1944, 64–65; "Toys for Sale," *Modern Plastics*, Aug. 1939, 21; "Rainbow Balls" of American Character Inc. ad, *TN*, Feb. 1954, 260; "Toys for Tomorrow," *Colliers*, March 16, 1946, 20–21; Doughboy ad, *TN*, March 1952, 165.

16. Cootie ad, *TN*, May 1953, 11.

17. "Toy Tycoon," *Readers' Digest*, Sept. 1946, 85–87; "Toys for Tomorrow," 21; American Radar Corp. ad, *PT*, June 1946, 33; Revell ad, *PT*, May 1955, 106.

18. Sears, Roebuck, *Catalogue* (Chicago, 1957), 231; Tom Engelhardt, *The End of Victory Culture: Cold War America and the Disillusioning of a Generation* (New York: Basic Books, 1995), 81–86.

19. "Toys are Terrific," *Life*, Dec. 5, 1949, 18–28; Tonka ad, *PT Toy Fair Issue*, March 1959; Asakawa and Rucher, *Toy Book*, 95–99.

20. Pressman ad, *TN*, Sept. 1953, 113; "1959 Transogram catalog," Warshaw Collection of Advertising, Smithsonian Institution, Box 4, File 2, 4; Gilbert ads, *PT*, March 1957, 6–7, and March 1958, 269.

21. Norton-Honer ad, *TN*, Feb. 1953, 71; Banner Plastics ad, *TN* Oct. 1954, 16; Jerry Scanton ad, *TN*, March 1953, 131; Inland Manufacturing ad, *TN*, March 1954, 383, and June 1954, 18; Sears catalog (1956), in Peter Fritz and John Mautner, *Presenting the Big Toy Box at Sears* (Auburn, Mass.: Toy Town Classics, 1987), 282.

22. "Into Orbit," *Time*, Oct. 21, 1957, 94–95; "A Safe Toy Missile," *Life*, April 7, 1958, 75–76; Kenner ad, *PT*, Feb. 1958, 145; Monogram ad, *PT*, Nov. 1958, 80.

23. Sears, Roebuck, *Catalogue* (Chicago, 1958), 379–381; Fritz and Mautner, *Presenting the Big Toy Box*, 267.
24. "Brand Name Toys Train Buyers Young," *Business Week*, July 25, 1953, 36–37; "Big Business Goes Tiny," *Life*, Nov. 9, 1952, 97–98; Amsco ads, *TN*, March 1952, 49, and May 1953, 23; Revere Ware ad, *Better Homes and Gardens*, Dec. 1955, 124–125; Ideal Toy ad, *PT*, March 1956, 104–105.
25. "Negro Dolls Undergo Transformation," *TN*, March 1952, 420–421; "Modern Designs for Negro Dolls," *Ebony*, 7 (Jan. 1952): 46–50.
26. Ideal Toy ad (Toni Doll), *TN*, March 1953, 342; Betsy McCall ad, *PT*, March 1955, 47; Vogue Doll ad, *PT*, March 1957, 81–92; Vogue Dolls, "Hi? I'm Jeff," and "Hi! I'm Ginny What Shall I Wear Today" (Medford, Mass., 1955); Vogue Dolls, "The Vogue Doll Family: Their Fabulous Clothes and Accessories for 1958" (Medford, Mass., 1958); Doll Bodies (Lingerie Lou) ads, *PT*, Feb. 1956, 213–216, and March 1956, 439–443.
27. *Life* ad, *TN*, Aug. 1953, 83–94; Cecil Munsey, *Disneyana: Walt Disney Collectibles* (New York: Abrams, 1974), 238, 250–252; Craftsmen's Guild ad, *PT*, Sept. 1946, 187; Walt Disney Character Merchandising Division ad, *TN*, Jan. 1952, 90; Joleen Robison and Kay Sellers, *Advertising Dolls* (Paducah, Ky.: Collector Books, 1980), 89; Grey Advertising ad for Campbell Kids licenses, *PT*, March 1956, 561; Ideal Toy ad, *PT*, Sept. 1957, 168.
28. Classy Productions ad, *PT*, March 1948, 311; Roy Rogers Enterprises ad, *TN*, Feb. 1954, 182.
29. Effanbee Dolls ad, *PT*, March 1949, 24–25; Parker Brothers ad, *TN*, Aug. 1953, 1; Sears Catalogue, 1956, 266–267; Elizabeth Whiting ad for Pinky Lee Game, *PT*, March 1955, 53.
30. "Frisbees, Yo-Yos, Goo-Goos, etc.," *New York Times Magazine*, Aug. 11, 1957, 27; "Small Fry Fads," ibid., Sept. 11, 1958, 29; Wham-O ad, *PT*, Sept. 1958, 135.
31. *Playskool Toy Catalogue: The Right Toy for Every Age* (Chicago, 1950), 1–2, 5, 13–17, 22–23, 33–35, 40.
32. Creative Playthings, *Toys: We Have Traveled the World to Bring You the Best in Toys* (Princeton, 1963), 7–9, 10–11, 24, 26–27, 30.
33. Fisher-Price ad, *PT*, March 1955, 21–24; "Chat with Herman Fisher, Toy Maker," *PT*, Jan. 1955, 117–118; Tinkertoy ad, *Parents' Magazine*, Dec. 1953, 97; Rainbow Crafts ad, *PT*, Sept. 1957, 23; Walco ads, *TN*, June 1954, 85, and Oct. 1954, 50–51.
34. Benjamin Spock, "Creative Use of Toys," *Ladies' Home Journal*, Dec. 1961, 36–37.
35. "Toys for the Children You Love," *Parents' Magazine*, Dec. 1947, 40–41, 82, 90; "Tops in Toys," ibid., Dec. 1949, 38–39; "The Experts Talk about Christmas Toys," *Look*, Dec. 16, 1952, 100–108.
36. J. Tarow, *Entertainment, Education, and the Hard Sell: Three Decades of Network Children's Television* (New York: Praeger, 1981), 16–17, 20–23, 44–60; Stephen Kline, *Out of the Garden: Toys and Children's Culture in the Age of TV Market-*

ing (New York: Verso, 1993), ch. 4; Halsam Products ad, *PT,* March 1951, 115; "TV Tips," *PT,* Oct. 1961, 53; "Playskool," *TN,* May 1953, 86–87; American Character Dolls ads, *TN,* Aug. 1953, 14–15, June 1954, 10, and Oct. 1954, 86; AMF ad, *PT,* Dec. 1957, 82.

37. Link Research Co. ad, *PT,* Feb. 1960, 17; French American Reed Corp. ad, *TN,* March 1952, 59; Emenee Industries ad, *PT,* March 1951, 17–18.

38. "Toy Trends," *PT,* April 1954, 96–97; A. and H. Doll Co. ad, *TN,* April 1952, 43; Adjust-a-Dyper ad; *TN,* Oct. 1954, 49; American Character Inc. ads, *TN,* May 1953, 54, and Sept. 1953, 164; Walt Disney Character Merchandising ad, *PT,* April 1955, cover; L. M. Eddy ad, *PT,* Aug. 1955, 90.

39. ABC-Paramount Character Merchandising Department ad, *PT,* Nov. 1957, 85.

40. Munsey, *Disneyana,* 294; Robert Heide and John Gilman, *Cartoon Collectibles: 50 Years of Dime Store Memorabilia* (Garden City, N.Y.: Doubleday, 1983), 233–235; Mattel ad, *PT,* March 1956, 413; ABC Paramount Character Licensing Dept. ad, *PT,* May 1956, 63; Knickerbocker ad, *PT,* Feb. 1956, 94; Gong Bell Manufacturing ad, ibid., 189.

41. Jerry Bowles, *Forever Hold Your Banners High* (Garden City, N.Y.: Doubleday, 1976), esp. 16–17.

42. Cy Schneider, *Children's Television: The Art, The Business, and How It Works* (Chicago: NTC Business Books, 1987), 23–37; Ruth Handler, *Dream Doll* (Stamford, Conn.: Longmeadow Press, 1994), chs. 4–5; "Mattel, Inc," in *Notable Corporate Chronologies,* ed. Martin, 668; Mattel promotion, *PT Toy Fair Issue,* March 1959, n.p.; "TV Tips," *PT,* June 1961, 61; Mattel ads, *PT,* March 1961, 314–318, Oct 1961, 25–26, and March 1962, n.p.

43. In *PT:* Transogram ad, March 1961, 69; Kenner ad, Sept. 1961, 41; Hasbro ad, March 1962, 290; Mattel ad, March 1963, 189–190; Ideal ad, Sept. 1963, 120; Marx ad, April 1962, 141; Gilbert ad, Aug. 1961, 15.

44. "Playthings Visits Trenton," *PT,* April 1958, 158; Dale Kunkel, "From a Raised Eyebrow to a Turned Back: The FCC and Children's Product-Related Programming," *Journal of Communications,* 38, no. 4 (1988): 92–100.

45. Figures exclude "durable" toys like wagons and sleds. I was unable to separate toys from sporting goods for this comparison. Department of Commerce, *National Income and Product Accounts, 1959–1988* (Washington: Government Printing Office, 1992), II, 70, 75; Department of Commerce, *Statistical Abstract of the United States* (Washington: Government Printing Office, 1995), 491.

46. "Playthings Annual Survey," *PT,* March 1964, 315–322; "Survey," *TN,* March 1964, 267–286; "Playthings Annual Survey," *PT,* March 1966, 282.

47. Kenner ad, *PT,* March 1967, 324; "Top 10 Toy Advertisers," *Toys,* Sept. 1972, 39–40.

48. Kline, *Out of the Garden,* esp. 174–208.

49. Asakawa and Rucher, *Toy Book,* 100–106, 57–64; Aurora Plastics ad, *PT,*

Aug. 1962, 51–52; Fritz and Mautner, *Presenting the Big Toy Box*, 447–450; Sears, Roebuck, *Sears Toy Book* (Chicago, 1964, 1970); Sears, *Wish Book for the 1977 Christmas Season* (Atlanta, 1977).

50. "The 1973 Dolls Never More Traditional," *PT*, Aug. 1973, 52; "Inside the Doll Market," *Toys*, May 1975, 23–25.
51. Tyco ad, *Toys*, March 1971, 1–16; "Mini-Collectibles," *PT*, Nov. 1975, 78–81; Schaper Plastics ad, *Parents' Magazine*, Nov. 1973, 85; Silly Putty Marketing ad, *PT*, Oct. 1960, 21.
52. Lego ad, *PT*, March 1962, 428–429; Lego ad, *Parents'* Magazine, Dec. 1964, 43; "Fisher-Price's Secret: Its Love Affair with American Mothers," *PT*, Nov. 1972, 68; Creative Playthings ad, *Toys*, May 1973, 46.
53. Hasbro ad, *PT*, March 1963, 15; Kenner ads, *PT*, Aug. 1963, 91–124, and March 1965, 69–70; Mattel ad, *PT*, Nov. 1961, 85.
54. "Television Toys," video produced by Video Resources N.Y., New York.
55. "Troubled King of Toys," *Saturday Evening Post*, March 5, 1960, 28–30, 54–57; "Inventing Toys Is No Mere Child's Play," *Business Week*, Dec. 21, 1963, 40–43; "Symposium on Toys," *TN*, Sept. 1969, 76–78.
56. "Child's World Is Overwhelming the Consumer," *TN*, Nov. 1970, 28–33; "Room for One More," *Toy and Hobby World* (hereafter *THW*), March 1978, 26; Toy Manufacturers of America, *Toy Fact Book* (New York, 1986), 16.
57. Bruegman, *Toys of the Sixties*, 170, 189; "General Mills," in *Notable Corporate Chronologies*, 427; "How Fisher-Price Sells All Those Toys," *Business Week*, March 3, 1973, 40–41.
58. Remco ad, *PT*, March 1970, 22–27; "Rap: Marty Abrams," *Toys*, Dec. 1974, 31–34; "Mego Makes It Big," *Business Week*, March 8, 1978, 27–28; Wallace Crouch, *Mego Toys* (Paducah, Ky.: Collector Books, 1995), 6; "Licensing," *PT*, April 1976, 23–28.
59. Handler, *Dream Doll*; Rebecca Harnmell, "To Educate and Amuse: Paper Dolls and Toys, 1640–1900" (M.A. thesis, University of Delaware, 1988, University Microforms International, Ann Arbor, 1989).
60. Handler, *Dream Doll*; A. Glen Mandeville, *Doll Fashion Anthology and Price Guide*, 4th ed. (Cumberland, Md.: Hobby House, 1993), 1–33; K. Westenhouser, *The Story of Barbie* (Paducah, Ky.: Collector Books, 1994), 5–15; Billy Boy, *Barbie: Her Life and Times* ((New York: Crown, 1987), 17–28, 40–44.
61. Mattel, "Barbie, Teen-Age Fashion Model," "Barbie, Teen-Age Fashion Model, and Ken, Barbie's Boy Friend (He's a Doll)," "Exclusive Fashions by Mattel," book 3 (Hawthorne, Calif.: Mattel, 1958, 1960, 1963). All in the Strong Museum.
62. "The Origins of the Barbie Doll (and Her 'Family')," Mattel Press Kit, Please Touch Museum, Toy Fair Collection, (hereafter TFC), Box 5.
63. "Inside the Doll Market," *Toys*, March 1975, 23–25.
64. Billy Boy, *Barbie*, 92; Mandeville, *Fashion Anthology*, 41–43, 69–71; Ron Goulart, *The Assault on Childhood* (Los Angeles: Sherbourne, 1969), 26.
65. "Fact Sheet: Hasbro's G.I. Joe, A Real American Hero," Hasbro Press Kit,

Feb. 1993, TFC, Box 3; Susan and Paris Manos, *Collectible Male Action Figures* (Paducah, Ky.: Collector Books, 1990), 8–9.

66. "G.I. Joe, Action Soldiers: America's Moveable Fighting Man" (Pawtucket, R.I.: Hasbro, 1964), Strong Museum.

67. Manos, *Male Action Figures*, 20–33, 38–43; Vincent Santelmo, *The Official 30th Anniversary Salute to G.I. Joe* (Iola, Wis.: Kreuse, 1994), 17–18, 66–72, 75–97, 325, 343, 412–413.

68. Bruegman, *Toys of the Sixties*, 89–97; Hawk Model ad, *PT*, March 1963, 206–208.

69. Carol Turpen, *Baby Boomer Toys* (Atglen, Pa.: Schiffer, 1993), 42–50, 83–92; Asawaka and Rucker, *Toy Box*, 149–151; "Monstrous Christmas to All," *Nation*, Dec. 14, 1964, 463–464.

70. Bruegman, *Aurora*.

71. Carol Markowski, *Tomart's Price Guide to Action Figure Collectibles* (Dayton, Oh.: Tomart, 1992), chs. 1–2; Steven Kimball, *Greenberg's Guide to Superhero Toys* (Sykesville, Md.: Greenberg, 1988), 13–61; Ideal ad, *PT*, March 1967, 24; "Preview 1977," *PT*, Feb. 1977, 256; Mego ad, *PT*, July 1977, 1; "Neil Saul," *Toys*, Aug. 1976, 65.

72. "Bernard Loomis," *Toys*, April 1976, 51.

73. Kline, *Out of the Garden*, 170–171, 187–195.

74. "Seymour Gartenberg," *Toys*, Sept. 1973, 27–28; Creative Playthings ad, *PT*, Feb. 1977, 147–151; Playskool ad, *PT*, Feb. 1974, 113.

75. "Sesame Street Expands POP Image," *PT*, Nov. 1973, 71; Kline, *Out of the Garden*, 159.

76. "Who Bombed Santa's Workshop," *New York Times Magazine*, Dec. 12, 1968, 87, 98; "I Turned Mine In," *Time*, Sept. 6, 1968, 94; "Retired Sears Buyer Reflects," *PT*, March 1969, 214–215.

77. Bruegman, *Aurora*, 24; Edward Swartz, *Toys That Don't Care* (Boston: Gambit, 1970); "The Swartz Affair," *PT*, Aug. 1971, 58–59.

78. "Should Toymakers Worry about Their Image?" *PT*, March 1970, 68–69; "TMA at Boca Raton, How to Survive in '75," *PT*, June 1975, 39–40; "TMA Girds for a Consumer Offensive," *PT*, Jan. 1972, 56–59; "TMA Urged to Meet the Consumer," *PT*, Jan. 1973, 75–85.

79. "Birth Rate at New Low," *PT*, May 1974, 37; "Christmas Bringing Mixed Tidings for Toys," *Business Week*, Dec. 12, 1977, 54; Handler, *Dream Doll*, chs. 4–5; "What Retailers Are Saying," *PT*, March 1971, 165.

80. Scott Cohen, *Zap! The Rise and Fall of Atari* (New York: McGraw-Hill, 1984), 1–80; Richard Levy and Ronald Weingartner, *Inside Santa's Workshop* (New York: Henry Holt, 1990), 63–65.

81. "TV and Toymakers—Present and Future Conditions," *PT*, Aug. 1974, 56–70; Evelyn Kay, *The Act Guide to Children's Television*, rev. ed. (Boston: Beacon, 1979), 221–222; William Moody, *Children's Television: The Economics of Exploitation* (New Haven: Yale University Press, 1973), 83–116; "Children's Telly," *Toys*, Aug. 1972, 52–53.

82. "Special Report," *Toys, Hobbies and Crafts* (hereafter *THC*), Aug. 1978, 16–17; "The Thorny Issue of Toy Advertising," *PT*, March 1978, 57; Federal Trade Commission, *FTC Staff Report on Television Advertising to Children* (Washington, 1978), 11, 20, 243, 267.

83. "Are Government Efforts Mischannelled?" *THC*, Aug. 1978, 64, 16–17; "No TV Advertising," *THC*, Feb. 1978, 304; "Toy Industry Goes to Washington," *THC*, May 1979, 18–19; D. Kunkel and D. Roberts, "Young Minds and Marketplace Values: Issues in Children's Television Advertising," *Journal of Social Issues*, 47, no. 1 (1991): 57–72.

7. Spinning Out of Control

1. "Advertisers Woo Kids with a Different Game," *Media and Marketing Decisions*, 18 (Sept. 1983): 72–73.

2. Data from the Toy Manufacturers of America (hereafter TMA), excluding video games and equipment. Department of Commerce, *Statistical Abstract of the United States* (Washington: Government Printing Office, 1996), 253, found that personal consumption per child in nondurable toys and sports supplies rose by 65% from 1980 to 1993.

3. Richard Levy and Ronald Weingartner, *Inside Santa's Workshop* (New York: Henry Holt, 1990), 137, 101.

4. TMA, *Toy Industry Fact Book* (New York, 1992), 11, (1995), 12, 23; "Mattel Expects '85 Sales to Exceed $1 Billion," *Toy and Hobby World* (hereafter *THW*), Feb. 1986, 14.

5. P. M. Hirsch, "Processing Fads and Fashions," *American Journal of Sociology*, 77 (Jan. 1972): 639–659.

6. TMA, *Toy Industry Fact Book* (1993), 20–21.

7. Kenneth Brown, "The Collapse of the British Toy Industry, 1979–1984," *Economic History Review*, 46 (Aug. 1993): 592–606; Sydney Stern and Ted Schoenhaus, *Toyland: The High-Stakes Game of the Toy Industry* (Chicago: Contemporary Books, 1990), pp, 23–37, 155–171.

8. "The Rise and Fall of Coleco," *THW*, Sept. 1988, 12–15; "Toymakers: Playing to Win," *Economist*, Oct. 19, 1985, 85–86; "Toymaker on the Teeter-Totter," *Business Week*, Aug. 5, 1991, 77.

9. "Hasbro: Blazing New Business Trails," *Playthings* (hereafter *PT*), Aug. 1970, 92; "Hasbro: Merging with Milton Bradley," *Business Week*, May 21, 1984, 90; "Hasbro," *Advertising Age*, March 9, 1992, 41; Stern and Schoenhaus, *Toyland*, 247–262.

10. "How Quaker Oats Got Rolled," *Fortune*, Oct. 8, 1990, 129; "Mattel Gets All Dolled Up," *U.S. News and World Report*, Dec. 13, 1993, 74–77.

11. Business Trend Analysts, *The U.S. Market for Toys and Games* (New York, 1989), 262.

12. "Licensing Programs Flourish," *THW*, April 1983, 1; "Licensing Letter,"

plush Teddy bear

furlike exterior

Change people's opinion about bear

THW Marketing Report, Feb. 1983; TMA, *Toy Fact Book* (1987), 15; "Licenses No Substitute for Sound Merchandising," *PT*, April 1984, 62.

13. Disney Character Licensing ad, *THW*, Feb. 1983, 6.

14. "FCC Won't Force Child Programs," *Boston Globe*, Feb. 12, 1983, 35.

15. "Children and Television," Hearing of Subcommittee on Telecommunications, March 16, 1983, U.S. Congress, serial no. 98-3, 13; TMA, *Toy Industry Fact Book* (1993), 23; Cynthia Alperowicz, "Toymakers Take Over Children's TV," *Business and Society Review*, 49 (Spring 1984): 49.

16. See Alperowicz, "Toymakers Take Over," 47–51; "ACT Wants Guidelines for TV Advertising," *Broadcasting*, July 12, 1982, 49; "Feds Urge Another Look at Toy/Program Linkups," *Advertising Age*, Aug. 12, 1985, 58.

17. Hal Katz, "Alternatives in Advertising to Children," *PT*, Aug. 1983, 102.

18. Dale Kunkel, "From a Raised Eyebrow to a Turned Back: The FCC and Children's Product-Related Programming," *Journal of Communications*, 38, no. 4 (1988): 91; Nancy Carlsson-Paige and Diane Levin, "Saturday Morning Pushers," *Utne Reader*, Jan. 2, 1992, 68–69; Alan Wolf, "Toying with Television," *THW*, Nov. 1985, 1, 17–20.

19. "Is the Toy Business Taking Over Kids' TV?" *TV Guide*, June 12, 1987, 5–7; "TMA Meeting," *THW*, Feb. 1985, 49; Tom Engelhardt, "Saturday Morning Fever: The Hard Sell Takeover of Kids' TV," *Mother Jones*, 11, no. 6 (1986): 36; "Are the Programs Your Kids Watch Simply Commercials?" *Business Week*, March 25, 1985, 54–55; Wolf, "Toying with Television," 18–20; Cy Schneider, *Children's Television: The Art, The Business, and How It Works* (Chicago: NTC Business Books, 1987), esp. chs. 4, 6.

20. Patricia Bauer, "Babe in Toyland," *Channels of Communication*, 7 (July 8, 1987): 48–51.

21. See, e.g., "Manufacturers Double as Licensors," *PT*, June 1984, 64–65.

22. "Economics and Your Business," *PT*, Feb. 1984, 166.

23. "TV Special to Kick off Defenders," *Character Licensing*, Feb. 1986, 14.

24. "Panelists Peer into Licensing and Video," *PT*, May 1983, 3.

25. Mattel Press Kit, Feb. 1983, Please Touch Museum, Toy Fair Collection (hereafter TFC), Box 3/6a; Care Bear Ad, *THW*, Feb. 1985, 84–85; "Licensed Products Gain Major Role," *THW*, April 1983, 1.

26. "Star Wars," *THW*, June 1983, 24, 26; "'Star Wars' Summer Awaits Marketers," *Advertising Age*, April 11, 1983, 1; Kenner Press Kit, Feb. 1983, TFC, Box 3/13A.

27. Vincent Santelmo, *The Official 30th Anniversary Salute to G.I. Joe* (Iola, Wis.: Kreuse, 1994), 94–101; "G.I. Joe vs. Rambo," *Advertising Age*, Aug. 5, 1985, 31.

28. William Woods, "The Littlest Arms Race," *Harper's*, April 1983, 6, 8, 10; Ellen Sweet, "G.I. Joe on the March," *Ms Magazine*, Dec. 1983, 103; "What's On Your Mind? An Interview with Stephen Hassenfeld," *THW*, Feb. 1984, 14–15.

29. *Hasbro* (Pawtucket, R.I., Hasbro, 1984), 74–75; "Hasbro Annual Report," 1983, TFC, Box 4; Tom Engelhardt, *The End of Victory Culture: Cold War America and the Disillusioning of a Generation* (New York: Basic Books, 1995), 81–86, 300.

30. *Mattel Delivers* (Hawthorne, Calif.: Mattel, 1983), 102–103, in TFC, Box 3/6b; *Mattel Sets the Pace* (Hawthorne, Calif.: Mattel, 1986), 166–189; "Top TV Toys," *THW*, July 1983, 4; "Licensing Spotlight," *THW*, Jan. 1983, 12; "Suppliers Predict Another Boom Year for Action Figures," *THW*, April 1984, 13–14.

31. "Transformers," *PT*, Feb. 1984, 32; Hasbro Press Kits, Feb. 1986, TFC, Box 5/6a.

32. Tonka ad, "GoBots," *PT*, Feb. 1984, 32; Tonka Press Kit, Feb. 1986, TFC, Box 7/38; "Robotics Help Transform Retail Shelves into Profit Centers," *PT*, April 1985, 46–49; "Merchants Ponder Robots' Fate," *THW*, Dec. 1985, 44–45.

33. James Korkan, "Toy Counterterrorists vs. Toy Counter Terrorists," *Advertising Age*, May 5, 1986, 43–45; Kenner Press Kit, Feb. 1984, TFC, Box 4/6A; Coleco Press Kit, June 1986, Box 5/2.

34. "Who Are Those Characters from Cleveland?" brochure published by American Greeting for the Toy Fair in 1984; Kenner Press Kit, Feb. 1983, both in TFC, Box 3/13A.

35. "American Greetings Sees $250M in First Year of Care Bears," *PT*, Dec. 1982, 54; "Zoo Story," *Wall Street Journal*, Sept. 24, 1982, 56; "Plush Buyers Bullish for 83," *PT*, June 1983, 24–28, 66–70; Kenner Press Kit, Feb. 1983, TFC, Box 3/13a; "Those Characters from Cleveland," *THW*, Feb. 1983, 74; Hasbro Press Kit, Feb. 1986, TFC, Box 5/6B.

36. "New Properties," *THW*, Feb. 1984, 169; Mattel Press Kit, Feb. 1983, TFC, Box 3/6a; *The Winners Keep Coming from Kenner* (New York: Kenner, 1984), 110–113, TFC, Box 4/6; Kenner Press Kit, Feb. 1985, TFC, Box 6/28; "Taking Toyetic License in 1985," *Toys, Hobbies, and Crafts* (hereafter *THC*), Feb. 1985, 44–45.

37. William Hoffman, *Fantasy: The Incredible Cabbage Patch Phenomenon* (Dallas: Taylor, 1994), 1–13; Stern and Schoenhaus, *Toyland*, ch. 10; "Cabbage Patch Dispatch" (Fall 1982), a publicity brochure, and Coleco Press Kit, Feb. 1983, TFC, Box 3; "Oh, You Beautiful Dolls!" *Newsweek*, Dec. 12, 1983, 78–85.

38. John Jacob, "The Benign Exploitation of Human Emotions: Adult Women and the Marketing of Cabbage Patch Kids," *Journal of American Culture*, 10 (fall 1987): 61–71.

39. "How Long Can Cabbage Patch Kids Keep Coleco Afloat?" *Business Week*, Oct. 24, 1984, 41; Coleco Press Kit, Feb. 1984, TFC, Box 4/3; Coleco Press Kit, June 10, 1986, TFC, Box 5/2.

40. Hasbro Press Kit, Feb. 1986; *Hasbro '86*, (Pawtucket, R.I., 1986), 2–13, both in TFC, Box 7/24–25; Hasbro Ad for Jem, *THW*, June 1986, 40–41; *THW*,

feature called "Hit Parade" (a listing of top-selling toys), from March 1986 to June 1987.

41. "Contending for Barbie's Crown: Hasbro's Maxie Is California Cool," *Business Week*, July 18, 1988, 78.

42. Mattel ad for Barbie and the Rockers, *Toy Fair News*, Feb. 9, 1987.

43. *Kenner Has Hot Stuff for a Sizzling 1986* (Cincinnati: Kenner, 1986), TFC, Box 6; *Tonka Takes You There* (catalog, 1988), TFC, Box 9; statistics derived from TMA, *Toy Industry Fact Book*, various issues.

44. Tonka Press Kit, Feb. 1986, TFC, Box 7/38; Galoob Press Kit, Feb. 1986, TFC, Box 7/23; Pamela Tuchscherer, *T.V. Interactive Toys: The New High Tech Threat to Children* (Bend, Ore.: Pinnaroo, 1988), esp. ch. 5.

45. *Coleco 1985* (New York, 1985), 86–97; Coleco Press Kit, Feb. 1985, TFC, Box 6/18.

46. Tyco Press Kit, Feb. 1988, TFC, Box 8; Tyco Press Kit, Feb. 1989, TFC, Box 9; Stern and Schoenhaus, *Toyland*, chs. 5, 11, 14, 17; Tom Engelhardt, "The Morphing of the American Mind," *New York Times*, Dec. 24, 1994, A25.

47. "Female Action Figures Demand Equal Time," *PT*, March 1985, 56, 57, 120.

48. Carol Markowski, *Tomart's Price Guide to Action Figure Collectibles* (Dayton, Oh.: Tomart, 1992), 43–45, 76–77; Mattel, *Setting the Pace*, 152–165, and Mattel Press Kit, Feb. 1985, TFC, Box 8/9.

49. *Galoob 1985* (South San Francisco:, 1985); Galoob Press Kit, Feb. 1985, TFC, Box 5.

50. Playmates Press Kit, Feb. 1987, TFC, Box 6/1; "Heroes in a Half Shell," *Forbes*, Oct. 28, 1991, 49–55; Playmates Press Kit, Feb. 1989, TFC, Box 8/7.

51. *Playmates '89* (La Miranda, Calif., 1989), 5, TFC, Box 9.

52. Playmates Press Kit, Feb. 1989, TFC, Box 9; Playmates Press Kit, Feb. 1991, TFC, Box 14; Matthew Grimm, "Playmates Prepare for Post-Turtle Life," *Adweek Marketing Week*, Nov. 26, 1990, 17; Hasbro Press Kit, Feb. 1989, TFC, Box 14.

53. Fisher-Price Press Kit, Feb. 1983, and *The Excitement Is Building* (East Aurora, N.Y.: Fisher-Price, 1983), TFC, Box 3; Fisher-Price Press Kit, Feb. 1986, TFC, Box 6; Fisher-Price Press Kit, Feb. 1988, TFC, Box 8/2.

54. Playskool Press Kit, Feb. 1985, TFC, Box 6; Playskool Press Kit, Feb. 1987, and *Playskool '87: Feeling Good about the Playskool Years*, TFC, Box 8/21; *Playskool Promises Fun, 1990*, TFC, Box 12.

55. Worlds of Wonder Press Kit, Jan. 1987, TFC, Box 8/25; Galoob Press Kit, Feb. 1986, TFC, Box 7/23.

56. Fisher-Price Press Kit, Feb. 1990, TFC, Box 11; Playskool Press Kit, Feb. 1991, TFC, Box 14; Mattel Press Kit, Feb. 1983, and *Mattel Delivers*, (1983), 50–53, TFC, Box 3/6A; Kenner Press Kit, Feb. 1986, TFC, Box 6; *Galoob* (1986), 54–73, TFC, Box 7/23.

57. "Little Tikes," *Adweek Marketing Week*, Sept. 10, 1990, 18–19; *Childcraft* (New York, 1980), 99, TFC, Box 2.

58. Gund, Inc. Press Kit, Feb. 1983, TFC, Box 3; Playmobil Press Kit, Feb. 1989, TFC, Box 10; *Brio 1983* (Milwaukee, 1983), TFC, Box 3; Peter Reynolds, "The 'White Papers' on Toys and Play" in Brio Press Kit, Feb. 1990, TFC, Box 11.
59. Lego Press Kit, Jan. 1988, TFC, Box 10.
60. "Legos," *Adweek*, March 16, 1987, 20–21; "Down and Dirty," *THW*, Feb. 1984, 16.
61. Toys advertised in the Feb. 1986 issue of *Licensing Book;* "More Action Figures Battle for Shelf Space," *PT*, April 1986, 35–36.
62. "Licensing Lesson," *Licensing Today*, 2 (1988): 143; "Tube Talk," *THW*, Feb. 1988, 138; "Tube Tales," *THW*, March 1987, 18–19; "Licensing's Profitable but Saturated," *PT*, Feb. 1986, 288–291; "Retailers Advise Licensors to Cut Back," *PT*, Feb. 1987, 262–265; "Action Figures Battle for Position," *PT*, April 1987, 38–39.
63. "The Good, The Bad, and the Ugly," *THW*, Feb. 1991, 29.
64. "Wham! Zap! You Just Made a Million," *Economist*, Aug. 18, 1990, 60; "Nintendo Crowned Top Toy for '88," *PT*, Dec. 1988, 28; Stephen Kline, "Virtual Toys: Video Games and Post-Modern Play," International Toy Research Conference, Halmstad, Sweden, June 1996.
65. Children's Television Act of 1990, publication no. 101–437, 101st Congress, 1st sess., *Children's Television Hearing*, Subcommittee on Telecommunications and Finance, March 10, 1993, serial no. 103–127, 10–19; "ACT Challenges Children's TV Rules," *Broadcasting*, May 20, 1991, 62; "ACT Seeks Reimposition of Ad Guidelines," *Broadcasting*, Aug. 31, 1987, 35–36.
66. "Fight Heats Up Against Kids' TV 'Commershow,'" *Marketing News*, Oct. 9, 1989, 2, 6.
67. Matchbox Press Kit, Feb. 1988, TFC, Box 9/26; Galoob Press Kit, Feb. 1988, TFC, Box 8/20; Galoob Press Kit, Feb. 1991, TFC, Box 13; Kenner Press Kit, Feb. 1988, TFC, Box 8/3; Fisher-Price Press Kit, Feb. 1991, TFC, Box 12; "Building Blocks," *THW*, April 1987, 38; "Meccano Reintroduces the Erector Set," *PT*, Jan. 1991, 16.
68. "Character Licensing," *Licensing Book*, Feb. 1988, 16; "Character Licensing," *Licensing Book*, Feb. 1989, 69; "Viacom Licenses Images from Yesterday, Today, and Tomorrow," *THW*, June 1991, 32–33; "Toys," *Licensing Book*, Feb. 1991, 18.
69. "Dolls on the Rise Again," *THW*, May 1989, 25–26; Ideal Press Kit, Feb. 1989, TFC, Box 9/6A; "Oopsie-Daisy, Guess Who's Tops in Toyland Now?" *Business Week*, Dec. 18, 1989, 102; Tyco Press Kit, Feb. 1990, TFC, Box 12; Hasbro Press Kit, Feb. 1990, TFC, Box 11.
70. "Girl Talk," *THW*, March 1990, 21; *Kenner 1988* (New York:), 1–10, TFC, Box 8/3; Kenner Press Kit, Feb. 1988, TFC, Box 8/4; Kenner Press Kit, Feb. 1989, TFC, Box 9; Mattel Press Kit, Feb. 1989, TFC, Box 9.
71. Mattel Press Kit, Feb. 1987, TFC, Box 7/7; Mattel Press Kit, Feb. 1990, and *Corolle Collection, 1990* (Mattel, 1990), TFC, Box 12.

72. American Girl Collection on line, www.pleasantco.com. Note also *The American Girl*, a quarterly magazine published by the Pleasant Company. Susanne Alexander, "Doll Line Is History—And a Pleasant Hit," *Wall Street Journal*, Aug. 22, 1991, B1.

73. "The Ties That Bind," *THW*, April 1991, 29–31; "Licensing Scope," *PT*, Feb. 1994, 102–103.

74. Kline, "Virtual Toys"; TMA, *1991–1992 Toy Industry Fact Book*, 6, and *1994–1995 Toy Industry Fact Book*, 10.

75. "Toy Sales," *PT*, June 1995, 27; "1994 Best Selling Toys," *PT*, Dec. 1994, 25–27; "What's Up Doc? Retail!" *Time*, May 9, 1995.

76. "Mattel's Barbie's Got a New Billion-Dollar Figure," *Brandweek*, Feb. 8, 1993, 32; "Mattel," *Forbes*, Jan. 7, 1991, 66.

8. Making Sense of the Modern Toybox

1. William Marbach, "I'm Dreaming of a Robot Hamster," *Newsweek*, Dec. 8, 1986, 83; Henry Rudnitsky, "Bang, Mom, You're Dead," *Forbes*, June 16, 1986, 86–87; "For Boys, Ugly Is In," *Public Relations Journal*, 43 (Feb. 1987): 11.

2. Toy Manufacturers of America, *Toy Fact Book 1994–1995* (New York, 1994), 28, and *Toy Fact Book, 1987 Edition* (1988), 14.

3. Marilyn Brandbard, "Sex Differences in Adults' Gifts and Children's Toy Requests at Christmas," *Psychological Reports*, 56 (June 1985): 969–970.

4. Judith Waldrop, "More Toys for Girls and Boys," *American Demographics*, Dec. 1991, 1, 40.

5. Neil Postman, *The Disappearance of the Child* (New York: Dell, 1982), 46, 89–90; Ron Goulart, *The Assault on Childhood* (Los Angeles: Sherbourne Press, 1969), 1, 3, 15, 28–29.

6. Nancy Carlsson-Paige and Diane Levin, *Who's Calling the Shots? How to Respond Effectively to Children's Fascination with War Play and War Toys* (Philadelphia, New Society, 1990).

7. Crawford Woods, "The Littlest Arms Race," *Harper's*, 266 (April 1983): 6; D. G. Green, "Toy Soldiers and War Games," *Dissent*, 32 (winter 1985): 115–118; Ken Schroeder, "Barbie Doesn't Add Up," *Educational Digest*, 58 (Dec. 1992): 72–74; Fara Warner, "The New Barbie-Bashers," *Adweek's Marketing Week*, Dec. 9, 1991, 10; Press Packet from the Barbie Liberation Organization, Aug.–Dec. 1993, Strong Museum Collection.

8. Joan Robie, *Turmoil in the Toy Box* (Lancaster, Pa.: Starbruster, 1989), ch. 6.

9. "The 'Happy' Doll," *Marketing News*, Sept. 30, 1991, 21; Robie, *Turmoil*, 195.

10. Diana Green, *Parents' Choice: A Sourcebook of the Very Best Products to Educate, Inform and Entertain Children* (Kansas City: Andrews and McMell, 1993), 1–22.

11. DeAndiran Mellin, "Is Barbie a Threat to Three-Year-Olds?" *Public Inquiry,*

March 22, 1989, 1A; Brian Sutton-Smith, *Toys as Culture* (New York: Gardner, 1986), 9, 11, 28, 65, 75; Jerome and Dorothy Singer, *Television, Imagination, and Aggression: A Study of Preschoolers* (New York: LEA Publishing, 1981), 217.

12. Toy Manufacturers of America, *Toy Fact Book* (New York, 1987), 7; Robert Steck, "The Checkered Game of Life," *Dun and Bradstreet Report*, Sept. 10, 1992, 46.

13. Stephen Kline, *Out of the Garden: Toys and Children's Culture in the Age of TV Marketing* (New York: Verso, 1993), 2, 12, 18–20, 214.

CREDITS

1. Noah's Ark. Library of Congress, Stereograph, 1896
2. German doll. Courtesy Peter Pluntky, Stockholm, Sweden
3. Miniature kitchens. Courtesy The Strong Museum, Rochester, N.Y.
4. Cast-iron horse and wagon. Courtesy The Strong Museum, Rochester, N.Y.
5. Jolly Nigger bank. Courtesy Peter Pluntky, Stockholm, Sweden
6. Acrobats. Courtesy The Strong Museum, Rochester, N.Y.
7. Humpty Dumpty Circus. Courtesy The Strong Museum, Rochester, N.Y.
8. American Flyer ad. *Youth's Companion*, Dec. 4, 1919, p. 695
9. Knapp Electric Toys ad. *Youth's Companion*, Oct. 10, 1925, p. 722
10. Butterick Rag Doll ad. *Delineator*, Dec. 1907, p. 1085, Library of Congress
11. Patsy and Patsy Ann dolls. Courtesy Kathy George, photographed by Benjamin Reeder, State College, Pa.
12. Bye-Lo Baby ad. *Playthings*, April 1924, p. 41, Library of Congress
13. Brownies. Courtesy The Strong Museum, Rochester, N.Y.
14. Billiken doll. Courtesy The Strong Museum, Rochester, N.Y.
15. Mickey Mouse Hand Car. Courtesy The Strong Museum, Rochester, N.Y.
16. Daisy Air Rifle ad. *Youth's Companion*, Dec. 7, 1922, p. 711
17. Buck Rogers pistol. *Playthings*, Jan. 1935, p. 17, Library of Congress, Courtesy Daisy Manufacturing Company
18. Shirley Temple doll. Courtesy Peter Pluntky, Stockholm, Sweden
19. Quintuplet dolls. Courtesy Peter Pluntky, Stockholm, Sweden
20. Playskool Institute ad. *Parents' Magazine*, Dec. 1930, p. 47, Playskool® is a trademark of Hasbro, Inc., copyright Hasbro, Inc., all rights reserved, used with permission

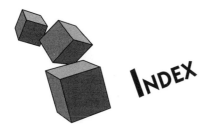

INDEX

American toy industry *(continued)*
197, 170–171, 181; reaction to criticism
(1970s), 182–187; emergence of charac-
ter-toy lines, 190–196; use of TV
(1980s), 197–202. *See also* Character li- ·
censing; Retailing of toys
Amos 'n' Andy (radio series), 100, 157
Amsco, 157
Ancient toys, 12–13
Arcade toys, 32, 55
Armstrong, Louis, 169
Arnaz, Desi, 163
Atari, 184, 221. *See also* Video games
Aunt Jemima, 84
Aurora Plastics, 151, 177, 178, 179, 181,
183
Automata, 15, 22. *See also* Clockwork
toys; Windup toys
Autry, Gene, 163

Baby boom, 147, 149, 172, 222
Baby dolls. *See* Dolls
Baby Snookums, 90
Back-to-Basics, 225
Ball, Lucille, 163
Banner Plastics, 155
Barbie dolls, 1, 2, 5, 76, 158, 166, 190; ori-
gins, 171–173; significance, 172–175; im-
pact on doll market, 174; changes
since 1980, 195, 211, 212, 213, 219, 226,
229, 236; opposition to, 231, 232; de-
fense of, 232. *See also* Dolls, fashion
Barnyard Commandos, 216. *See also* Ac-
tion figures
Barrie, J. M., 86
Batman (TV series), 179. *See also* Comic-
strip toys
Battery toys, 55, 59
Beecher, Catharine, 67
Bergen, Edgar, 108, 109
Berle, Milton, 149
Berryman, Clifford, 94
Berwick dolls, 75
Betsy Wetsy, 158, 187
Bicycles, 23
Billikens, 92–94, 109
Birth rates, 184. *See also* Family size
Blocks, building, 4; before 1900, 35, 37,
38; as an educational toy, 121, 129, 134,
135, 148, 160; and Luther Gulick, 132
Boehm, Edith, 141, 142

Borgfeldt, Georges, 95, 104
Boy Problem, 125
Boy's Life, 168
Brio toys, 219, 220
Brownies, 88–89, 177
Bryan, Anna, 131
Buck Rogers (radio and movie series), 82,
107, 114
Buddy "L" toys, 52, 55, 56–57, 76, 155
Bush, George, 222
Bushnell, Horace, 122
Buster Brown, 89
Butler Brothers Co., 33, 96
Bye-Lo Baby, 77, 168

Cabbage Patch Kids, 195, 210–211
Caillois, Roland, 12
Camera toys, 59
Campbell Kids, 73, 84, 85, 89, 159. *See
also* New Kid dolls
Captain Action, 179, 187. *See also* Action
figures
Captain Kangaroo (TV series), 163, 198
Captain Power (TV series), 213
Care Bears, 9, 191, 199, 202, 207, 209
Carroll, Lewis, 36, 86, 209
Cast-iron toys, 11, 22
Celebrity toys. *See* Character licensing
Centurions, 206. *See also* Action figures
Chain stores. *See* Variety stores
Chan Tai Ho, 216
Chaplin, Charlie, 91
Character licensing: before 1930, 40, 84–
85, 89–90, 91, 103; and the Depression,
103–107; from movies (1930s), 103–107,
117; from radio (1930s), 107–109, 114–
115, 118–119; in the 1950s, 156, 159;
from TV (1950s–1970s), 159–160, 171,
179, 182; from TV (1980s–1990s), 197–
198, 201, 202, 207–209, 221, 223, 226.
See also Fantasy toys; Trademark toys
Charlie McCarthy dolls and toys, 100,
101, 107–108, 109
Charren, Peggy, 184, 186, 199
Chase, Martha, 77, 140, 145
Chemistry sets, 53, 64, 72, 154
Child Craft Co., 219
Child experts, child psychologists, 3, 123,
124, 125, 126, 131; attitudes toward parents, 123, 135. *See also* Educational
toys; Play

Milton Bradley Co.: origins, 60, 66, 87, 91, 111; and educational toys, 134; post-1945, 170, 181, 192, 196, 234
Minidolls, 207–209, 217–218, 221
Missile toys, 156
Mitchtom, Benjamin, 150
Mitchtom, Morris, 94
Model-T Ford, 53, 55, 57
Monogram toys, 155
Monster toys, 178, 179
Montessori, Maria, 131
Montgomery Ward, 27, 66, 97, 168
Mothercraft School, 132. *See also* Read, Mary
Mouse Trap Game, 170
Movie star toys. *See* Character licensing
Mr. Machine, 170
Mr. Potato Head, 5
Mumblety-peg, 21. *See also* Folk toys
Musical toys, 39, 152, 163, 164
My Buddy doll, 217
My Little Pony, 208, 210, 215, 218. *See also* Minidolls

Nabisco, 183
Nash, Maude, 127, 128
National Education Association, 131
New Kid dolls, 73, 74, 84, 95, 119
New York Times, 101, 150
Nintendo, 221
Noah's Ark, 15, 20, 21, 168
Novelty industry, 87–88. *See also* Fads; Fantasy toys
Nuremberg, 16, 17; Nuremberg Kitchen, 17
Nurseries, 35
Nutty Mads, 178

Ohio Art Co., 105, 151
O'Niell, Rose, 73, 85, 94
Outcault, Richard, 89

Pajeau, Charles, 60
Palmer, Luella, 137, 138, 143
Parents: ambiguity toward novelty, 3, 116, 189, 228, 230–231; attitudes toward contemporary toys, 1, 2, 9, 13, 228–233; nostalgia for old toys, 1, 2, 148, 159, 221, 224–225. *See also* Child experts; Childrearing and childhood; Consumer culture; Educational toys

Parents' Magazine, 2, 4, 43; impact of educational toys, 123, 141, 153, 161, 169
Parker, Fess, 163
Parker Brothers Inc., 87, 196. *See also* Games
Patsy dolls, 52, 75–78, 189
Penney, J. C., 27, 33
Pershing, John, 111
Peter Pan, 32, 86
Pet's Toy Grocery Store, 72–73
Piaget, Jean, 126. *See also* Child experts
Ping Pong, 88
Plasticine, 140
Plastics, 153–154, 155
Play: anthropology of, 12–14; of adults, 14, 15, 17; in medieval Europe, 16–17; 19th-century, 20–21, 36; during holidays, 34; instinct for, 124, 126, 127; and child development, 125–127; as child's work, 127–128, 143; street games, 148. *See also* Childrearing and childhood; Male-bonding toys; Play theory; Recreation movement
Play Doh, 151
Playground Association, 125
Playground equipment, 128, 139
Playmates toys, 195, 216
Playmobil toys, 219, 220
Playrooms, 128, 131
Playskool Inc., 4, 5, 6, 7; origins, 140, 142; 1950s–1960s, 160, 170; abandonment of educational toys, 181, 196, 217, 218, 219
Play theory, 124–125. *See also* Play; Recreation movement
Playthings Magazine: origins, 29, 30, 88; promoting toy sales, 32, 48, 51, 85; toy advertising in, 56, 62, 85, 88, 96, 149. *See also* Advertising toys; Retailing of toys
Plush toys, 94–95, 218, 219. *See also* Teddy bears
Pocahontas (film), 229, 236
Pogo sticks, 88, 160
Polly Dolly, 39, 40
Popeye, 8, 108, 115
Popular Mechanics, 53, 63, 156
Popular Science, 63
Postman, Neil, 231
Pressman Inc., 155

Product safety, 183
Program-length commercials, 199–201, 206, 208, 211–212; decline of, 221–222. *See also* Advertising; Television
Puritans, 43, 234

Quaker Oats Co., 5, 171

Racist toys: 1870s–1900, 41, 68, 88, 97–99; since 1900, 99–100
Radio, children's, 103, 107–108, 114–115
Raggedy Ann dolls, 74, 224
Rainbow Brite, 191. *See also* Minidolls
Rambo toys, 206. *See also* Action figures
Rapaport Brothers (Junior Caster Sets), 113
Rat Fink toys, 178
Rattles, 3, 20, 132
Read, Mary, 127, 132, 135, 144
Reagan, Ronald, 203, 222
Recreation movement, 125, 127
Religion and toys, 13–14, 232. *See also* Christian toys
Remco (models), 171, 178
Retailing of toys: 2, 4, 6, 7; 19th century, 23, 24–25, 27, 29; 1900–1945, 29–33, 101–103; post-1945, 152, 167, 170, 193–194. *See also* Advertising; American toy industry; Seasonal sales
Revell Co., 150, 154, 177, 178
Revlon cosmetics, 158
Rice, Enoch, 24
Ringling Brothers' Circus, 184
Rites of passage, 192
Roach, Hal, 91
Roberts, Xavier, 210
Robie, Joan, 232
Rocking horses, 35
Rogers, Roy, 156, 168; Roy Rogers toys, 197
Roller skates, 23
Roosevelt, Theodore, 8, 40, 41, 69, 78, 87, 94, 99, 150
Roth, Ed, 178
Rousseau, Jean-Jacques, 19, 35
Rowland, Pleasant, 225

Sales of toys: to 1945, 7, 29, 31, 101, 119; post-1945, 153, 166, 170, 189, 226, 229
Santa Claus, 39, 46–48, 181, 230. *See also* Christmas

Sarson, Evelyn, 184
Saturday Evening Post, 28, 153
Saul, Neil, 180
Schaper Plastics, 168
Schimmel, Wilhelm, 20
Schneider, Cy, 165
Schoenhut, Albert (toymaker): origins, 24, 37, 39; Schoenhut dolls, 40–42, 96, 101, 194; educational toys, 140
Schwarz, F. A. O. (toy store), 29, 48, 142, 152
Science-fiction toys. *See* Action figures; Fantasy toys; Space toys
Scientific toys, 22, 57–58, 150, 154, 155, 156
Sears, Roebuck and Co.: origins, 27, 29; 1910s–1920s, 55, 61, 66, 68; 1930s, 99; post-1945, 155, 168, 197
Seasonal sales, 32, 142, 193, 196. *See also* American toy industry; Christmas; Retailing of toys
Sectaurs, 213, 214. *See also* Action figures
Sesame Street (TV series), 2, 182, 187
Sewing cards, 129
Sewing patterns, 68
Sheehy, Emma, 153
She-Ra, 214–215. *See also* Action figures
Shimmer dolls, 218
Shneider, Sid, 170, 183
Silly putty, 168
Simone, Rose, 112
Skipper doll, 6, 173–174. *See also* Barbie dolls
Slinky, 151, 160
Sloan, Alfred, 65
Smurfs, 88, 222
Snow White and the Seven Dwarfs (film), 106–107, 108, 158, 193, 198
Soldiers, toy, 13, 17, 111–113, 176. *See also* Guns, toy; Military toys
Space toys: 1930s, 114–115; 1950s–1960s, 155, 156, 163, 168; 1970s, 180, 181. *See also* Action figures
Spock, Benjamin, 140, 161, 176, 183
Steam engine toys, 58–59, 149
Steiff, Margarete, 94–95
Stevens and Brown toys, 24, 25, 58, 98
"Story of a Sandpile" (G. Stanley Hall), 133
Strawberry Shortcake, 200, 207, 212. *See also* Minidolls